Music of
the Great Depression

Recent Titles in
American History through Music
David J. Brinkman, Series Editor

Music of the Counterculture Era
James E. Perone

Music of the Civil War Era
Steven H. Cornelius

Music of the Colonial and Revolutionary Era
John Ogasapian

Music of
the Great Depression

William H. Young and Nancy K. Young

American History through Music
David J. Brinkman, Series Editor

GREENWOOD PRESS
Westport, Connecticut • London

Library of Congress Cataloging-in-Publication Data

Young, William H., 1939–
    Music of the Great Depression / William H. Young and Nancy K. Young.
      p. cm.—(American history through music)
    Includes bibliographical references (p.) and index.
    ISBN 0–313–33230–4 (alk. paper)
    1. Popular music—United States—1921–1930—History and criticism. 2. Popular
music—United States—1931–1940—History and criticism. 3. Depressions—1929—
United States. I. Young, Nancy K., 1940– II. Title. III. Series.
ML3477.Y68 2005
780'.973'09043—dc22   2004022530

British Library Cataloguing in Publication Data is available.

Library of Congress Catalog Card Number: 2004022530
ISBN: 0–313–33230–4

First published in 2005

Greenwood Press, 88 Post Road West, Westport, CT 06881
An imprint of Greenwood Publishing Group, Inc.
www.greenwood.com

Printed in the United States of America

The paper used in this book complies with the
Permanent Paper Standard issued by the National
Information Standards Organization (Z39.48–1984).

10 9 8 7 6 5 4 3 2 1

To
Gwen and Doug,
Good friends
and
Splendid fellow travelers

Contents

Series Foreword

The elements of music are well known. They include melody, rhythm, harmony, form, and texture. Music, though, has infinite variety. Exploring this variety in the music of specific time periods, such as the Colonial and Revolutionary Period, the Roaring Twenties, and the Counterculture Era, is the purpose of the "American History through Music" series. The authors of each volume describe the music in terms of its basic elements, but more importantly, focus on how the social, economic, political, technological, and religious influences shaped the music of that particular time. Each volume in the series not only describes the music of a particular era but the ways in which the music reflected societal concerns. For these purposes, music is defined inclusively; this series considers such diverse musical genres as classical, folk, jazz, rock, religious, and theater music, as each of these genres serve as both reflections of society and as illustrations of how music influences society.

Perhaps the most important conclusion that readers will draw from this series is that music does not exist independently of society. Listeners have enjoyed music throughout time for its aesthetic qualities, but music has also been used to convey emotions and ideas. It has been used to enhance patriotic rituals, and to maintain order in social and religious ceremonies. The "American History through Music" series attempts to put these and other uses of music in an historical context. For instance, how did music serve as entertainment during the Great Depression? How did the music of the Civil War contribute to the stability of the Union—and to the Confederacy? Answers to these and other questions show that music is not just a part of society; music *is* society.

The authors of "American History through Music" present essays based in sound scholarship, written for the lay reader. In addition to discussing important genres and approaches to music, each volume profiles the composers and performers whose music defines their era, describes the musical instruments and technological innovations that influenced the musical world, and provides a glossary of important terms and a bibliography of recommended readings. This information will help students and other interested readers understand the colorful and complex mosaics of musical history.

David J. Brinkman
University of Wyoming

Acknowledgments

Thanks and appreciation go to Chris Millson-Martula for all the capable assistance he and the staff at the Lynchburg College Library have freely provided. Especially prominent in that effort was Ariel Myers, archivist and interlibrary loan specialist; she located those obscure texts no one else could find. As always, the Library of Congress Prints and Photographs Division, and Jan Grenci and the staff for newspaper collections in particular, went beyond the call of duty. Danny Givens and everyone connected with Givens Books in Lynchburg, Virginia, likewise provided invaluable help in tracking down materials. Naomi Amos, herself a musician, made sure our descriptions of pop songs and standards were accurate. Bryan Wright, the possessor of a remarkable collection of old 78 rpm records and an encyclopedic knowledge about them, generously shared both with us. In a similar manner, Al Harris and Susan Vaughn gave us access to a selection of sheet music from the era. Books require many drafts, and Ed Canada again rose to the occasion with reams of usable scrap paper. And a tip of the hat to all those others who, through conversation and comments, have assisted in the creation of this text. Any errors of omission or commission of course remain ours.

Introduction

How did music of such quality emerge in a time of economic and social disequilibrium? A fair question. Different forces influence the course of popular music over any time span, but in the 1930s, several factors combined to have a disproportionate effect on the music of the era. In particular, record manufacturing, radio broadcasting, and sound film production worked in many ways—some subtle, some obvious—to chart the course of much American music. People had hundreds of recordings from which to choose, radio stations grew in number and boasted varied schedules, and a changing marquee at the local theater enticed everybody to go to the movies. What people purchased at record stores, what they heard on their radios, and what they viewed in theaters had interconnections little realized at the time.

Prior to the 1930s, much American music carried with it an aura of elitism. To be good, to have quality, it had to appeal to genteel tastes. It often tried to be patrician, or nondemocratic, a music for the select few. Anything that attracted a mass audience aroused suspicion, and many critics contemptuously dismissed it. In fact, some historians see parallels between the popularity of swing and the simultaneous rise of the New Deal. Both unified the country, bringing people together during a difficult time.

The traditional popular song reached its peak in the 1930s, a decade when composers like George Gershwin, Jerome Kern, Richard Rodgers, and dozens of others routinely created one classic song, or standard, after another. The

1920s had been labeled "the Jazz Age," and jazz contributed an important component to the music played during those years. But many other choices presented themselves to listeners and dancers in the thirties and "Swing" emerged as the nominative term. The Swing Era replaced the Jazz Age.

In 1932, Duke Ellington penned a little ditty called "It Don't Mean a Thing (If It Ain't Got That Swing)." Hardly his greatest composition, its title nevertheless sums up the music scene for much of the ensuing decade. Swing ruled, and all other music had to follow in its footsteps. In no period, before or since, has one musical form so captured the popular fancy. Legend has it that pianist Fats Waller said, after being asked to explain "swing," "If you have to ask, you'll never understand it." Like most legends, credit for this rejoinder has gone to others as well, but the point remains: swing is as much a feeling as it is a particular type of music; it speaks of pluralism, of equality.

Perhaps the best way to describe the swing phenomenon is to say that it involves a contagious rhythmic feeling, a desire to snap the fingers, tap the toes, and get up and dance. That definition of course transcends time and focuses on the physical side of swing. Historically, the Swing Era usually refers to the emergence of innumerable large bands during the 1930s that played primarily for dancers. Small groups and vocalists could likewise "swing," but when talking about the 1930s—especially the later 1930s—the big dance bands serve as the main attraction. Like a teapot simmering on a stove, the big band revolution did not come about in a flash. It took time, patience, a realization that swing would evolve out of what had come before.

This book examines the rise of radio, along with the continuing influence of Broadway and sound movies, on the nation's musical landscape. The remarkable number of enduring popular songs and standards the decade produced receives particular attention. Of course, any study of music and the 1930s demands some concentration on the emergence of swing, especially the big bands and their leaders. Despite the predominance of the swing phenomenon, alternative formats, such as folk, country, ethnic, and protest music, also merit discussion. Finally, classical composition, often ignored in the social ferment of the time, shares a chapter with the pioneering federal music program.

The decade witnessed the dramatic rise of recordings at the expense of sheet music, the interdependency of recordings and radio, and finally the impact swing had on all facets of the music business. The audience also underwent shifts of its own. Listeners began to divide along lines like race, gender, age, education, location, and many other variables that sociologists delight in employing when explaining change. Young people preferred up-tempo swing to lugubrious ballads. Women liked crooners better than blues belters. The more educated wanted sophisticated lyrics, not raw emotion, whereas rural folks leaned more toward country singers. These sweeping generalizations were all correct and all open to debate. On one thing people did agree: the music of the 1930s clearly pointed to the future and continued change.

For musicians and music lovers alike, and even with the momentary triumph of swing, American musical choices and tastes had splintered; no one "style" or "type" would ever again define the music or the audience.

Music and Media: Radio, Sheet Music, and Recordings

When it came to music in the 1930s, millions of Americans found whatever they wanted right in their own homes: radio. What had begun as a novelty in the early 1920s had evolved into the most popular, the most pervasive, medium ever. When not listening to their radios, Americans tended to learn about new musical artists and trends through sheet music and phonograph recordings. Both sheet music and record sales, however, plummeted during the Great Depression, while radio continued its steady growth.

RADIO

At the beginning of the decade, slightly over 600 AM (Amplitude Modulation) stations broadcast to almost 14 million receiving sets, or 46 percent of American homes. By the mid-1930s, the actual number of stations had dropped slightly because of the economic situation, but people continued buying new radios. In 1935, over 21 million sets could be found in 67 percent of homes. At the close of the 1930s, the industry had recovered from its minor slump, and 765 stations sent their signals to over 51 million receivers in 81 percent of homes. In addition, many families had multiple sets, a clear reflection of radio's vast popularity.

Car radios, introduced to the driving public in 1927, initially had a long way to go to capture the public's fancy. Less than 1 percent of all vehicles had a receiver in 1930, but interest in them showed signs of growing, despite the Depression. Apparently, a growing percentage of consumers found a car radio just as necessary as one in the home. By 1935, over 2 million cars boasted radios, and at the close of the decade the number had leaped to 7 million sets, a quarter of all automobiles. Amid continuing economic woes, the ubiquitous receiver established itself as a household and automotive necessity that most people considered "Depression-proof."

Network radio, which drove the business on a national scale, had grown spectacularly since its inception in the 1920s. In 1926, the National Broadcasting Company (NBC) went on the air with 25 stations. The following year, to diversify its programming and attract the maximum number of affiliates, the network divided into NBC Red and NBC Blue, each with separate stations, schedules, and shows. That same year, 1927, the Columbia Broadcasting System (CBS) came into being with two stations. By 1930, NBC (Red and Blue together) claimed 71 affiliates, and CBS boasted 60. Ten years later, NBC controlled 182 stations, and CBS stood not far behind with 112.

The Mutual Broadcasting System (MBS, but usually referred to as "Mutual") went on the air in 1934 with four stations; by 1940, it had 160. The Mutual network, however, functioned primarily as a cooperative venture and offered little original programming. Most of its affiliates already had limited associations with NBC or CBS, and they used Mutual to provide further connections among them. In addition, the Mutual shows tended to go to regional or rural markets that attracted small audiences, so it never had the influence or popularity of an NBC or CBS, despite its seemingly impressive numbers. Musically, the importance of the Mutual network proved negligible.

Even with Mutual's unique status, at the end of the decade, 464 stations— 60 percent of the 765 then on the air—had some network affiliation, a fact that would have enormous implications for the music business. One song, played over the networks, had the potential to be heard by a majority of the population. As an acknowledgment of the power and popularity of radio, in 1932 Hollywood released a film entitled *The Big Broadcast*; instead of movie celebrities, it features radio personalities almost exclusively. Instead of fighting the medium, the studios courted the new stars of the airwaves, hoping their fame would draw more patrons to the movies.[1]

Radio exists as a medium of communication, a carrier, and in theory should not influence the content of anything being broadcast. In reality, however, the opposite occurred. Radio receivers, or "sets," as they came to be called, sig-

Many musical personalities owed their popularity to radio. The Boswell Sisters (left to right: Helvetia, or "Vet," Connee, and Martha) commenced broadcasting at the beginning of the decade. Their bouncy, energetic renditions of pop hits gave them a wide following; the trio's first big hit was "Life Is Just a Bowl of Cherries" (1931; music by Ray Henderson, lyrics by Lew Brown), a number they recorded in 1933. They also appeared in *The Big Broadcast* (1932), a film that used radio stars as its primary cast. Connee Boswell later gained additional fame as a solo artist. [Library of Congress, Prints & Photographs Division]

nificantly affected how listeners heard programming, especially popular music. The technology of radio helped define the qualities of broadcast music. The sound produced by radio amplifiers and speakers emanates as sharper, "tinnier," than the older-style sound produced by acoustic reproduction such as would be found in early phonographs. In the first days of recording, a time that predates radio, acoustical reproduction had been the only means available. Large horns, like oversized megaphones, reproduced sounds through large diaphragms. A singer had to project his or her voice into these horns; otherwise it would come out as muffled. Thus a strong tenor, like Enrico Caruso (1873–1921), proved a great favorite on acoustic recordings because his voice came across clearly. Similarly, brass instruments, instead of strings, provided better sound for instrumental passages because of their sharper timbre.

All of that would change, however, with the introduction and popularization of radio. Electrical amplification, the basis for radio sound, proved more efficient and more economical than the acoustic variety, and it could easily fill a room with sound while at the same time picking up subtleties that acoustic amplification missed. Both highs (a bit shrill at first) and lows (somewhat boomy) came across far more audibly, and so small, amplified electrical loudspeakers soon replaced the bulky horns of old. A performer required an electrical microphone, or "enunciator"; he or she need stand only six inches from this device to achieve the best effects. For their part, listeners came to accept—and want—this clear but mechanical sound. With its heightened clarity, electrical amplification served as an example of how technology, not the music itself, dictated the way sounds would be reproduced.

In the mid-1920s, the sound qualities of phonographs lagged behind that of the new radio receivers, since they had been manufactured for acoustical recordings. As electrically amplified recordings became available, people found that their now-outdated acoustic record players made them sound shrill; to enjoy the new recordings, they had to purchase newer electrical models. Thus did planned—or forced—obsolescence create both a new market and a new aesthetic standard. In a sly move, RCA even included radios—since broadcasting had from the outset reproduced the electronic sound—in their "Orthophonic" phonograph consoles, thereby reassuring consumers that their new record players could aurally match anything their radios produced.[2]

Technology and the Rise of Crooning

Thanks to these innovations, a new style of singing had come about. Called "crooning," the word probably derives from Scottish roots. Originally, it meant "to bellow"—like a bull or cow. Over time, however, meanings shifted, and it went from bellowing to "lowing," again for cattle. But in terms of modern usage, lowing possesses little similarity to bellowing. From there, crooning moved to the human voice, meaning to hum or sing softly, first in a melancholy way, but finally just singing without putting much force behind it, be it sad or happy. In the later nineteenth century, "crooning" took on racial overtones and became a word employed in minstrel shows to suggest a black "Mammy" (a nursemaid) humming or singing to a child, presumably white.

Al Jolson, in characteristic blackface, used the term in a 1918 hit, "Rock-a-Bye Your Baby with a Dixie Melody" (music by Jean Schwartz, lyrics by Sam M. Lewis and Joe Young). As he sings, Jolson invokes the image of a person (whom he refers to as "mammy") crooning to her charge a "tune from Dixie."

Then, sometime in the early 1920s, and with its rich linguistic history, "crooning" took on a broader, more contemporary meaning. "Crooning" evolved as the term to identify a new style of vocalizing, one that meant singing softly and directly into an electrical microphone. Among the first to utilize the new technology was a woman named Vaughn De Leath (1900–1943), dubbed by promoters as "The First Lady of Radio," "The Original Radio Girl," and "The Sweetheart of the Radio." Heard on thousands of broadcasts from the early 1920s to the late 1930s, De Leath achieved great popularity by projecting a soft, intimate style of singing. A soprano, she usually performed unaccompanied except for a ukulele.

De Leath developed her distinctive manner almost inadvertently. During a pioneering 1919 experiment dealing with electrical amplification, she sang, *a cappella*, into a prototype electrified microphone. Intuitively sensing that too much volume could lead to distortion, she got close to the microphone and barely spoke into it, initiating a new musical form for the medium, and one that would come to dominate much vocalizing in the 1930s.

She became a featured soloist on *The Voice of Firestone* in 1928, an NBC network program that led to her having her own fifteen-minute musical shows in the 1930s. She performed for all three networks, and her intimate, breathy intonation made her come across as everyone's "friend." Given her innovative approach to the medium, plus her uncounted appearances on a variety of shows during the somewhat chaotic days of early commercial broadcasting, Vaughn De Leath earned her title of "The First Lady of Radio." She also paved the way for a generation of crooners who would utilize a similar manner of singing.[3]

Seldom heard in concerts and dance halls, which tended to be too big and too noisy, crooners at first existed on and for radio. And, as electrical amplification grew in popularity and importance, crooning likewise dominated the recording industry. People like Cliff Edwards (better known as "Ukulele Ike"), Art Gillham ("The Whispering Pianist"), Little Jack Little ("The Friendly Voice of the Cornfields"), "Whispering Jack" Smith ("The Whispering Baritone"), and Joe White ("The Silver-Masked Tenor") became stars in the later 1920s and early 1930s, their names known to millions of avid listeners. Probably the most popular of the group was Gene Austin. By crooning directly into the microphone, he made singing seem both intimate and effortless. In 1927 he recorded "My Blue Heaven" (music by Walter Donaldson, lyrics by George Whiting), and it soared to unanticipated success. Although accurate figures do not exist, it gained the reputation of being the best-selling American recording of all time, or at least until another crooner, Bing Crosby, unseated it with his rendition of "White Christmas" (words and music by Irving Berlin) in 1942. Austin remained popular well into the 1930s, his casual style appealing to audiences everywhere.

With crooning a well-established mode of singing by the beginning of the 1930s, radio audiences took to such personalities as Morton Downey (1901–1985), Singin' Sam (1899–1997), and Arthur Tracy (1899–1997). Downey, a light Irish tenor, could be found on the air almost constantly throughout the decade, appearing mainly on variety shows. Dubbed "The Irish Troubadour" and even "The Irish Thrush," Downey's career lasted until the demise of most network programming in the early 1950s.

"Singin' Sam," the radio name given Harry Frankel, a vaudevillian turned balladeer, enjoyed widespread success beginning in 1930. Frankel sang on innumerable fifteen-minute network shows; he usually performed old-time, nostalgic tunes in a soft bass voice. For much of the decade, Barbasol shaving cream sponsored him, which led to his being christened "Singin' Sam, The Barbasol Man." His advertisements for Barbasol, probably as well known as anything he sang, made Frankel one of the first to do singing commercials, and put him in league with other celebrities who became identified with specific products.

Finally, Arthur Tracy, better known as "The Street Singer," serves as another personality who rose to radio fame during the crooning craze. Cloaking himself in some mystery as to his identity, Tracy appeared on *Music That Satisfies* in the early 1930s, a musical show sponsored by Camel cigarettes. In a clever but clear display of commercialism, Camels parlayed its slogan, "They Satisfy," into the title. But mysteries, no matter how tantalizing, cannot last forever. Listeners learned his identity, and Tracy moved on to a succession of shows, including several series in England, the "Street Singer" nickname a reminder of earlier popularity.[4]

Radio audiences maintained that crooning humanized the singer, making him (or her) more approachable and believable. Plus, by virtue of performing over the radio or on records, the medium made the vocalist invisible, an ethereal voice. For many, this fantasy quality only reinforced the latent sexuality of many of the songs of the era, but what would not be appropriate in reality became allowable when coming through a loudspeaker. For several years, however, arguments raged among critics and other gatekeepers about the morality of crooning, a discussion that might seem incomprehensible for contemporary listeners.[5]

When talking about crooning, American popular song, and the 1930s, three names, however, tower above the rest: Rudy Vallee, Russ Columbo, and Bing Crosby. They dominated the field, defined the style for millions, and had the greatest popular acclaim.

Rudy Vallee

Born Hubert Pryor Vallee in 1901, Rudy Vallee, often categorized as a "crooner," became more a popular entertainer than a vocalist. His singing, however, initially caught the public's attention. He rose to early fame in the 1920s as a bandleader, fronting a group called The Connecticut Yankees. Because he had a thin, nasal voice that did not project well, Vallee developed a routine of performing his vocal numbers through a large megaphone. In the days before electric amplification, the device allowed him to croon and be heard above background noise.

The megaphone almost immediately became a standard prop and people expected it. As a consequence, Vallee retained it, although he no longer needed it when microphones and electrification allowed even the weakest voices to be heard. He eventually had his megaphone wired so audiences would both see it and hear him as he sounded on similarly amplified recordings. Once again, the technology of the period influenced artistic performance.

In 1928, NBC offered Vallee a contract to do his own variety show. The first great radio variety program, *The Fleischmann Yeast Hour* lasted until 1936, when it changed sponsors and became *The Royal Gelatin Hour*. It continued on NBC in one form or another until 1950. As he did in his night club performances, Vallee opened his radio broadcasts with "Heigh Ho, Everybody," a reference to the Heigh Ho Club, a New York bistro where the band had once played.

Vallee's style set the pattern for most other important singers of the 1930s. He favored simple songs that listeners could remember, and often skipped the verse and went straight to the chorus—the melodic portion that people usually associate with a particular song. Among the first performers to feature singing as part of the band's package of dance music, Vallee put his primary emphasis on the lyrics, and his vocal solos frequently replaced what traditionally had been instrumental ones. In this way, the band took second stage to the singer, a shift in roles. For the first half of the 1930s, this approach to vocalizing dominated; only with the rise of swing and the importance placed on instrumentalists would the pendulum swing back toward the orchestra.

Throughout his radio days, Vallee enjoyed a continuing string of hits. Numbers like "My Time Is Your Time" (1929; music by Leo Dance, lyrics by Eric Little), "A Little Kiss Each Morning (A Little Kiss Each Night)" (1929; words and music by Hillary Woods), "I Guess I'll Have to Change My Plan (the Blue Pajama Song)" (1929; music by Arthur Schwartz, lyrics by Howard Dietz), "Stein Song" (1930; University of Maine, original music by E. A. Fensted in 1901, words by Lincoln Colcord), "You're Driving Me Crazy! (What Did I Do?)" (1930; words and music by Walter Donaldson), "Let's Put Out the Lights" (1932; words and music by Herman Hupfield), "Just an Echo in the Valley" (1932; words and music by Harry Woods, James Campbell, Reg Connelly), and "Everything I Have Is Yours" (1933; music by Burton Lane, lyrics by Harold Adamson) kept him in the musical spotlight throughout the first years of the decade, and he reigned as one of the top male stars in show business.

Despite his admittedly weak voice, Vallee struck a chord with listeners, especially women. On the radio, he sounded intimate, as if he were singing di-

Posed before his customary NBC microphone, Rudy Vallee (1901–1986) epitomized the sophisticated radio crooner of the 1930s. The amplification made possible by radio and recordings allowed singers with otherwise weak voices to project their songs effectively. Vallee landed his first
NBC show, *The Fleischmann Yeast Hour*, in 1928; he would remain with the network until 1950.
[Library of Congress, Prints & Photographs Division]

rectly to the listener. This approach made some people uneasy, and they viewed Vallee and his counterparts as effeminate, as "sissies" who did not project traditional masculinity into their music. But his legions of fans felt otherwise; they loved the image of a man confessing his weaknesses in a romantic relationship. Radio proved Vallee's medium: he got to do some singing, lead the Connecticut Yankees, and clown with celebrities of the day. After a long, varied, and successful career, Vallee died in 1986.

Russ Columbo

Russ Columbo (1908–1934) followed close behind Vallee both in popularity and time. A strikingly handsome man, cut in the mold of film idol Rudolf Valentino, Columbo emerged as something of a minor Hollywood personality in the late 1920s. He played uncredited roles and bit parts (*The Wolf Song*, 1929; *The Texan*, 1930) at first, but his good looks, plus an ability to write and sing, got him noticed. Nothing memorable resulted from his brief film career other than a few "B" movies. If remembered at all, his best pictures would also be his last ones. *Broadway Through a Keyhole* (1933) and *Wake Up and Dream* (1934) gave him a chance at acting, and *That Goes Double* (1933), a short, allowed him to sing. In that film, he performs two of his biggest hits, "Prisoner of Love" (1931; music by Russ Columbo and Clarence Gaskill, lyrics by Leo Robin) and "You Call It Madness (But I Call It Love)" (1931; words and music by Con Conrad and Russ Columbo).

As Columbo's career sputtered and sparked but never truly burst into flame, composer Con Conrad envisioned bigger things for the singer and became his agent around the beginning of the decade. The two co-wrote "You Call It Madness (But I Call It Love)" in 1931 and, thanks to radio and recordings, the song catapulted the singer to fame. In appreciation, he took it as his theme. Much more than Rudy Vallee, Columbo projected an erotic quality in his breathy, intimate manner of singing. People started to tout Columbo as a star crooner, someone who could rival, maybe surpass, anyone then on the scene. He enjoyed a stint with NBC radio from 1931 to 1933; a contract with RCA Victor recordings; and several more hits, including "Lies" (1931; music by Harry Barris, lyrics by George Springer), "Too Beautiful for Words" (1934; words and music by Russ Columbo, Bennie Grossman, and Jack Stern), and the aforementioned "Prisoner of Love."

But the "Romeo of Radio," the "Vocal Valentino," as publicity agents would have it, died mysteriously in 1934 when only 26 years old. Although his death brought him more fame than he had experienced in life, the excitement soon disappeared. His legacy consists of a handful of recordings and some mediocre movies, the promise of his short life unfulfilled. For a brief moment, however, Russ Columbo actually stood shoulder to shoulder with Rudy Vallee and Bing Crosby.[6]

Bing Crosby

It would remain for Bing Crosby (1904–1977) to emerge as the top crooner of them all. Working with friends Al Rinker and Harry Barris, Crosby in 1926 formed The Rhythm Boys, a vocal trio. Good luck came their way when bandleader Paul Whiteman, always with an eye for talent, spotted them. Soon the threesome was singing with Whiteman and also the Gus Arnheim orchestra. In time, Crosby took more and more solo vocals, and scored his first big hit with "I Surrender, Dear" (music by Harry Barris, lyrics by Gordon Clifford) in 1931. That success led Crosby to break with the group in the early 1930s and become a single; he achieved almost instantaneous acclaim as a crooner.

When Whiteman originally hired Crosby and The Rhythm Boys, he had limited experience with vocalists. He instead saw his orchestra as a group of instrumentalists much more interested in the composition of a song than in its lyrics. If someone took a solo, everyone assumed that it would be instrumental. Now arrangements would have to include vocals. The trio of singers posed some additional problems. During a recording session or in a radio studio, no outsiders saw the band. But at a public dance, what did a singer do when he had nothing to sing? Whiteman solved the problem by giving Crosby an instrument to hold while the band played, so he would not appear idle. In time, of course, that all changed and, "idle" or not, the vocalist attained a status equal to that of the band members. Singers like Bing Crosby became important in their own right, and not just on records or radio. The band vocalists of the 1930s achieved a significance never before accorded them, to the point they often overshadowed the very orchestras with which they performed.

Most male vocalists in the popular field at that time tended to be tenors, but Crosby possessed a warm baritone. In addition, he displayed skill with many different kinds of lyrics and rhythms. He made direct references to the

Depression with "I Found a Million-Dollar Baby in the Five and Ten-Cent Store" (1931; music by Harry Warren, lyrics by Billy Rose and Mort Dixon) and the poignant "Brother, Can You Spare a Dime?" (1932; music by Jay Gorney, lyrics by E. Y. Harburg); both proved big hits. Most of his output, however, remained more romantic than topical, and included such best sellers as "It's Easy to Remember" (1935; music by Richard Rodgers, lyrics by Lorenz Hart), "Sweet Leilani" (1937; words and music by Harry Owens), and "Too Marvelous for Words" (1937; music by Richard Whiting, lyrics by Johnny Mercer). Crosby's unending flow of recordings—he eventually cut over 2,600 titles—coupled with their widespread acceptance and sales, made him the dominant male vocalist of the period.

His success with Whiteman led CBS to offer him his own show in 1931. At first called *Fifteen Minutes with Bing Crosby*, the series went through name and sponsor changes, but he nevertheless stayed with CBS until 1935. The following year, however, found him with rival NBC, where he took over *The Kraft Music Hall* from Al Jolson. Already a successful show during Jolson's tenure, it soon became a Thursday night ritual for millions of radio listeners, and Crosby would remain there until 1946.

Crosby's radio personality came over the airwaves as that of a nice, easygoing guy, someone people would like for their neighbor. The casualness might be practiced and studied, but it worked. His success allowed him to invite his favorite musicians as guests on the show, and that translated as popular standards, good jazz, some swing, and fine vocalists. Although *The Kraft Music Hall* might seem as relaxed as its host, Crosby demanded high levels of professionalism. A significant part of the show involved comedy, and that meant frequent visits from Bob Hope, later to be Crosby's co-star in the famous "Road" pictures. Of course, the main ingredient remained music, whether performed by Crosby himself or one of the many talented guests.

In addition to the continuous radio exposure, Crosby churned out numerous films, some first-rate, but most mediocre, that capitalize on his easygoing crooning style. Probably only the most die-hard Crosby fans can recall *Too Much Harmony* (1933) or *Here Is My Heart* (1935), two typical products of his popularity. Sustained by wafer-thin plots, the movies gave Crosby ample opportunity to sing such ditties as "The Day You Came Along" (1933; music by Arthur Johnston, lyrics by Sam Coslow) and "Love Is Just Around the Corner" (1935; music by Lewis E. Gensler, lyrics by Leo Robin). The pictures did reasonably well, and demonstrated how different media—radio, recording, and film—can interconnect.[7]

Radio star, recording star, and movie star—but with all those accomplishments, many still characterized Bing Crosby as merely a crooner. In the late 1920s and early 1930s, he had sung the lush romantic ballads with the best of them, his throaty baritone instantly recognizable. He possessed the right vibrato, the proper intonation, and breathless quality so desired by crooners. His first big film—a short, actually, but one in which he played a strong role— even bore the title *I Surrender, Dear* (1931). The perfect vehicle for a crooner, it also happened to be the name of his first recorded hit. But he had become aware of the mixed feelings people had about crooners and crooning, and he determined to do something about it.

In later recordings, he lowered his pitch slightly, dropped some of the vibrato, and branched out into other genres. He recorded Western songs ("Home on the Range"—1933; song composed 1885; music by Daniel Kelley, words by Brewster Higley), blues ("St. Louis Blues"—1932, with the Duke Ellington orchestra; song composed 1914; words and music by W. C. Handy), and jazz ("Sweet Georgia Brown"—1932, with the Isham Jones orchestra; song composed 1925; words and music by Ben Bernie, Maceo Pinkard, and Kenneth Casey), and moved away from straight crooning. He even injected some humor into the style with "Learn to Croon" (1933; music by Arthur Johnston, lyrics by Sam Coslow), a tune that almost denies crooning.

By the mid- to later 1930s, people might still refer to Bing Crosby as a crooner, a singer of sad or saccharine ballads, but they perceived him as a nice, all-American fellow. No one would ever accuse him of being effeminate or getting too emotional about a failed love affair. His manner took those things in stride, and his lighthearted banter, always a part of his personality, laughed off his troubles. The crooner label stuck, but the mannerisms that bothered some had by this time become foreign to Crosby's persona.

Despite Crosby's successful distancing from any negative connotations about crooning, the subject still aroused interest and debate. In light of that, a 1932 movie, directed by Lloyd Bacon, used the title *Crooner*; the producers knew full well it would draw attention. Russ Columbo had been cast for the crooner lead, but after a studio disagreement blocked his getting the role, the part went to David Manners, a little-known actor who played in dozens of "B" pictures throughout the decade. Not much of a picture, it nevertheless reflects the ongoing popularity of crooning. In fact, in a tip of the hat to Rudy Vallee, the main character sings so softly he uses a megaphone (see Chapter 3 for more on this movie).[8]

Radio Programming and Popular Music

Of course, not every crooner used a megaphone, but they all sang about love and romance. And what they sang came to be what the public wanted in the 1930s. The attention lavished on crooners demonstrated in part a growing interest in popular music, one that accompanied the meteoric rise of radio as a mass medium. By the early 1930s, well over two-thirds of total radio programming consisted of music-based shows, with a large proportion of that figure—about 40 percent—focused on genres other than straight popular selections, such as classical, operetta, ethnic, or regional. Plus every day, stations broadcast a great deal of incidental music that served as background or brief features on variety shows, comedy series, and the like. Wherever people turned their radio dials, they could pick up music, and most likely, popular music.

As the 1930s progressed, not quite so much of the broadcast day offered music, but the change proved slight. Thus, by the end of the decade, music programming still constituted 57 percent of all broadcasting, down only about 10 percent from ten years earlier. More significant, however, the programming of popular music to the exclusion of other formats displayed a marked increase. By 1939, approximately 75 percent of all the music on the air consisted of popular songs. Clearly, a decision to stress popular music had become the rule during this period.[9]

With so much emphasis being placed on broadcasting popular music to the exclusion of other types, the way of the future became clear: radio would continue to carry vast amounts of music, but the proportion of time devoted to nonpopular formats would decline. American radio had narrowed its range of choices, with the overwhelming first choice being to play popular songs. In the succeeding years, classical selections all but disappeared from regular AM schedules; not until the rise of FM (Frequency Modulation) in the 1950s would alternative musics be again heard with any regularity. The popular song, the "hit," had come to dominate the airwaves.

Your Hit Parade

When dealing with pop music and what is good and what is mediocre, people instantly see themselves as experts. Without quantitative data, any attempt to list "the best" becomes a subjective exercise and will not be to the liking of all. But that did not stop a group of radio producers in April of 1935. On that date *Your Hit Parade* premiered over the NBC network on Saturday evenings. "We don't pick 'em, we just play 'em," was its slogan, and the hour-long show became an immediate favorite, to the mutual delight of its cigarette sponsor and NBC. In fact, *Your Hit Parade* enjoyed sufficient popularity that in March of 1936 two different networks shared broadcasting rights to the show. CBS scheduled it on Wednesday evenings, and NBC remained with its Saturday hour. Finally, CBS gained both programs, retaining them until 1947, when NBC recaptured the show. *Your Hit Parade* would play on radio until 1957; a television version also covered the hits; it ran from 1950 until 1959, an unusual radio-television overlap.

By surveying weekly record and sheet music sales, the show's promoters claimed to have a scientific estimate of the nation's popular preferences. They professed to favor no one—Broadway and Hollywood tunes, current hits, standards, revivals—whatever sold during the week they made note of. They also contacted band leaders about their most requested numbers, although that must have been a less-than-scientific poll. After completing the polling, the show promised listeners it would perform the fifteen top-selling songs for the last seven days. Contrary to popular memory, the format at first had those fifteen songs played in random order; the breathless counting down to "number one" came later.

The sponsor's advertising agency tabulated what was popular and what was not in great secrecy. Representatives from the agency delivered the results to the studio each week in an armored truck. Of course, such procedures generated considerable publicity, something everyone involved wanted. Amid all the hyperbole, the orchestra had to come up with weekly arrangements of the chosen songs, varying repeat performances from prior weeks enough to keep things from getting repetitious or boring.

As the show matured, the producers tinkered with the program's organization. In 1936, fifteen songs got reduced to seven. Then in 1937, seven went to ten (the number most people seem to remember), staying with that figure until 1943, when nine became the new total. The numbers kept shifting until *Your Hit Parade*'s demise in 1957—at which time the band and singers performed only five songs. As an additional treat, and time permitting, there might be a "Lucky Strike Extra" on the show, usually a well-known song or standard not in the running for top honors.

Over the years, the performers on *Your Hit Parade* seemed to change almost as quickly as the latest hits. Between 1935 and 1940, the house band had no less than fourteen different leaders fronting it, most for just weeks at a time. They ranged from fairly well-known figures like Lennie Hayton (July–November 1935), Harry Sosnick (September 1936), and Raymond Scott (November 1938–July 1939), to relative unknowns like Richard Himber (June 1937) and Peter Van Steeden (July 1937). The vocalists likewise made for a mixed group, with nineteen different singers interpreting the hits of the day. Few achieved much fame; Kay Thompson (1935), Buddy Clark (1936), Georgia Gibbs (then known as "Fredda Gibson," 1938), Lanny Ross (1939), "Wee" Bonnie Baker (1939), and Bea Wain (1940) perhaps remain the best-remembered.

An accurate indicator of public preferences or not, audiences loved the suspense, and of course they got to hear some of their favorites performed each week. It proved a winning formula; *Your Hit Parade* outlasted most music shows of any kind. Unlike disc jockeys and the popular band remotes on radio, *Your Hit Parade* focused on the songs themselves, not the performers. "Number One" always meant a particular tune, although several interpretations of the same song by different artists might be competing on the marketplace. With its large, enthusiastic audience, a tantalizing question arises: how closely did the show reflect the public's tastes, and how much did it influence them? No definitive answer has ever been provided, but *Your Hit Parade* doubtless had its effects on both sides of the issue. Like many elements of popular culture, it functioned as both influence and reflector.[10]

The Disc Jockey

Americans had no shortage of new music; Broadway continued to supply new shows and new hits, the movies flourished, and radio boomed. And there to play the records sat the "radio jockey." Some time in the late thirties he— virtually no women spun records on the air then—was dubbed a "disc jockey," and the name stuck. The first well-known disc jockey, Al Jarvis, broadcast from Los Angeles on KFWB in "The World's Largest Make-Believe Ballroom." Jarvis's show began in 1932; in 1935 Martin Block had his own "Make-Believe Ballroom" on New York City's WNEW, a show that eventually could be heard nationally. Block entitled one of his features "Saturday Night in Harlem," a segment that gave precious exposure to black bands and singers, then a rarity on radio. Others across the land picked up on his successful format—chatter, records, chatter, commercials—and the disc jockey soon occupied a major portion of the broadcast day.[11]

Sheet Music

As more people acquired radios and recordings during the first third of the twentieth century, this new technology did not have an immediate, significant impact on either instruments or sheet music; sales of both remained impressive until the mid-1920s. Sheet music, the oldest of the three media, dates back to colonial times when the outlet for musical performance could often be found in the home. The sales of pianos, organs, and stringed instruments followed the popularity of various musical formats, and sheet music provided the instruction necessary to perform the latest songs.

Following the end of World War I in 1918, however, sheet music suffered declining sales as more and more people purchased phonograph recordings. In order to stabilize the industry, publishers decided on a set price of thirty cents a copy, a figure they felt would be competitive with the prices for recordings, which ranged from less than fifty cents a disc for some imports to well over a dollar for certain classical discs. Canny consumers quickly noted that a single recording yielded two sides and two songs, therefore halving the price per song, a considerable saving. One copy of sheet music, on the other hand, provided just that: one copy of a particular song, giving recordings a price advantage sheet music could never overcome.

Performances by specific artists doing a particular song began to dominate the popular market during the 1920s. In addition, jazz and the blues had become rising favorites, especially on record. Each of these formats proved virtually impossible to transcribe to sheet music, and consumers increasingly opted to purchase a recording of what they had heard instead of the music that they might play. The nuances of a particular singer, along with the improvisations characteristic of jazz and the blues, could be captured on discs, something printed musical notation might never convey. As the decade progressed, recordings of popular tunes, along with jazz and blues, established a permanent lead over sheet music in total sales, although paper copies of other musical formats continued to sell briskly.

Sheet music did possess longevity, an advantage over recordings. A popular hit could sell 500,000 or more printed copies, provided it remained available for a sufficiently long time. As a rule, much sheet music could be purchased months or even years after its initial publication. A recording, on the other hand, had a more limited shelf life; three to six months totaled the average availability of a recording before being replaced by new releases. Thus a short-lived record might not equal the sales of its more long-lived sheet

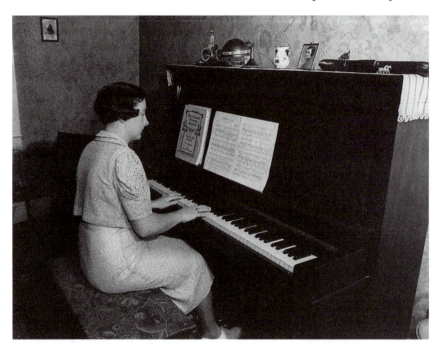

Although sales plunged during the Depression years, sheet music continued to attract a few buyers, especially those who could play an instrument. Here a pianist plays in a rural Pennsylvania home in 1938. But radio, recordings, and sound movies continued to make inroads on this venerable musical medium, and many traditional venues no longer carried sheet music by the advent of World War II. [Library of Congress, Prints & Photographs Division]

music counterpart. But the various record labels released many more titles than did the music publishers, and this also accounted for the lead they established.

The longer life of sheet music led to discrepancies about what the music industry saw as popular with the public. The record companies tracked their sales closely, and knew within just a couple of weeks what records sold well and which releases moved more slowly. But a time lag of ten weeks or more existed in the sheet music business. As a rule, people did not rush to purchase new sheet music as readily as they did new recordings. Publishers therefore allowed their printed music to remain with outlets much longer, and so a song declared a hit by record manufacturers might barely have made a dent in sheet music sales.

The bottom fell out of both the sheet music and the record business with the onset of the Depression. Sheet music publishers had to cut their prices when the full force of the economic collapse made itself felt. Twenty-five cents, sometimes less, became the common price for sheet music in the 1930s, although that climbed back to 1929 prices around 1938–1939. In the meantime, the industry considered any song that boasted sheet music sales of over 200,000 copies in a year a real success, but those tunes came along infrequently. Discouraged by this declining market, the mighty Woolworth's chain of five-and-dimes, once a primary carrier, closed its sheet music departments, leaving rival Kresge's as the main outlet. Aside from a brief spurt in sales during World War II, brought on by a recording ban, sheet music would never again be a major component of the popular music business.[12]

RECORDINGS

Coping with the Depression proved no easier for the recording industry than it had for sheet music publishers. Mass production of phonographs and recordings had commenced in the 1890s; by 1910, records emerged as the primary means of reproducing music in homes. The Columbia, Victor, and Edison labels dominated the business in the early twentieth century, but Brunswick, Gennett, Okeh, Paramount, Perfect, HMV, and Vocalion established themselves as strong competitors, introducing many Americans to contemporary dance music, along with popular jazz and blues.

The increasing competition of radio in the early 1920s initially drove down record sales, but the general prosperity of the decade had them rising again by 1929. For example, in 1921 the recording industry could boast income in excess of $100 million, a figure never before achieved. Then radio commenced its spectacular rise in popularity, and by mid-decade record sales had fallen to $59 million, or just over half of the 1921 total. By 1929, the industry's income had risen to $75 million—along with record player sales of almost 1,000,000 units—and then the Depression reversed everything. The succeeding years reveal just how hard the economic collapse affected the industry.

Table 1 illustrates how, at the beginning of the decade, the recording industry had been dealt a triple blow: economic depression, the rise of sound movies, and the omnipresent radio. As a point of contrast, in the late twenties, the sale of over 350,000 records qualified a song as a hit. By 1930, that figure had declined to 40,000 records, and showed no signs of improving. In the darkest days of the Depression, 1931–1933, the average sales for a hit

Table 1

The Recording Industry during the 1930s

Year	Annual Sales	Number of Records Sold	Comments
1929	$75 million	About 70 million discs.	High sales can be attributed to general prosperity until October and the stock market crash.
1930	$46 million	About 40 million discs.	Most movie theaters now have sound, and most homes have radios.
1931	$18 million	About 15 million discs.	Sound movies and radio continue to have negative effects on the industry, coupled with the economic impacts of the Depression.
1932	$11 million	About 10 million discs.	Only 40,000 record players sold, but radio sales tripled.
1933	$5 million	Just over 4 million discs.	The depth of the Depression, but Prohibition ends and bars and nightclubs begin to flourish again.
1934	$7 million	About 5 million discs.	The first industry turnaround, coupled with partial economic recovery and lower record prices.
1935	$9 million	Almost 7 million discs.	Recovery and lower prices continue.
1936	$11 million	About 8 million discs.	Swing begins to affect record sales positively.
1937	$13 million	About 10 million discs.	A recession slows the economy, but thanks to swing, record sales continue to improve.

(continued)

Table 1 (Continued)

Year	Annual Sales	Number of Records Sold	Comments
1938	$26 million	About 40 million discs. *By label*: Victor: over 13 million discs; Decca: over 12 million discs; Columbia/ARC: over 9 million discs. *Independent labels*: the remaining 6 million discs.	Swing is king and Americans listen to jukeboxes and buy large numbers of records.
1939	$36 million	About 55 million discs.	The swing phenomenon shows no letup, and record sales rise sharply.
1940	$52 million	About 80 million discs.	Sales continued to climb into the early 1940s.

Source: Joseph Csida and June Bundy Csida, *American Entertainment: A Unique History of Popular Show Business* (New York: Watson-Guptil Publications, 1978), 216–323.

record totaled 3,500 copies in the first three months of its release, and an additional 1,500 copies in the remaining three months prior to its disappearance from retailers' inventories. That reflected a decline of some 35,000 copies per title just since 1930. And those figures represent hit records; less popular songs did proportionally worse, to the point that basic recording costs might not even be met.

In 1932, Victor introduced a new product, the Duo. This gadget consisted of a 78 rpm turntable and not much else; it had no tubes or speakers. The Duo jacked into a radio, sold for a rock-bottom $16.50, and enjoyed immediate success. The Duo, however, served only as a stopgap; it could not prevent record sales from declining further. The music business needed a tonic, not another record player, but not until 1934 did record sales again begin a long, slow climb to their former levels.

Thomas Edison, despite his considerable reputation as a pioneer in recording technology, realized the plight of the industry and stopped marketing
records altogether, turning his back on his own invention. He had stubbornly
persisted in manufacturing acoustic recordings, and his market simply disappeared. Clinging to a straw, Edison continued to manufacture his already-
obsolete phonographs and cabinets, along with radios and dictating equipment.
Shortly thereafter, he admitted defeat on all fronts and ceased manufacturing
phonographs.

While the record industry seemed mired in insoluble problems, radio exhibited ever-growing strength. As evidence, the Radio Corporation of America (better known as RCA) bought the struggling Victor Record Company in
1929. Victor, which had been part of the Victor Talking Machine Company
since 1901, early on established itself as one of the premier recording firms,
but lacked the financial resources to withstand the straitened economy. RCA,
owned by AT&T, General Electric, and Westinghouse, already controlled the
National Broadcasting Company, and the acquisition of the Victor label gave
the radio giant a vast archive of recorded music. In a related move, RCA had
also created the RKO (for Radio-Keith-Orpheum) studio, a film production
company, thus providing it access to movies, recordings, and of course, radio.
In short order, RCA had entrée to all of the electronic mass of the day, a feat
that provided it some insulation from most of the economic fluctuations and
troubles of the period. If recordings faltered, the movies might prosper, and
radio seemed impervious to anything.

This brief history of Victor records gives but a hint of the byzantine trans-
actions that occurred throughout the American recording industry during the
1930s. Brunswick Records, a part of the Brunswick-Balke-Collender Company
of Dubuque, Iowa, had come into being shortly after the parent firm began
manufacturing phonographs in 1916. Previously noted for pool tables and pianos, the Iowa firm saw great potential in the whole phonograph industry.
Its recording subsidiary, boasting the latest technology, bought the once-
prosperous Aeolian and Vocalion catalogs in 1924 and seemed poised to become a major label. Brunswick also owned a budget line called Melotone.
Even with its acquisitions, the company saw overall sales continue an inex-
orable decline, and the Warner Brothers film studios purchased Brunswick
in 1929. When it made the purchase, Warner Brothers enjoyed high profits
and seemed poised to expand. But then the moviemakers, like the rest of the
nation, fell on hard times after the market crash. Thinking Brunswick was
doomed to being a money-losing proposition, Warner Brothers turned around

and in 1931 sold the label to the American Record Company (ARC), an up-start group that had been organized in 1929 with the express purpose of buying out destitute companies and retailing bargain discs in five-and-dimes and cheap variety stores.

With Edison out of the picture, Victor a part of RCA, and Brunswick absorbed by the American Record Company, only Columbia Records remained as a major independent label. But even mighty Columbia, which at the time of the Depression the huge English EMI (for Electric & Music Industries) firm owned, went on sale. EMI unloaded the label to the company manufacturing Majestic radio receivers. The economic crisis continued, however, and the sales of Majestic receivers dropped, a situation that placed Columbia once more on the auction block. This move resulted in the always-alert American Record Company picking up the once-prestigious label in 1934 for next to nothing.

The Columbia Phonograph Company, one of the original parents of Columbia Records, had, in the 1920s, grown rich during those Jazz Age boom times. In its heyday, it manufactured not only Columbia discs and phonographs, but also Silvertone and Supertone records for Sears, Roebuck and Company, from 1905 to 1931. In addition, from 1925 to 1931 it produced Diva Records for the W. T. Grant chain of five-and-ten-cent stores. Okeh Records, another division within Columbia, produced considerable jazz and dance music; it continued as a semi-autonomous branch from 1926 until 1935. The Columbia Phonograph Company's wealth allowed it to assist in the creation of the Columbia Broadcasting System in 1928. What no one foresaw, of course, was how radio would prosper, while the formerly thriving recording industry would stumble.

In an ironic turnaround, CBS in 1938 thus acquired not just the namesake Columbia label, but the entire American Record Company operation, giving NBC's primary rival a significant stake in the recording industry. CBS promptly sold one of its acquisitions, Brunswick, once ARC's prestige line, to American Decca in 1940. As a final indignity, CBS dropped the remaining ARC listings that same year, retaining only the Columbia imprint. In addition, it should be noted that Paramount Studios, another Hollywood giant, owned 49 percent of CBS as a result of a deal finalized in 1929; this arrangement further cemented the film-radio-recording connections and made the network a worthy rival to NBC.

Before falling on its own hard times, the American Record Company, by virtue of its sharp discounting—its discs sold from 25 to 50 cents apiece, and often retailed at three for a dollar—became a force in popular music. Formed in 1929 by the merger of Regal Records, Cameo Records, and the Scranton Button Company, the new firm built an extensive catalog overnight by taking over many smaller, financially straitened recording companies. ARC quickly acquired the inventories of independent labels like Banner, Conqueror, Medallion, Pathe (U.S. only), and Perfect. Some of these little-known labels also featured subsidiaries. Cameo owned Romeo Records, a brand sold by the S. H. Kress variety stores. It also held the Lincoln brand, a label that featured dance music and jazz.

To stay in business, these firms sometimes obtained masters from the bigger labels like Victor and Brunswick and stamped cheap copies from them. For ARC's Banner Records, almost the entire line consisted of reissues. To keep manufacturing costs at an absolute minimum, the smaller labels recorded on surfaces like waxed or chemically treated paper, and also on metal or tin foil. As might be expected, fidelity was minimal, and the recording seldom lasted much beyond a handful of plays. They also specialized in what the industry disingenuously called "hick discs," performances by little-known rural bands and singers playing songs that required no copyright fees. Conqueror Records, another ARC acquisition, typified the small recording company of that era and provides a good illustration of the practice: Sears, Roebuck sold the label's records from 1926 until 1942, and Conqueror utilized mail-order marketing, trafficking in rural areas of the country. By owning a number of these firms, the American Record Company became one of the largest distributors of phonograph records in the thirties, exceeded only by England's EMI group.

ARC's 1931 purchase of Brunswick Records from Warner Brothers finally gave the group a well-known label. Instead of pricing Brunswick selections at their prevailing 25- to 50-cent rates, ARC made Brunswick its prestige line and retailed the label at a premium 75 cents a disc. This move may have cost ARC some sales, but it gave the company stature in the market.

While the American Record Company wheeled and dealed, the other surviving record firms dropped artists, cut back on recording sessions, and reduced individual takes on a particular number to just one, provided no obvious defects could be detected. They also slashed prices for their products and experimented with various marketing schemes. Seventy-five-cent records went on sale at two for a dollar, and fifty-cent discs could be bought at three for a dollar. Victor, which had stubbornly held prices to its 1920's levels, created the Bluebird label in 1933 as a response to ARC's pricing policies; the new Bluebirds sold for thirty-five cents. Others struck deals with large retailers like Woolworth's and Sears, Roebuck and Company to sell miniature

Boasting a bargain price of fifteen cents and often retailed at newsstands, "Hit of the Week" records could be found between 1930 and 1932. Their "Durium" surface gave listeners three to five minutes of poorly recorded music and wore out quickly. With record sales down sharply during the Depression, they served as one of several attempts to lure buyers with cheap recordings. [Photograph by author; from the Bryan Wright Collection]

(eight inches in diameter, instead of the traditional ten) records of dance music for a dime. One label, Oriole Records, was owned by McCrory Department Stores, and could only be obtained at this chain.

Between 1930 and 1932, "Hit of the Week" Records tried selling discs at newsstands. The one-sided records, boasting a bargain price of fifteen cents and made of "Durium," a concoction of paper and resin, gave a listener three to five minutes of scratchy music. Aside from presaging radio's *Your Hit Parade* by a few years, "Hit of the Week" fared poorly.

Despite all the gloom and doom surrounding the recording industry, a few individuals saw prosperity beckoning and took advantage of it. In 1934, a British investor by the name of Ted Lewis (not to be confused with the popular entertainer of the same name) started American Decca, a new label and the offshoot of English Decca, a well-established label. Lewis persuaded Jack Kapp, then the head of Brunswick Records, to lead the new operation, and Kapp brought with him many of Brunswick's leading performers, including crooner Bing Crosby. American Decca also gained the catalog of Gennett Records in this move. An old (1917) label that had built a rich trove of blues and jazz sides, Gennett's list included the first recorded version of Hoagy Carmichael's classic "Star Dust" in 1927. To battle ARC's low prices, Kapp decided to sell Decca recordings for a bargain 35 cents, making them strong competitors in the marketplace. In a short time, Decca's cheap discs, along with their roster of stars, especially Crosby, made the company one of the sales leaders for the decade.[13]

"Race Records"

The Depression hurt jazz and black music particularly hard. Most of the small independent labels failed, which meant the disappearance of many companies that had recorded black musicians and catered to black audiences. Their recordings carried the term "race records," meaning that they usually could be obtained only in predominantly black neighborhoods. Larger distributors, fearful of a white consumer backlash, refused to carry them. Coupled with the restraints of Prohibition, the small clubs and bars that once dotted neighborhoods shut their doors, effectively closing another avenue for black musicians, and for musicians of every stripe as well. Not until the late 1930s and the explosive growth of swing (along with the popularity of jukeboxes) did musicians again find widespread employment opportunities.

The story of Black Swan Records, a subsidiary of Paramount Records (no connection to the movie studio), illustrates the dilemma of black musicians. The label had specialized in recording black artists, which meant Black Swan discs, or "race records," had little entrée into white markets. The Depression finally caught up with Black Swan in 1935, forcing it out of business just before swing brought about a renewed interest in jazz and dance bands. The label would, however, be reactivated in the early 1940s.

Swing and the Recording Industry

Swing did indeed prove the tonic the industry needed. It re-invigorated many struggling companies, especially the fortunes of three labels. Columbia (including its Brunswick and Okeh subsidiaries), Decca, and RCA Victor (including its Bluebird subsidiary) dominated the American recording field in the later years of the decade. Other companies continued to issue purely pop sides and music geared to more specialized tastes, but these three monopolized the big bands.

Ever optimistic, several new independents entered the growing field for swing and jazz. In 1938, Milt Gabler, the owner of New York City's Commodore Music Shop, a favorite hangout for jazz fans, created Commodore Records. Clearly jazz-oriented, the label survived, but remained popular primarily with dedicated collectors searching for specific artists or songs. Following a similar path, Blue Note Records came into being in 1939. Founded by Alfred Lion and Francis Wolff, Blue Note also catered to the true jazz aficionado. Neither label became a major player in the swing mass market, but instead remained on the sidelines, catering to the wants of specialists.

Record companies vied for recording rights to specific bands as swing captured the public imagination. The players found themselves in the position of rushing into recording studios and having to play a new number on first sight. This required a high level of professionalism and mastery of both music and instruments, something musicians had in remarkable quantity during this hectic decade. The vast majority of sidemen had studied hard and played with numerous aggregations, so reading new arrangements had become second nature. Recording four or more new sides in a single session of just a few hours' duration might be challenging, but in the Big Band Era seldom seemed impossible. In just a couple of takes (playing the same number two times, usually with only slight changes), a new classic might emerge, or certainly a recording suitable for airplay and wide distribution.

Because audio technology at that time lacked the sophistication later taken for granted, the bands recorded directly onto wax or acetate. Tape played no role, so splicing did not exist as an option, and digital editing had not entered even the most vivid imaginations of engineers; the take consisted of "all or nothing." More often than not, complete songs were recorded in a single session, often in memorable versions that have come down to the present as definitive renditions.

A popular hit promised big money to the band recording the preferred version, so arrangers worked hard to alter tempos, vocalists stylized their renditions, soloists improvised on the written score, and the leaders themselves added touches of their own. As a result, hit songs like "One O'Clock Jump" (1937; music by William "Count" Basie) and "I'll Never Smile Again" (1940; words and music by Ruth Lowe) might exist in several interpretations at the same time; it rested with the audience as to which version sold the best.

In the case of the two songs mentioned, "One O'Clock Jump" at first enjoyed its biggest sales by the Basie band, but their success proved short-lived. Instead of one overriding favorite, many bands—Harry James and Benny Goodman, for example—soon had competing versions, and they sold well also. Often the public liked a particular band, and individual songs carried less importance than the orchestra itself. In the case of "I'll Never Smile Again," the tune "belonged" to the Tommy Dorsey aggregation and his impressive new vocalist, Frank Sinatra. Other versions existed, but consumers demanded the Dorsey/Sinatra rendition.[14]

Jukeboxes

The etymology of "jukebox" remains a murky one. In West Africa, a "juke" meant a house of prostitution. With slavery, the word made its way to the United States and took on new meanings. In the South, a "juke" (sometimes spelled "jook") signified a dance hall, especially a lower-class one, and then even some of the dances themselves. To "juke" meant to dance, but in a suggestive way at a roadside joint. In the late 1920s and on into the 1930s, coin-operated record machines began to replace the small bands and combos that had traditionally played in these dance halls, or "juke joints." It did not take long for the word to make the transition from dance and locale to the machine supplying the music. A "jukebox" played in juke joints for juking. Over time, "jukebox" has clearly evolved into an innocent term with few connections to its colorful past. The manufacturers of these machines, in a futile attempt to disassociate their products from any such past, insisted on calling them "Multi-Selector Phonographs," "Automatic Coin-Operated Phonographs" or "coin machines," but the public stuck with "jukeboxes."

Regardless of any linguistic roots, crude jukeboxes first appeared in the 1880s. By 1920, these primitive forerunners had all but disappeared. Then, in 1921, a patent was issued for an efficient and durable record changer; by

1927, a coin-operated model had been perfected. The Automatic Instrument Company, or AMI, began to manufacture these early models. By the beginning of the 1930s, J. P. Seeburg, Rudolph Wurlitzer, and the Rockola (later Rock-Ola) Manufacturing Company had also entered the business.

In 1933, Americans rejected Prohibition in no uncertain terms; Repeal said people could legally consume alcohol once again. The reopening of lounges, bars, and nightclubs meant they had to have music, either live or recorded, and jukeboxes sprang up everywhere, becoming standard fixtures. They sported names like "Night Club," "Streamliner," "Singing Tower," "Throne of Music," and "Peacock," and appealed to a youthful market. They spread to ice cream parlors, soda fountains, and restaurants—places where music might boost business. Customers saw them as a form of cheap entertainment; proprietors saw them bringing in more customers.

About 25,000 jukeboxes could be found scattered across the country by the end of 1933. That number jumped to over 100,000 by the mid-1930s, 225,000 by 1937, and it just kept climbing: in excess of 400,000 jukeboxes played the latest hits to millions of listeners and dancers with nickels in their pockets (or six tunes for a quarter) when the thirties drew to a close. Coupled with the rise of swing and a limited economic recovery, jukeboxes had lost any negative connotations and could be found just about anywhere by 1940.

With their sinuous curves, shiny chrome and plastics, neon tubes and flashing lights, 1930s jukeboxes served as a kind of summation of the popular Streamline design of the era. They represented modern architecture, skyscrapers in miniature. More importantly, they made money, both for the establishments having them and for the music business in general. In the Swing Era, jukeboxes devoured over half of all records on the market and helped to encourage fads and fashions in music. Because of their ubiquity, they went a long way in determining a record's popularity.

For the record business, jukeboxes represented a godsend. These insatiable machines consumed 720,000 records a week, 30 million a year, toward the end of the 1930s, and went a long way toward saving the flagging record industry. Wurlitzer, the leading manufacturer of coin-operated machines, was turning out 45,000 a year by 1939, and its competitors boasted equally impressive numbers.

What sold on a jukebox got repeated—endlessly, both in its original format and by imitators. This led to repetition and musicians getting stuck in stylistic ruts. They had to keep sounding like their most recent hit, thus stifling creativity. But hidden benefits emerged for one group of musicians. Color-

By the mid-1930s, the jukebox had established itself as a ubiquitous part of the American music scene. From dilapidated road houses to ritzy nightclubs, the chrome and neon boxes dispensed the latest hits and favorites of audiences everywhere. In this 1939 photograph, the jukebox has replaced the live musicians, and someone even moved it to a prominent place in front of the bandstand. It appears the dancing couple voiced no objections. [Library of Congress, Prints & Photographs Division]

blind, jukeboxes provided black musicians the best possible outlet for a mass audience to hear their music. In its mechanical way, the jukebox served as an equalizer in a segregated world. Of course, they only played records, and so they replaced live musicians who might otherwise be performing at a dance hall or club. Like so much modern technology, a curse accompanied the blessing.[15]

Many musicians, along with songwriters, objected to the use of recordings on radio and, by extension, in jukeboxes. They felt—justly—that radio and coin-operated devices deprived both musicians and songwriters of income, since most of them received no royalties when stations played their recordings or a patron's nickel keyed a song. In an attempt to remedy the situation, ASCAP (the American Society of Composers, Arrangers, and Producers), an organization dedicated to protecting the performing rights of musicians and songwriters, stepped into this debate. Founded in 1913 to take advantage of revised U.S. copyright laws, ASCAP wanted to raise the licensing fees charged to radio stations for the privilege of playing music on the air. In late 1939, broadcasters retaliated by forming BMI (Broadcast Music Incorporated) as an alternative. This split would result in a long fight over musicians' rights, a recording ban, and finally some resolution in the mid-1940s. Another story, another decade, but its roots lay in the 1930s and the proliferation of both radio and recording.

Some mechanically reproduced music took an unusual turn in the thirties. In 1934, Muzak, a service that went directly to restaurants, dancehalls, factories, and offices, made its debut in Cleveland, Ohio. It piped in soothing background music with no attempt made to copy the latest hits or dance numbers. This consisted of packaged music just below the level of consciousness, a kind of subliminal sound massage, and it had little impact on the popular music business. Despite the Depression, music flourished during the 1930s, available to millions easily and cheaply.

2

Popular Hits and Standards

Although many people associate the 1930s with swing and all the dance bands of the time, the decade also stands as the golden age of American songwriting. During these turbulent years, composers and lyricists like Harold Arlen, Irving Berlin, Hoagy Carmichael, Duke Ellington, Dorothy Fields, George and Ira Gershwin, Jerome Kern, Jimmy McHugh, Cole Porter, Leo Robin, Richard Rodgers and Lorenz Hart, Harry Warren, and Alec Wilder collectively defined American popular music. And those names make up just the short list; many other distinguished songwriters also deserve a spot on any such compilation. They took the popular music format and turned it into an art form; at the same time, the big bands were creating dance classics with similar materials.

Almost weekly, it would seem, new songs appeared by these consummately talented people. Destined to become standards—songs known by a large audience that remain popular for generations—their compositions have endured, still vibrant for listeners of all ages. In 1930, the Gershwins penned "Embraceable You," Hoagy Carmichael "Georgia on My Mind" (lyrics by Stuart Gorrell), just as Rodgers and Hart put the finishing touches on "Ten Cents a Dance," and Cole Porter "What Is This Thing Called Love?" In 1935, Irving Berlin wrote "Cheek to Cheek," Vernon Duke composed "Autumn in New York," Harry Warren and Al Dubin collaborated on "Lullaby of Broadway," and Duke Ellington added "Solitude" to his repertoire. The sheer number and variety of songs that came along during the 1930s quickly grew to remarkable proportions. For whatever reasons, the decade produced some of the finest, most lasting, music in the history of American popular song.

THE POPULAR SONG

The inroads of jazz, swing, and, later, rhythm 'n' blues and rock 'n' roll, cannot be denied, but for sheer longevity and uniformity, the American popular song remained recognizably unchanged for much of the twentieth century. Such classics possess a deceptively simple structure: almost always written in a verse-chorus form (see below), the verse sets the scene or poses a situation and then the chorus, or refrain, brings about a resolution. During the 1930s, jazz and swing, for all their appeal, had to adapt more to the verse-chorus format than it to them. In many ways, the thirties marked the apotheosis of the popular song in American musical culture.

As a rule, these songs are built on discrete units called *phrases*. Following a brief instrumental opening, listeners will usually hear an introductory section, or *verse*, normally a sixteen-bar phrase. The verse introduces the tempo, or rhythm, of the music, although it will not be found in every instance, since some songwriters chose deliberately to omit it. The verse section was, however, extremely important to most songwriters and lyricists of the 1930s; what it establishes will be expanded and/or resolved in the succeeding phrases, or *choruses*.

When dealing with words set to music, many composers and lyricists use the verse for an introductory comment, a kind of preface to the story the choruses, or refrain, will cover. Many contemporary listeners, however, do not know these little stories that so often opened the standards of the decade. The three- to four-minute time constraints of radio broadcasts and recordings, coupled with a sharp drop in sheet music sales, brought about a decreased emphasis on the verse, so what people heard might not include all that the songwriters had originally included. In time, popular songwriting witnessed the decline, if not outright disappearance, of the verse. By the last years of the twentieth century, few popular songs deemed the verse a necessary component in musical structure. Today, many orchestras and performers, especially when recording a song, leave out the opening verse, preferring to move straight to the choruses. Although radio and recording might dictate this omission, a simple, crowd-pleasing reason also plays an important role in this decision: the choruses, or refrain, contain those lyrics and melody most likely to be remembered by listeners. The song usually concludes with a *coda*, a short summing-up of what has gone before.

For example, the classic Hoagy Carmichael (music)/Mitchell Parish (lyrics) "Star Dust" (1927, 1931), clearly illustrates this basic verse/chorus construction.

First comes the verse, in which an unresolved situation is described:

> . . . And now the purple dust of twilight time
> Steals across the meadows of my heart,
> High up in the sky the little stars climb,
> Always reminding me that we're apart.
>
> You wandered down the lane and far away,
> Leaving me a song that will not die,
> Love is now the star dust of yesterday,
> The music of the years gone by.

Those eight lines complete the verse. It is then followed by the *refrain*, in this case consisting of two choruses. They contain the familiar melody and lyrics that people everywhere recall, and the situation presented in the above verse reaches a resolution.

> Chorus #1:
>> Sometimes I wonder why I spend
>> The lonely night
>> Dreaming of a song?
>> The melody haunts my reverie,
>> And I am once again with you,
>> When our love was new,
>> And each kiss an inspiration,
>> Ah, but that was long ago:
>> Now my consolation
>> Is in the star dust of a song.
>
> Chorus #2:
>> Beside a garden wall,
>> When stars are bright,
>> You are in my arms,
>> The nightingale tells his fairy tale
>> Of paradise, where roses grew.
>> Tho' I dream in vain,

In my heart it will remain:
My star dust melody,
The memory of love's refrain.

At the completion of the second chorus ("The memory of love's refrain"), many recorded versions of the song then instrumentally repeat the music of the choruses, and this repetition serves as the coda, the summation of what has gone before.

As to the age-old question, "Which came first, words or music?" the answer depends on who composed the music and who wrote the lyrics. For "Star Dust," when Hoagy Carmichael first composed the melody in 1927, he created a slightly up-tempo piece that contained no lyrics. A modest success at best, this original version certainly cannot be thought a standard. In 1931, lyricist Mitchell Parish slowed down the tempo of Carmichael's tune and contributed the now-famous words, making it into a contemplative love song. Only then did "Star Dust" start its climb toward immortality as a great American standard.

The creative process thus varies among individuals and writing teams. For example, when working on a production for stage or screen, a playwright or a director will have an idea or a concept. He or she might ask a composer to score some "sad" (or "happy," "inspirational," etc.) music. If the songs include vocal components, a lyricist then fits appropriate words to them.

On the other hand, a lyricist may have some lines that need music to accompany them. In that case, the writing of the music follows the words. Occasionally—Irving Berlin or Cole Porter, for example—the same person handles the two tasks. No definitive answer can be given, but for the 1930s there existed no shortage of either inspired music or equally inspired words.

In popular American song, therefore, lyricist and composer stand as co-equal. Many of the great songs of the 1930s owe their longevity to an outstanding composer–lyricist team: Richard Rodgers and Lorenz Hart (the Rodgers and Hammerstein collaboration would come later), George and Ira Gershwin, Jerome Kern and Dorothy Fields, Harold Arlen and Johnny Mercer, Fats Waller and Andy Razaf, James Van Heusen and Johnny Burke, and so on through a distinguished line of such pairings. But whether one creator or two, the abundance of enduring songs during the decade serves as a testament to the musical richness of the period. That so much popular music achieved a stunning level of variety, sophistication, and maturity while employing the same format as a starting point suggests that these writers found, within its confines, ample room to improvise, to bend the "rules," so to speak, and put their personal stamp upon their creations.[1]

Creating Popular Hits

Economic ups and downs color the history of American music in the early decades of the twentieth century. Popular songs usually came from one of four sources: the theater (i.e., musicals), sound movies (musicals again), dance bands, and Tin Pan Alley. This last term identifies a geographical section of New York City where composers, lyricists, arrangers, and song pluggers (people trying to sell a particular song or an idea for one; see Chapter 3 for more on this profession) congregated and interacted with various music publishers. Geographically, the "alley" signified Manhattan's Twenty-eighth Street, the section between Fifth Avenue and Broadway. As these people mingled, often in tiny offices equipped with no more than a desk, a couple of chairs, and an upright piano, a body of popular music developed—indeed flourished—remarkably well.

In the Roaring Twenties, the hopes of independent composers and lyricists had never been higher; the decade witnessed the greatest number of popular songs published in history. But sheer numbers of songs do not guarantee hits, and this volume of music failed or survived not just on the whims of popular taste, but also on the effectiveness of distribution. As a rule, the products of Tin Pan Alley seldom enjoyed movie or stage performances, but relied instead on a direct connection with consumers for their success. These songs usually went straight into sheet music and recordings. If stores lacked sufficient copies, either printed or recorded, people would turn to something else. Keeping local outlets stocked with all the latest numbers could determine a tune's fate, not just public taste. As those in the business knew—or quickly learned—the public displayed little patience, and would turn to other music if it could not purchase a specific song.[2]

With the growth of commercial radio in the 1920s, the mix added airplay. Among those who labored in Tin Pan Alley, a widely held belief said that popular taste determined a hit; the public exercised free will and the merits of a piece of music decided its success or failure. In the 1930s, however, this somewhat naïve point of view underwent considerable revision, and radio in particular forced the reevaluation: well over 40 percent of American homes had receivers by 1930 and the percentage kept growing.

Most people saw radio as free; once the set had been purchased (no one thought much about the connections between radio usage and the monthly electric bill), the shows themselves cost nothing. On the other hand, sheet music and recordings cost money at the time of purchase. Because cash was scarce and had to be allocated to meet needs, people faced a heightened awareness about expenses. After the traditional food, clothing, and shelter, buying music, either printed or recorded, might be thought a luxury few families could afford. Thus the precipitous drop in sheet music and record sales, and the rise of radio as a primary purveyor of popular music.

Sound films also exerted an effect on the music business. Millions attended the movies each week, which meant a featured song reached an audience larger than anything previously envisioned. That exposure, coupled with repetitive airplay, could make the most innocuous tune a hit. Popularity begat popularity; songs became hits because millions of consumers knew about them, and they knew about them through radio and the movies.

In the case of songs written by tunesmiths working in the traditional Tin Pan Alley fashion—writing a song, finding a publisher, seeing it printed in sheet music form, and also getting it recorded—an important part of the process involved effectively "plugging" the composition. Many individuals earned their livings by song plugging. They circulated a new song among sheet music publishers and record companies, showed it to potential performers (vocalists, band leaders), visited as many radio stations as possible with recorded copies, and generally made the song known among their networks of contacts. As radio and movies took on increased importance in the success or failure of a song, the plugger's job assumed greater importance. Film studios had to be made aware of the song, and more stations required copies for airplay. With the rise of swing in the later 1930s, convincing noted band leaders to add the song to their repertoire also proved vitally important.[3]

For the 1930s, a typical week in the music business meant the release of some thirty-five to forty new songs. Figures collected by the Federal Communications Commission for 1938 indicated that, with any luck, a handful of tunes—maybe five to eight out of the total thirty-five or so—received a disproportionate amount of airplay. Over a year's time, the same statistics apply: a few songs, a tiny minority, received over 80 percent of all airplay. The remainder went into a kind of musical limbo, a place where only the most determined searchers could find them. Those looking for specific artists or specific versions of a song might locate what they wanted at a record store or

through friends who also collected music. Tunes that lacked any effective promotion simply disappeared in time, unheard and unsold.

Distribution and airplay therefore became key in a song's success or failure. Estimates suggest that the effective life of most new music ranged between ten and twenty weeks. A novelty number usually peaked more quickly
than a traditional romantic ballad, thus the disparity in time. If a tune did become a hit, it still possessed a limited lifespan. In the past, a hit might retain
its popularity for as long as eighteen months or so; by the 1930s, and with
the insistent repetition of radio, about four months served as the maximum
life for a number to be considered a hit. Anything "undiscovered" after twenty
weeks was probably doomed to obscurity. To become a hit also meant, within
those narrow limits, sales of 75,000 copies of sheet music and 250,000
records. For most of the decade, those in the business considered anything
that exceeded such modest totals as extraordinarily successful indeed.[4]

Other factors changed the face of American popular music. For the first
half of the 1920s, the rise of the phonograph signaled a proportionate decline
in the sales of sheet music. People listened to their favorites instead of playing them on home instruments. By the middle of the decade, the growing
popularity of radio cut into both sheet music and record sales. Improved technology, especially the introduction of electrical amplification, and widespread
prosperity gave a momentary boost to the recording industry, so that by the
end of the 1920s recordings again sold at a phenomenal clip, but sheet music
continued its slump. The onset of the Great Depression slowed the recording recovery, plunging the industry once more into a sharp decline. By 1933,
the depth of the economic downturn, record sales totaled only about $5 mil-
lion, a paltry sum compared to years past.

For the denizens of Tin Pan Alley, this situation spelled disaster. Those
consumers able to afford sheet music frequently demanded folios of songs
made popular by a particular radio or movie star, not necessarily the latest
hits. The same held true for recordings, although individual songs by particular singers or bands, not collections, drove the business. Oftentimes, the
music played on radio consisted of old favorites in new wrappings: vocalists
and orchestras performing the tried-and-true at the expense of fresh compositions. This situation created tough economic times for composers and lyricists attempting to make a living at their craft.

If the 1930s witnessed a decline in the output of Tin Pan Alley, an upsurge
in the production of songs for stage and screen, particularly the latter, coun-

terbalanced the situation. Hollywood, cranking out hundreds of new films each year, proved insatiable in its demands for music. Rather than relying on East Coast composers and lyricists, the studios bought established publishing firms and relocated them 3,000 miles west. In this way, they enjoyed the services of some of the best songwriters in the country, as well as access to the vast catalogs of already-established popular numbers these companies had produced over the years. And they thereby owned the rights to the music, an important financial consideration. The early 1930s found a number of old Tin Pan Alley firms with new quarters in the film capital. Back in New York, many of the remaining song publishers had to consolidate in order to stay profitable. An era had passed.[5]

A new generation of composers and lyricists, people like Arthur Freed and Nacio Herb Brown, Mack Gordon and Harry Revel, Leo Robin and Ralph Rainger, Sidney D. Mitchell and Lew Pollack, Ned Washington and Victor Young, rose to the challenge of scoring for films and not the traditional stage. Although the bulk of the era's movie music may not have achieved the distinction bestowed on many Broadway songs written at the same time, much of it stood a step or two above the usual pop tunes ground out for mass consumption.

Other events also changed the face of the music business. The rise of swing in the latter half of the decade meant that new music often originated not with old-fashioned songwriters, but with the bands themselves. As the many orchestras grew and competition stiffened, arrangers, those individuals who took the compositions of others and organized (i.e., arranged) them in a distinctive manner, achieved a new importance. They had the responsibility of creating music to fit the qualities of a particular orchestra or group, of giving an aggregation a singular sound. During the Swing Era, arrangers frequently emerged as important as the songwriters themselves (see Chapter 7 for more on prominent arrangers).

HITS AND STANDARDS

Over time, many songs have become "hits," and the supposition is made that people know the piece and have purchased the sheet music or a recording of the number in question. But hits tend to be ephemeral—although a few, to be sure, endure. They exist as the popular music of a given moment, music that enjoys a burst of popularity and then usually fades away. Guy Lom-

bardo and His Royal Canadians had a big hit in 1931 called "(There Ought to
Be) Moonlight Saving Time" (words and music by Irving Kahal and Harry
Richman). On the strength of Bing Crosby's singing, "Little Dutch Mill"
(1934; music by Harry Barris, lyrics by Ralph Freed) briefly reigned as a big
seller. Even a powerhouse orchestra like Glenn Miller's could have a hit with
"The Man with a Mandolin" (1939; music by Frank Weldon, lyrics by James
Cavanaugh and John Redmond). All three of these tunes have largely disappeared, momentary flashes in the musical firmament instead of lasting
melodies that continue to captivate listeners.

For all the songs that briefly made *Your Hit Parade*, there also exists a body
of popular music that never got designated as "hits," but music that has
somehow survived the passage of time and still attracts performers and listeners. These songs finally receive the highest accolade of all: they become
"standards." At the time of their composition and release, the majority of
songs recognized today as standards sold in far smaller quantities than might
be assumed. Instead, they insinuated themselves into the nation's musical
consciousness by virtue of lyrics, melody, and the overall quality of composition. Their audience eventually far exceeded anything that yearly sales figures
might suggest, and they carry over from year to year. A standard has stood
the tests of time.

As a rule, a hit gets associated with a particular performer; a standard, on
the other hand, may be performed by various musicians and yet retains its
popularity on its own merits. Think of "Star Dust" (1927, 1931; music by
Hoagy Carmichael, lyrics by Mitchell Parish); vocalists as diverse as Frank
Sinatra and Willie Nelson have sung its lyrics, bands from Artie Shaw to the
Dave Brubeck Quartet have tackled it instrumentally. Hundreds of interpretations of "Star Dust" exist, and no one singer, no one instrumentalist, can
claim an exclusive association with the song. The same case holds true for
"Dancing in the Dark" (1931; music by Arthur Schwartz, lyrics by Howard
Dietz), "Yesterdays" (1933; music by Jerome Kern, lyrics by Otto Harbach),
"September in the Rain" (1937; music by Harry Warren, lyrics by Al Dubin),
and dozens of other songs that today hold the honor of being standards from
the 1930s. Who first recorded it? Whose version sold the most copies? Whose
rendition is "best"? stand as academic questions that have little impact on the
enduring popularity of a standard.[6]

As a point of contrast, "When the Moon Comes Over the Mountain" (1931;
music by Harry Woods, lyrics by Howard Johnson) will always "belong" to
Kate Smith; it matters little that she died in 1986, and had not publicly per-

Kate Smith (1907–1986) reigned as the undisputed queen of the airwaves. She enjoyed almost immediate success on CBS radio, beginning in 1931 with *Kate Smith Sings*; she would continue with the network throughout the 1930s, earning the nickname "The Songbird of the South." "When the Moon Comes Over the Mountain" (1931; music by Harry Woods, lyrics by Howard Johnson) became her well-known theme song, but she achieved her greatest renown singing Irving Berlin's "God Bless America" (originally written in 1918); her energetic rendition made it an unofficial national anthem in the days before and during World War II. [Library of Congress, Prints & Photographs Division]

formed for ten years before that. Similarly, perhaps others have tried "Where the Blue of the Night (Meets the Gold of the Day)" (1931; music by Fred E. Ahlert, lyrics by Roy Turk and Bing Crosby), but the song remains irrevocably tied to Bing Crosby. On the instrumental side, "Sing, Sing, Sing" (1936; music by Louis Prima; arrangement by Jimmy Mundy) is so identified with Benny Goodman and his orchestra that few other bands have even had the temerity to attempt it.

Although many standards receive instrumental performances, a set of lyrics usually lurks at the back of the listener's mind. Some people recall a classic song because of its melody, others because of its words. When both work smoothly together, the two combine to trigger the memory. By extension, the same holds true for almost any song categorized as a standard; the lyrics may not always be sung, but they remain an integral part of the total work.[7]

When discussing the popularity of music from the early 1930s, accurate information is notoriously difficult to come by. As radio grew in popularity, something called "the Sheet" attained almost legendary status. Actually, several "sheets" existed, since they consisted of playlists cobbled together by *Variety* and *Billboard*, two music trade publications. They provided weekly tabulations of how many times the three major networks (NBC-Blue, NBC-Red, and CBS) played a song between 5:00 P.M. and 1:00 A.M. daily. Since the Sheets listed only those tunes receiving ten or more performances for the week, song pluggers strove to see that their particular artists and songs made these lists. Not terribly scientific, nor a real reflector of popular preferences, the Sheets nevertheless gave some indication of what songs received extensive network airplay.

At the same time the Sheets circulated, other sources tracking music included individual agencies like music publishers, periodicals, record companies and their distributors (record shops, department stores), radio stations, and even bars and restaurants with jukeboxes. All, however, shared a tendency to create impressionistic pictures of popularity. The rise of shows like *Your Hit Parade* and more specialized research provided the industry with some degree of statistical accuracy (see Chapter 1 for more on *Your Hit Parade*).

Perhaps the most scientific, and therefore the most reliable, among these efforts was the "Top 10," a list issued weekly by *Billboard* magazine that first appeared in 1940. This compilation replaced the so-called "Sheet." *Billboard*, widely read and respected, had been published since 1894; it first focused on the activities of carnivals, but it soon devoted more and more of its attention to the growing field of popular music, first covering sheet music, then vaude-ville, and adding radio in the early 1930s. As noted above, the magazine had begun tracking the airplay of pop songs, and added jukebox figures in 1938. Two years later, the magazine commenced publishing comprehensive charts that covered sheet music, disc jockey airplay, jukeboxes, and the retail sales of single records. Unfortunately too late for this study of the 1930s, the *Bill-board* "Top 10" nevertheless demonstrated the interest that had developed in accurately following the field of popular American music.[8]

In the year-to-year survey that follows, some of the major hits of the decade have been tracked, along with some of the enduring standards that also made a splash at the time of their release. Absent are many songs that appeared without any fanfare, songs that worked their way into popular memory and have survived to the present. Generally, these sleepers sold, but in a slow, steady way. The fable of the tortoise and the hare resembles the stand-off be-tween most standards and pop hits: the hare creates a lot of fuss and garners immediate attention, but standards, like the tortoise, slowly make their way, gaining new listeners here and there, and finally end up far ahead of the hits. It all occurs in a process that takes time.

REPRESENTATIVE HIT SONGS OF THE DECADE

1929

Most of 1929 basked in prosperity; not until October did the infamous Crash occur. It therefore may come as no surprise that "Tip-Toe Thru the Tulips with Me" (music by Joe Burke, lyrics by Al Dubin), an innocuous lit-tle love song, ranked as the biggest single hit of the year. Audiences first en-countered "Tip-Toe Thru the Tulips with Me" in the film *Gold Diggers of Broadway* (1929). An indicator of things to come and the first of several such films, *Gold Diggers of Broadway* also brought about widespread familiarity with the term "gold digger," a phrase dating from the 1900s that describes a woman out to snare a wealthy man.

Another inoffensive number called "Honey" (1928; words and music by Seymour Simons, Haven Gillespie, and Richard A. Whiting) claimed second place. Released as both a recording and sheet music, the recorded version fea-tured Rudy Vallee, one of the most popular vocalists of the decade, crooning the song. The tune's primary distinction rests with the fact that "Honey" came from neither a play nor a movie. (For more on Vallee, see Chapter 1.)

For the remainder of 1929, several future classics failed to enjoy that brief moment of public acclaim that distinguishes the hit from the standard. As noted, hits tend to have little staying power, whereas standards may not be chart-busters, but instead survive over the long haul. For instance, comedian Eddie Cantor's interpretation of "Makin' Whoopee!" (1928; music by Walter Donaldson, lyrics by Gus Kahn) has come down to the present as his and his alone. But in 1929 it ranked sixteenth for the year, not a bad showing, but far behind the leaders.

Similarly, the Fats Waller/Andy Razaf standard, "Ain't Misbehavin'," finished 1929 at twenty-eighth place, but has long since established itself as one of the all-time classics, especially in the realm of jazz piano. Throughout the song lists of the 1930s, this kind of story gets repeated over and over again. A fickle public often does not recognize greatness at the moment, but usually redeems itself by virtue of continuing sheet music and record sales.[9]

1930

The leading song of 1930, the year the Great Depression began to affect every aspect of American life, hardly serves as a sociological commentary on the economy. "Stein Song," from the University of Maine (1910; original music by E. A. Fensted in 1901, words by Lincoln Colcord), led the way for the year, a tune as far removed from topicality as could be. Another vehicle for crooner Rudy Vallee, it revolved around drinking and college life, and perhaps reflected a lingering escapism more appropriate to the 1920s and the Jazz Age than to the grim 1930s. But that in itself might constitute a muted response to the times.

"Dancing with Tears in My Eyes" contained music by Joe Burke and lyrics by Al Dubin, the same team that had created "Tip-Toe Thru the Tulips with Me" the previous year. Performed by the Nat Shilkret band, this romantic number followed "Stein Song" in popularity. A bit more serious than Rudy Vallee's hit, it nonetheless avoided anything topical, instead focusing on the eternal problems faced by lovers.

An economic downturn hardly provides fertile ground for composers and lyricists. Since popular music mainly functions to entertain, it would take a daring (or cynical) songwriter to attempt anything topical. But a tiny minority nevertheless tried commenting on the Great Depression, usually in metaphorical terms. Sharp-eared listeners, however, immediately picked up on the real subject matter, or what they interpreted the metaphors to mean.

"Happy Days Are Here Again" definitely were not yet here again when this Milton Ager (music) and Jack Yellin (lyrics) number achieved hit status in 1930. Popular in the depths of the Depression, it challenged any pessimism growing out of the national economic collapse. Determinedly cheerful, this upbeat number came to be the theme song of the resurgent Democratic Party and President Roosevelt's New Deal. [Photograph by author; from the Bryan Wright Collection]

For example, lyricist Jack Yellin (1892–1991) has come down to the present as the author of the ironic words to "There's No Depression in Love" (1931; music by Dan Dougherty) and "Happy Days Are Here Again" (1929; music by Milton Ager). "There's No Depression in Love" soon disappeared, but "Happy Days Are Here Again" has enjoyed a completely different history. Yellin and Ager actually wrote the song months prior to the great Crash of October 1929, planning to use it as filler for a film called *Chasing Rainbows.* The movie ultimately got shelved, but in the meantime "Happy Days Are Here Again" took on a life of its own, eventually becoming a 1929–1930 hit. Its seemingly upbeat lyrics laughed off the Depression; better days had to be coming. Of course, those same lyrics could be read as sarcastically acknowledging the hopelessness of the situation, but most people chose not to interpret them that way. In fact, the Democratic Party, under the leadership of Franklin D. Roosevelt, gave the tune a new lease on life two years later. The party adopted the song as its theme in the 1932 election—happy days really are here again!—and even today, loyal Democrats haul out the old warhorse and play it for their conventions and gatherings.

1931

By 1931, unemployment had soared to almost 16 percent of the work force, and the enormity of the crisis struck home with citizens everywhere. "Life Is Just a Bowl of Cherries" (1931) spoke to the era in ironic terms. It first appeared in the *George White Scandals, 11th Edition* (1931–1932), a periodic Broadway revue. The popular Ethel Merman sang it, and its infectious lyric—life *will* get better—struck a responsive chord. Consumers bought both the sheet music and recorded versions.

> "Life Is Just a Bowl of Cherries"
> Music by Ray Henderson, lyrics by Lew Brown
>
> Life is just a bowl of cherries;
> Don't make it serious;
> Life's too mysterious.
> You work, you save, you worry so,
> But you can't take your dough when you go, go, go
> So keep repeating it's the berries;
> The strongest oak must fall.
> The sweet things in life
> To you were just loaned,
> So how can you lose what you've never owned?
> Life is just a bowl of cherries,
> So live and laugh at it all.

Other "happy" songs that challenged these dark days included "Get Happy" (1930; music by Harold Arlen, lyrics by Ted Koehler), a tune that advised listeners to forget their troubles and simply sing "Hallelujah!" Similarly, "On the Sunny Side of the Street" (1930; music by Jimmy McHugh, lyrics by Dorothy Fields) first appeared in *Lew Leslie's International Revue* for that year. "I Found a Million Dollar Baby—In the Five and Ten-Cent Store" (1931; music by Harry Warren, words by Billy Rose and Mort Dixon) showed up in *Billy*

Rose's Crazy Quilt (1931); its bouncy lyrics suggested that being down at the heels could not quench love.

The biggest hit of 1931, however, ignored all that. A Spanish-influenced tune, "The Peanut Vendor" (1930; music by Moises Simons, lyrics by Marion Sunshine and L. Wolfe Gilbert)—it carried an original title of "El Manisero"—received a performance by the hitherto unknown Don Azpiazu. A flash in the pan for Azpiazu, it nonetheless had people trying out some unfamiliar Latin steps on the dance floor.

The peppy "Peanut Vendor" competed with a syrupy ballad for the public's favor. "Goodnight, Sweetheart" (1931; words and music by Ray Noble, James Campbell, and Reg Connelly) closed many a dance, especially in the recorded version by Guy Lombardo and His Royal Canadians. Originally introduced in *Earl Carroll's Vanities* that year, it has of course become the immediately recognizable final number for dance bands ever since.

A special musical event also occurred on March 3, 1931, when the U.S. Congress declared "The Star-Spangled Banner" the National Anthem. Written in 1814 by Francis Scott Key to the tune of "To Anacreon in Heaven," its selection reflected a desire for national unity in troubled times. Two other contenders vied for the title: "America" (1832; words by Samuel Francis Smith, set to "God Save the King," attributed to Henry Carey) and "America the Beautiful" (1895; words by Katherine Lee Bates, set to the tune of "Materna" by Samuel Augustus Ward).

Had the competition been held a few years later, Irving Berlin's "God Bless America" might well have won. In 1918, at the close of World War I, Berlin wrote the number for a musical entitled *Yip, Yip, Yaphank*. He dropped it from the score and it languished in his files for twenty years. In 1938, with World War II on the horizon, he dug it out and gave the popular singer Kate Smith exclusive rights to the song. For his part, Berlin turned over any royalties he might receive to the Boy and Girl Scouts of America. Smith's strong, optimistic rendition of the song lifted people's spirits, and "God Bless America" emerged as a kind of second, unofficial national anthem.

1932

Only a few songs looked at the darker dimension of the Depression, and one 1932 composition in particular stands out. A powerful story of confusion and loss unfolds in "Brother, Can You Spare a Dime?"

"Brother, Can You Spare a Dime?"
Music by Jay Gorney, Lyrics by E. Y. Harburg

Once I built a railroad, I made it run
Made it race against time
Once I built a railroad, now it's done
Brother, can you spare a dime?

Once I built a tower up to the sun
Brick and rivet and lime
Once I built a tower, now it's done
Brother, can you spare a dime?

Once in khaki suits, gee we looked swell
Full of that Yankee-Doodly-dum
Half a million boots went sloggin' through Hell
And I was the kid with the drum

Say, don't you remember, they called me "Al"
It was "Al" all the time
Why don't you remember, I'm your pal
Say buddy, can you spare a dime?

Originally featured in a short-lived musical called *New Americana* (1932), not many people saw singer Rex Weber perform "Brother, Can You Spare a Dime?" in the stage production. Millions, however, eventually heard Bing Crosby's recorded rendition, and the number stood among the top twenty songs of 1932.

Ted Lewis, the veteran vaudevillian, also had a surprise hit in 1932 with "In a Shanty in Old Shantytown" (music by Little Jack Little and John Siras, lyrics by Joe Young), the second-place finisher. It had appeared in the film *Crooner*. Despite the very real existence of shanties in Depression-era America, this particular song had nothing in it about poverty, other than the stereotyped image of the happy-go-lucky poor. Chances are, no one regarded the tune as subversive, but instead thought of it as a nostalgic look back to simpler, less threatening, times.

For much of 1932, people hummed the irresistible, pulsating melody of Cole Porter's "Night and Day," the top-ranked song of the year. It had been an important part of the play *Gay Divorce* (1932), and Fred Astaire, the popular dancer and vocalist, sang it on Broadway and provided the recorded rendition so vital to the success of the song. In the 1934 movie adaptation, *The*

Gay Divorcee, Astaire got to reprise the tune (see Chapter 3 for more on Porter and Astaire).

Part of this obliviousness toward the economic crisis came about because the focus of American popular music narrowed during the 1930s. The songs might grow in sophistication, but the subject increasingly became that of romantic love. Very little music that reached large audiences addressed the issues of the day; instead, it talked of romance and relationships. The Depression seemingly preoccupied everyone but songwriters.

1933

In 1933, cartoonist Walt Disney released a movie short entitled *The Three Little Pigs*. As cartoons go, it serves as an amusing retelling of the classic children's tale, but does not rank with his later classic animated features like *Snow White and the Seven Dwarfs* (1937) or *Fantasia* (1940). But *The Three Little Pigs* contains a classic all its own on the soundtrack: "Who's Afraid of the Big Bad Wolf?" (music by Frank E. Churchill, lyrics by Ann Ronell). Another Depression-era anthem, just like 1932's "Brother, Can You Spare a Dime?" the song presents a jauntiness missing in the weariness of the Gorney/Harburg work. Reports suggest that *The Three Little Pigs* showed in more theaters across the nation than any other film.

Only a year separates the two compositions, but "Who's Afraid of the Big Bad Wolf?" posits the idea that by working together, people can conquer any outside threats, in this case, the marauding wolf, who clearly represents the Depression. Not surprisingly, both the song and the cartoon came out at the time Franklin D. Roosevelt had taken office and was establishing the New Deal. Hopes ran high the new administration could somehow overcome the economic chaos in which the country found itself, and that if all the alphabet agencies and legislative groups worked in harmony, they could jointly build a sturdy foundation and lead the nation to recovery.

Other attempts at topicality include "Are You Makin' Any Money?" (1933; words and music by Herman Hupfield), but the tune went nowhere, suggesting the public did not want too many musical reminders about the crisis. Hupfield had previously written "Sing Something Simple" in 1930; he went on to compose "When Yuba Plays the Rhumba on the Tuba," a minor hit in 1931, and "Let's Put Out the Lights and Go to Sleep," another small hit from 1932. Despite these less than smashing successes, Herman Hupfield

(1894–1951) will endure in the annals of American popular song. He wrote the music and lyrics for "As Time Goes By," the romantic song featured in the movie *Casablanca*, a 1942 production. Few people realize Hupfield composed "As Time Goes By" in 1931 as part of a play entitled *Everybody's Welcome*. The play proved a moderate success (139 performances), but "As Time Goes By" fell by the wayside of forgotten songs. The music got recorded a few times in the 1930s, most notably by Rudy Vallee, but thanks to the Humphrey Bogart–Ingrid Bergman pairing in *Casablanca*, it will probably live forever as a soundtrack classic. Thus did a 1930s song emerge as a major hit of World War II.[10]

At another end of the musical spectrum altogether, a Western-tinged lament entitled "The Last Roundup" (1933; words and music by Billy Hill) topped the list of popular songs for 1933. Better known to many as "Git Along, Little Dogie," this big hit had absolutely nothing to do with the Depression, Broadway, or the movies, although after its success it would be interpolated into the score for the 1934 edition of *Ziegfeld Follies*. At the time, most people treated Western tunes as a kind of subcategory of popular American music, and so the success of "The Last Roundup" must be seen as a momentary fluke. George Olsen, a little-known singer, had the biggest hit for the number, but Guy Lombardo and His Royal Canadians, Don Bestor, Bing Crosby, and Victor Young also competed for listeners with the same melody. That so many people would record a single song suggests the popularity it enjoyed, but it also presaged an awakening of interest in Western themes that would continue to grow throughout the decade.

One of those numbers destined for the "standards" category occupied second place. Composer Harold Arlen penned "Stormy Weather" in 1933 for a semi-annual revue called *Cotton Club Parade*. Ted Koehler added the pessimistic words, and bandleader Leo Reisman performed the instrumental duties on record—with Arlen himself doing the vocal. But "Stormy Weather," unlike "The Last Roundup," proved no passing phenomenon. More durable than a single interpretation, Ethel Waters, who had sung it in the show, released her vocal version and created a classic. Duke Ellington provided a reading, as did Guy Lombardo and Ted Lewis. The tune had taken off, selling almost 8,000 copies a week, and becoming one of 1933's biggest sellers. Paramount Pictures even asked Ellington to film a short featuring the song, which resulted in *A Bundle of Blues* (1933), with the band's Ivie Anderson doing the vocal on screen.

Since 1933 marked the depth of the Depression, with unemployment hovering at 25 percent and bread lines a fact of life in many cities, the lyrics to "Stormy Weather" can be read as a commentary on the times and not just as another song about unrequited love. In that interpretation, the stormy weather of the title becomes the unending Depression and all the hardships it brings to people. Either as love song or topical observation, the number appealed to a large, diverse audience, and it has since become a standard for several generations of vocalists.

1934

Bing Crosby, one of the most important entertainers of the decade, demonstrated his popularity by claiming both first and second places in the hits for 1934. His version of "June in January" (from the 1934 film *Here Is My Heart*, words and music by Leo Robin and Ralph Rainger) claimed the coveted top position, and his "Love in Bloom" (from another 1934 film, *She Loves Me Not*, words and music again by Robin and Rainger) took #2. If that were not enough, Crosby also occupied #7 with "Little Dutch Mill" (music by Harry Barris, lyrics by Ralph Freed), #24 with "Good Night, Lovely Little Lady" (music by Harry Revel, lyrics by Mack Gordon), and #32 with "Love Thy Neighbor" (from the film *We're Not Dressing*, music by Harry Revel, lyrics by Mack Gordon). So it would go for Crosby the remainder of the decade: top hits followed by several also-rans. Almost anything he recorded climbed the charts, and he cut some 500 sides in the period 1929–1940 alone.[11]

Another important entertainer from the period was Shirley Temple (b. 1928). Not yet a teenager during the 1930s, Temple annually ranked as one of the most popular stars in Hollywood, and she served as the focus of a nonstop marketing extravaganza of dolls, toys, clothing, and books. Her celebrity carried into the recording studio; songs from her movies usually sold well. In 1934, she failed to make the year's charts, but she nonetheless performed a song that has become a classic for her: "On the Good Ship Lollipop" (1934; music by Richard Whiting, lyrics by Sidney Clare).

First heard in the film *Bright Eyes* (1934), "On the Good Ship Lollipop" allows the child star to mug and dance, as well as sing, talents her audiences loved. In all, Shirley Temple appeared in over forty movies during the decade—eleven in 1934 alone—and almost all of them did well at the box office. Her take-charge demeanor, coupled with simple plots that always allowed her to rise above any adversity, made Temple an ideal model for those troubled years. It might be escapism and hokum, but millions of moviegoers, young and old, flocked to her pictures.

As an aside for 1934, just before the Christmas holidays, singer/comedian Eddie Cantor introduced on his radio show a seasonal song entitled "Santa Claus Is Coming to Town" (music by J. Fred Coots, lyrics by Haven Gillespie). It has long since entered the rolls of timeless holiday hits, especially among parents who liked the theme running throughout the lyrics, imploring children everywhere to be on their best behavior. Bing Crosby's version, recorded some years later with the Andrews Sisters, gave him yet another big hit.

1935

Although he towered over most vocalists of the day, Bing Crosby did face some competition, Fred Astaire among them. Noted as a splendid dancer, Astaire could also sing, and well. He possessed a somewhat thin, high-pitched voice, but chose his songs carefully and displayed impeccable phrasing. Over time, he would introduce and record more standards than any other male vocalist, and major composers like Cole Porter, George Gershwin, and Irving Berlin often had him in mind when writing their music. As a result, in 1935 his rendition of "Cheek to Cheek" (from the film *Top Hat*, words and music by Irving Berlin), occupied the top slot. He also appeared at #31, with Berlin's "Top Hat, White Tie, and Tails" from the same movie.

During the same period, Crosby enjoyed four top recordings of his own: #15, "It's Easy to Remember" (from the film *Mississippi*, music by Richard Rodgers, lyrics by Lorenz Hart), #21, "Red Sails in the Sunset" (music by Hugh Williams, lyrics by Jimmy Kennedy), #25, "Soon" (1930; from the play *Strike Up the Band*, music by George Gershwin, lyrics by Ira Gershwin), and #37, "I Wished on the Moon" (from the film *The Big Broadcast of 1936*, music by Ralph Rainger, lyrics by Leo Robin). Not bad for someone who missed the year's top song.

Another escapist tune, "Isle of Capri" (1934; music by Will Grosz, lyrics by Jimmy Kennedy) came in at second place for 1935. A Tin Pan Alley composition, it endeared itself among both singers and musicians, allowing it to become, over time, a standard. It served as a hit for Ray Noble and his band, and also did well in a version recorded by the Freddy Martin Orchestra.

Farther down the ratings stood a song that would eventually eclipse "Isle of Capri" in long-term popularity: "Blue Moon" (1934; music by Richard

One of the finest dancers of the decade was also one of its most popular male singers: Fred Astaire (1899–1987). He danced his way to movie stardom during the 1930s, often teamed with Ginger Rogers. At the same time, Astaire showed an affinity for vocalizing many of his filmed dance numbers, and often they became hits under his name. [Library of Congress, Prints & Photographs Division]

Rodgers, lyrics by Lorenz Hart). The only non-movie, non-stage song penned by the songwriting team, it carries a curious history: Richard Rodgers originally wrote the melody for a tune he intended to title "Prayer." Plans had the song as a vehicle for Jean Harlow in a never-produced movie called *Hollywood Party*. The songwriters, however, did not discard "Prayer." Lorenz Hart wrote new lyrics and Shirley Ross performed it as "The Bad in Ev'ry Man" in *Manhattan Melodrama* (1934), a dramatic film. Still dissatisfied with their work, the two finally released the reworked song as a single entitled "Blue Moon" in late 1934.

Despite its lack of Broadway or Hollywood connections, "Blue Moon" slowly caught on. Eventually, even Elvis Presley attempted this standard as one of his first recordings in 1954. For 1935, however, those who chose to perform "Blue Moon" helped markedly in shaping it into a classic. Glen Gray and Benny Goodman, both up-and-coming bandleaders, led large aggregations that played for dancing and often featured mid- to up-tempo numbers with a decided jazz, or swing, flair. Both bands enjoyed success with "Blue Moon," their renditions hinting at things to come in dance music.

1936

With his omnipresent pipe, hat, and casual air, Bing Crosby continued his dominance in popular music. He held the year's #1 position with "Pennies from Heaven" (from the 1936 film of the same name; music by Arthur Johnston, lyrics by Johnny Burke), along with #30, "I'm an Old Cowhand" (1936; words and music by Johnny Mercer) and #33, "Robins and Roses" (1936; music by Joe Burke, lyrics by Edgar Leslie). Not quite so mushy as many of the things Crosby recorded, "Pennies from Heaven" has become a favorite of vocalists since its release.

Not to be outdone, Fred Astaire held four out of the top forty slots for the year, recording two numbers from the 1936 movie *Swing Time*, #3, "The Way You Look Tonight" and #6, "A Fine Romance" (both with music by Jerome Kern, lyrics by Dorothy Fields). He also had two hits from 1936's *Follow the Fleet*, #28, "I'm Putting All My Eggs in One Basket" and #32, "Let Yourself Go" (both with words and music by Irving Berlin). The Academy Award for Best Song in 1936 also went to "The Way You Look Tonight."

The #2 slot went to "Goody Goody," a Matty Malneck composition, with lyrics by Johnny Mercer. Benny Goodman, by this time the leader of one of the most successful and popular big bands, cut "Goody-Goody" and featured his fine vocalist, Helen Ward, on the recording. Well received by an increasingly swing-conscious public, its prestigious #2 position reflected a successful year for Goodman and his orchestra. Before the year had drawn to a close, he would occupy eight additional slots on the listings, ranging from a restrained "These Foolish Things Remind Me of You" (#16; from the 1935 play *Spread It Abroad*, music by Jack Strachy and Harry Link, lyrics by Holt Marvell) to an up-tempo cut of "You Turned the Tables on Me" (#22; from the film *Sing, Baby, Sing*, music by Louis Alter, lyrics by Sidney D. Mitchell). Both of these recordings also included vocals by Helen Ward, an indication of the growing importance a good vocalist had with a band.

While Messrs. Crosby, Astaire, and Goodman accumulated hit after hit, a 1936 novelty song also sold records by the thousands. The leaders of a small swing group, trumpeter Ed Farley and trombonist Mike Riley, wrote an infectious little number entitled "The Music Goes 'Round and Around." Red Hodgson concocted the silly lyrics. The music going "'round and around" refers to the music traveling through the sinuous curves of a French horn. Farley and Riley usually performed it with exaggerated gestures, concluding with the idea that the sound "comes out here" in the bell of the instrument. First issued on the new Decca label, the number proved an instant hit, selling over 100,000 discs in its first year of release. A kind of swing tune, it caught the public fancy, and even sheet music sales boomed as people played it at home. The song also had staying power, an important factor in the usually ephemeral music business, and it kept on selling, enough so that Hollywood rushed out a movie with that title late in the year. The popularity of "The Music Goes 'Round and Around" also presaged the coming Swing Era with its up-tempo rhythms.

1937

Virtually all the major hits for 1937 involved bands, and usually big, swing-oriented ones, with one exception: Bing Crosby. No matter how trite the song, when he recorded it, people listened—and bought. Thus "Sweet Leilani" (words and music by Harry Owens), about as superficial as pop music can be, took top honors, as did five additional songs by the popular crooner. "Sweet Leilani," a Hawaiian-inflected trifle from the movie *Waikiki Wedding* (1937), walked off with the Academy Award for Best Song in 1937, and Crosby's recording of it went to the top, eventually selling over 1 million copies. Other songs, possibly worthier ones, offered some stiff competition: Fred Astaire had recorded "They Can't Take That Away from Me" (music by George Gershwin, lyrics by Ira Gershwin) from the 1937 film *Shall We Dance*, and it too received a nomination. Today, "Sweet Leilani" has been largely forgotten, whereas "They Can't Take That Away from Me" has certainly attained standard status.

"Once in a While" (1937; music by Michael Edwards, lyrics by Bud Green), in a lush arrangement by the Tommy Dorsey band, took second place. Dorsey also captured the #3 position with "The Dipsy Doodle" (1937; words and music by Larry Clinton), a peppy little tune that likewise provided hits for bandleader Russ Morgan and composer/leader Clinton. Ironically, Larry Clinton had created "The Dipsy Doodle" as his own band's theme, but he could never achieve the commercial success with it that Dorsey and Morgan enjoyed. Dorsey, riding on a wave of hit songs, also listed four additional titles on the top-forty compilation for 1937.

Although most people usually do not think of comedian Bob Hope as a singer, he actually did a bit of passable vocalizing in several of his film efforts during the 1930s. When cast in the movie *Ziegfeld Follies of 1936*, he got to perform a number entitled "I Can't Get Started" (1936; music by Vernon Duke, lyrics by Ira Gershwin). Full of topical references, it proved an important stepping stone in his career. Hope's interpretation of the tune, however, never became a big hit; that honor rested with trumpeter Bunny Berigan, who recorded the song in 1937. Hope or Berigan, "I Can't Get Started" remains a classic of the era:

> I've flown around the world in a plane
> I've settled revolutions in Spain
> The North Pole I have charted
> Still I can't get started with you.
> On the golf course I'm under par
> Metro-Goldwyn has asked me to star
> I've got a house, a show place
> Still I can't get no place with you.
>
> You're so supreme
> The lyrics I write of you.
> Dream, dream day and night of you.
> And scheme just for the sight of you.
> But what good does it do?
> I've been consulted by Franklin D.

Even Greta Garbo had me to tea.
But still I'm broken hearted
I can't get started with you.

In 1929 I sold short
In England I'm presented at court
But you've got me downhearted,
'Cause I can't get started with you.

Hope introduced his signature theme song, "Thanks for the Memory" (1937; music by Ralph Rainger, lyrics by Leo Robin), in the film *The Big Broadcast of 1938* (released in 1937). He and Shirley Ross sing the number on screen, and their clever rendition made the song an instant hit. It impressed others, also; "Thanks for the Memory" earned an Academy Award for Best Song in the 1938 ceremonies.

The Big Broadcast of 1938 turned out to be so successful that Hope and Ross again shared the screen in the appropriately titled *Thanks for the Memory* (1939). The device of using the name of a hit song as a movie title was nothing new or original, although the song in question does not appear in the film. Instead, the two teamed up on "Two Sleepy People" (1938; music by Hoagy Carmichael, lyrics by Frank Loesser), a good song, but hardly "Thanks for the Memory." Audiences clearly enjoyed the Hope/Ross duets, because they were reunited yet a third time with *Some Like It Hot* (1939; retitled *Rhythm Romance* in deference to the popularity of swing). An innocuous little comedy that should not be confused with the hugely successful film of the same title that came out in 1959, it offered the two singing "The Lady's in Love with You" (1939; music by Burton Lane, lyrics by Frank Loesser).

The remainder of 1937's list contains one band after another; not even the reliable Fred Astaire, who had only one hit during the year (#30, "They Can't Take That Away from Me," with music by George Gershwin, lyrics by Ira Gershwin) could break the stranglehold. Guy Lombardo led the pack with six entries, Teddy Wilson had four, followed by Benny Goodman, Hal Kemp, and Eddie Duchin with two apiece—individually and collectively the bands ruled the day.

1938

A young singer who performed with Chick Webb's band at the Savoy Ballroom in New York's Harlem enjoyed a surprise 1938 best seller. The vocalist's name was Ella Fitzgerald and the song, a take-off on an old children's rhyme, was "A-Tisket, A-Tasket" (words and music by Ella Fitzgerald and Al Feldman). As the big bands proliferated, leaders like Webb, Teddy Wilson, Andy Kirk, Jimmie Lunceford, and Duke Ellington, along with singers such as Fitzgerald and Billie Holiday, attracted white audiences and consumers. The strict boundaries between white bands and their black counterparts had begun to crumble. Swing fans proved particularly color-blind; if someone could play good arrangements well, race played no role in popularity.

"My Reverie" (words and music by Larry Clinton) took the #2 position for the year. A smooth but swinging variation on Claude Debussy's "Reverie" (originally published in 1890) by the Clinton aggregation, vocalist Bea Wain sang Clinton's added lyrics. The adaptation of classical music to the sounds of a big band proved a popular practice during the 1930s. Tommy Dorsey jazzed up both Rimsky-Korsakov and Franz Liszt for, respectively, "Song of India" in 1935 and "Liebestraum" in 1937. Dorsey's brother Jimmy took a theme from Tchaikovsky's *Romeo and Juliet* and enjoyed some success in 1939 with "Our Love" (music adapted by Larry Clinton, lyrics by Buddy Bernier and Bob Emmerich). He then borrowed from Johann Strauss for a version of "The Blue Danube," also in 1939. Finally, Glenn Miller looked to Tchaikovsky—in this case, his Symphony No. 5—for 1939's "Moon Love" (music adapted by Mack David, lyrics by Mack Davis), and recorded an up-tempo version of Verdi's "Anvil Chorus" in 1940. For whatever reasons, sales suggested that people liked these adaptations of the classics, particularly the easily recognizable ones.

Hardly a classic in the traditional sense of the term, "Bei Mir Bist Du Schoen" (1932; music by Sholom Secunda, English lyrics by Saul Chaplin and Sammy Cahn), scored a big hit in 1938. Recorded by the Andrews Sisters (Patti, Maxine, La Verne), this traditional Yiddish song took off in the trio's rendition, making it to #7 for the year. In their happy, up-tempo style, the Andrews Sisters established themselves as the premier singing group of the late 1930s, a reputation they would burnish during the war years.

Not all the hit songs of 1938 came across as peppy, bouncy pieces. Composer Kurt Weill took a lyric written by dramatist Maxwell Anderson and created "September Song," a ballad about growing old destined to become an enduring standard. Originally a part of the play *Knickerbocker Holiday* (1938; music by Weill, libretto by Anderson), Walter Huston, a distinguished actor who lacked a singing voice, talked and sang his way through the number. But his rendition, despite other versions by dozens of "better" vocalists, remains the definitive one, as well as a surprise hit.

A 1938 picture of vocalist Ella Fitzgerald (1917–1996), just 21 years old at the time. Already something of a sensation because of her recording of "A-Tisket, A-Tasket" (1938; words and music by Ella Fitzgerald and Al Feldman), the 1930s marked the beginning of a legendary career; she would go on to international fame as one of the finest popular singers of the twentieth century. [Library of Congress, Prints & Photographs Division]

1939

In 1934, Peter DeRose composed a melody he called "Deep Purple" for solo piano. As far as commercial sales went, it did little. But songs never really die; they get rearranged, adapted, recast, and in the case of instrumentals, often have lyrics added. "Deep Purple" stands as a case in point. Lyricist Mitchell Parish, the same man who put words to Hoagy Carmichael's "Star Dust," refurbished DeRose's song and in the process created another standard. Larry Clinton's band had the #1 song of 1939 with their version of "Deep Purple." Vocalist Bea Wain took on Parish's new lyrics. The song assumed enough popularity that Jimmy Dorsey's rendition, with Bob Eberly doing the vocal honors, ranked #26 on the charts.

Hollywood gave the public two enormously popular movies in 1939: *Gone with the Wind* and *The Wizard of Oz*. Although "Tara's Theme" (1939; music by Max Steiner) has established itself over the years as enduring instrumental film music, nothing written for *Gone with the Wind* has ever equaled the remarkable music of *The Wizard of Oz*. The MGM studios hired composer Harold Arlen, along with the noted lyricist E. Y. Harburg, in 1938 to score the picture, paying the duo $25,000 in the process. This marked the first time a studio had employed a composer and lyricist in advance to do an entire feature-length film. MGM instructed them to match their music and lyrics to specific characters and situations, making the score more of an integral part of the total work, instead of simply functioning as background melodies.

As a result, audiences came away from the film humming "We're Off to See the Wizard," or "If I Only Had a Brain," or "Ding, Dong, the Witch Is Dead!" Most assuredly, those same audiences also recalled Judy Garland's touching interpretation of "Over the Rainbow," the centerpiece of the score, and a song thereafter associated with the young star. Almost dropped from the movie three separate times by MGM executives who feared it would slow the pace of things, "Over the Rainbow" went on to garner an Academy Award for Best Song and to become an enduring standard.

Since Judy Garland sang "Over the Rainbow" in the film, it might be assumed that her soundtrack version would be the big hit, but in the music business, the obvious is not always the case. The late 1930s marked the height of the Swing Era, and big bands ruled the charts. Thus, for "Over the Rainbow," Glenn Miller and his orchestra, with a vocal by Ray Eberle, occupied the #2 position. Miller's ensemble commanded such an enviable position with the record-buying public that they could place a total of seven songs on the listings for 1939. Bob Crosby, the younger brother of Bing, and his band also briefly made the charts with the Arlen/Harburg song. Ironically, the Judy Garland rendition, now accepted as the definitive one, did not break into the top-forty songs for the year. Only with time did her interpretation establish itself.

Novelty numbers have always attracted a share of the audience, as illustrated by the aforementioned "The Music Goes 'Round and Around" (1935; music by Ed Farley and Mike Riley, lyrics by Red Hodgson) and "A-Tisket, A-Tasket" (1938; words and music by Ella Fitzgerald and Al Feldman). Originally called "nut songs" or "nonsense songs," they gained a small measure of respectability with the term "novelty songs." The year 1939 proved no exception in this department. "Three Little Fishes" (1939; words and music by Saxie Dowell) came in as the big seller. Kay Kyser and his orchestra, with Ish Kabibble (Merwyn A. Bogue) singing this masterpiece of baby talk, ably accompanied by the Glee Club, Kyser's own vocal group, established the song as something of a minor classic for the era.

For the 1930s as a whole, the following titles (arranged chronologically) provide a representative sampling of novelty tunes:

"Goofus" (1932; music by Wayne King, lyrics by Gus Kahn)

"Inka Dinka Doo" (1933; music by Jimmy Durante, lyrics by Ben Ryan)

"Knock, Knock, Who's There?" (1936; words and music by Vincent Lopez, Bill Davies, Johnny Morris, and Jimmy Tyson)

"Flat Foot Floogie" (1938; words and music by Slam Stewart, Slim Gaillard, and Bud Green)

"Ti-Pi-Tin" (1938; music by Maria Grever, lyrics by Raymond Leveen)

Coleman Hawkins, a popular jazz saxophonist, recorded "Body and Soul" (1930; music by Johnny Green, lyrics by Edward Heyman, Robert Sour, and Frank Eyton) in October of 1939. Written for the 1930 Broadway play *Three's a Crowd*, "Body and Soul" had been put on records numerous times prior to Hawkins's interpretation. In the play, it gets performed as a "torch song"—a genre that usually has a vocalist lamenting a lost or departing love—in this case sung by the celebrated English actress Gertrude Lawrence. Such music usually receives a slow and sensual treatment, and "Body and Soul" proved no exception. With the word "body" and the implications of a physical (i.e., sexual) relationship, disc jockeys seldom mentioned the song's title when they played it on the air. The city of Boston, in a display of narrow-minded censorship, actually banned both the song and its title from the airwaves. But in Hawkins's instrumental rendition, a brilliant, transcendent improvisation on the melody, the tune took on new dimensions. No longer simply a torch song, it would become one of the most famous jazz solos of the decade, or any other decade, for that matter. It hinted at the modernism that would soon overtake jazz, and, to the surprise of everyone, it also became a hit.[12]

The remainder of 1939 saw the continued domination of popular music by swing and the big bands. Even the seemingly invincible Bing Crosby could manage only three hits in the rankings for the year. He recorded "What's New?" (1939; words and music by Bob Haggart and Joe Burke), a lovely ballad destined to be recorded again and again; "You're a Sweet Little Headache" (1938; music by Ralph Rainger, lyrics by Leo Robin), one of those trifles he frequently tackled; and "An Apple for the Teacher" (1939; music by James V. Monaco, lyrics by Johnny Burke), a novelty in which he teamed up with the popular Boswell Sisters. Instead, the listings tell it all: Tommy Dorsey, Benny Goodman, Glen Gray and the Casa Loma Orchestra, Kay Kyser, Glenn Miller, Red Norvo, Artie Shaw, and so on. Audiences and listeners wanted swing, they wanted the big bands, and individual entertainers at the time stood little chance with such a demanding public.

1940

With the end of the thirties and the onset of the 1940s, things changed little. Glenn Miller occupied the #1 position in the yearly ratings with his very danceable "In the Mood" (1939; music by Joe Garland, lyrics by Andy Razaf), a number that his arranger Jerry Gray made into a timeless Miller hit. Parts of this composition had surfaced off and on during the 1930s. The riff pattern had been played by trumpeter Wingy Manone in a jazz piece entitled "Tar Paper Stomp" (1930); bandleader Fletcher Henderson had arranged and performed its melodic line as "Hot and Anxious" in 1931, but neither of these antecedents ever caught the public fancy. Miller actually first recorded "In the Mood" in the fall of 1939, but the timing of its release made it a top song for 1940.

Fellow bandleader Artie Shaw stayed hot on Miller's heels. Enormously popular because of his 1938 smash "Begin the Beguine" (1935; from the play *Jubilee*, words and music by Cole Porter), he followed that number up with a string of hits, including the second-ranked song for 1940, "Frenesi" (music

One of the great—and most enduring—bandleaders of the Swing Era is clarinetist Artie Shaw (1910–2004). After playing with numerous orchestras during the first part of the decade, Shaw put together his own band and soon had climbed to the top in popularity. His 1938 rendition of Cole Porter's "Begin the Beguine" (composed in 1935 for the play *Jubilee*) serves as an anthem of swing's heyday, and has ensconced itself among the best-selling records of all time. [Library of Congress, Prints & Photographs Division]

by Albert Dominguez, lyrics by Ray Charles and S. K. Russell). Accompanied by a full string section, Shaw's lush arrangement brought legions of dancers to the floor.

Making his first—but certainly not his last—appearance on the charts was a young band vocalist working with the Tommy Dorsey Orchestra by the name of Frank Sinatra. Although Sinatra had first recorded with Harry James in 1939 doing "All or Nothing at All" (words and music by Jack Lawrence and Arthur Altman), this work lacked the impact of his later performances. He joined Dorsey in 1940 and cut his first sides with the band early that year. His interpretation of "I'll Never Smile Again" (1940; words and music by Ruth Lowe) skyrocketed him and the band to the #3 position. Sinatra/Dorsey also appeared on the charts at #34 with "We Three (My Echo, My Shadow, and Me)" (words and music by Dick Robertson, Nelson Cogane, and Sammy Mysels), a syrupy love song recorded later in 1940.

The overnight popularity of Sinatra presaged a groundswell of change that would alter the face of popular music as the 1940s progressed. Probably few realized it at first, but vocalists, male or female, had begun to upstage the bands. People now wanted their swing accompanied by singers. Even vocal groups—Glenn Miller had the Modernaires, Tommy Dorsey the Pied Pipers—came into intense favor. A look into the charts of popular hits for the year would still reveal a predominance of big swing orchestras, but most of the specific songs required a vocalist. The instrumental remained important, but audiences also expected numerous vocals along with their old favorites. In time, the singers themselves would begin to front many of the bands, and they certainly received top billing on record labels. But all that lay ahead in the 1940s.

Music from Broadway and Hollywood

Unlike today, a large proportion of the country's popular songs once originated on Broadway, home of the American musical theater. Only a small percentage of the population attended these shows, but effective promotion allowed many more people to experience this music. Most of the audience outside New York City knew about the latest theatrical hits through radio and recordings, although sheet music also remained a force, albeit a declining one. If a play was adapted for a movie version, then the potential audience size soared. But the real reason these songs gained popularity rests with the music itself. The Broadway songwriters of the 1930s turned out a remarkable number of enduring tunes that deserved popular attention. The corny, the mawkish, the just plain forgettable songs were there too, and some even had their moments, but when looking back over the decade, one cannot help but be struck with how many standards—those lasting melodies that come to mind, that continue to speak to the present—had their origins on stage.

Since the movie industry had by the late 1920s made the transition to sound, a growing proportion of hit tunes also came directly from film scores. Again, records and radio helped in the promotion of this music, but the quality of the songwriting also has to be a factor. Like their colleagues on Broadway, Hollywood tunesmiths created a lasting body of music. In many instances, the same people wrote for both film and stage, a coincidence perhaps, but a fortuitous one.

During this period, Tin Pan Alley, that old standby for popular songs, continued to churn out music, but its once-dominant influence waned. Then, as the swing phenomenon swept the country in the latter part of the thirties, everything changed; combos and big bands replaced Broadway, Hollywood, and traditional songwriters as the primary source of new hits. Record sales, while still dependent on radio, relied on the popularity of bands, bandleaders, and instrumentalists.

BROADWAY

The Great White Way suffered mightily during the Depression. With straitened times, theater attendance dropped, and not as many plays opened on Broadway as did during the prosperous 1920s. In 1930, twenty-eight musicals opened; by 1933, the total had dropped to only thirteen. Ticket prices stood at rock bottom in 1933, but attendance continued to be weak. The picture never really brightened for the remainder of the decade; in 1936, only ten new musical productions graced the stage—nothing like the halcyon days of just a few years earlier. Sound movies—"talkies"—further reduced the audience, with people choosing a cheap movie ticket over a more expensive one for a play. Then, with Hollywood's insatiable appetite for actors who also spoke (or sang) well, the pool of available stage talent shrank. No shows meant no work, and so actors, singers, composers, lyricists, and musicians once connected with the stage found greener pastures in Hollywood, and a virtual exodus of talented people moving from New York to California took place.

The flight to Hollywood hardly signified a cessation of creativity. A number of stage musicals that had the good luck to be produced in those grim days have gone down in theatrical history as towering examples of their art. Certainly, almost anything that Richard Rodgers and Lorenz Hart or George and Ira Gershwin collaborated on, or Jerome Kern, Cole Porter, or Irving Berlin penned, stood a better-than-average chance of being "big box office." These gentlemen, composers and lyricists of the first rank, had already established their reputations, and the Broadway musical stood as their forte.

Musicals generally come across to their audiences as bright and breezy, with a fair number of hummable tunes. They take people's minds off unemployment and discouraging economic news, and they have a better chance of succeeding than something that reinforces glum feelings. Thus it comes as no surprise that the bright, sophisticated songs the above writers and lyricists created easily found a receptive audience even in the worst years of the Great Depression. Other composers—for example, Harold Arlen, Vernon Duke, Jimmy McHugh, Ray Henderson, and Arthur Schwartz—could be mentioned, since they also achieved occasional successes during this time. Other lyricists—such as Lew Brown, Howard Dietz, Ted Koehler, Andy Razaf, and Jack Yellin—likewise spoke to audiences, but none could match the consistency achieved my Messrs. Berlin, Gershwin and Gershwin, Kern, Porter, and Rodgers and Hart.

Broadway mounted a total of 194 musicals between 1929 and 1940; of that total, thirty-nine, or 20 percent, boasted scores by these exceptional talents. Their collective contribution to popular American music during the 1930s has no equal, and the innumerable standards they penned continue to be played and sung generations after many of the plays in which their work first appeared survive only in memory. In light of such unparalleled success, a brief survey of their stage musicals from the 1930s should illustrate how many standards came from their collective talents and provide a sense of their importance in the history of American music.[1]

Irving Berlin (1888–1989)

Born Israel Baline in Siberia, Berlin and his family came to the United States in 1892, settling in New York City. Quickly acclimating himself to his new country, Berlin first made his mark on the American theatrical scene in 1908. He contributed a long-forgotten song, "She Was a Dear Little Girl," to an equally long-forgotten show, *The Boys and Betty*. But it proved a start, and Berlin quickly established himself as an up-and-coming young composer on Tin Pan Alley. By the time the 1930s rolled around, Berlin ran his own music publishing house, and he could claim authorship for dozens of songs.

Active on both Tin Pan Alley and Broadway during the early 1920s, Berlin turned to creating themes and interpolated songs for movies after the advent of sound in 1927. The theater called him back for a revue, *Face the Music*, in 1932. With a story (called a "book" in stage parlance) by playwright Moss Hart (not to be confused with the *Lorenz* Hart of the team of Rodgers and Hart), a gentleman with whom Berlin would work again, the show included "Let's Have Another Cup o' Coffee." A carefree little tune, it summed up the attitudes of many toward the Depression: When times are tough, have another cup of coffee and wait things out. It quickly became a favorite, suggesting the resiliency of Americans during crises.

Face the Music also included one of Berlin's less well-known pieces, the humorous "I Say It's Spinach (and I Say the Hell with It)." Hardly a standard, but nonetheless it gives an insight into the many directions his inventive mind might take.

In 1933, the low point of the Great Depression, Berlin again collaborated with Moss Hart for *As Thousands Cheer*. Designed like a daily newspaper, different sections of the revue are introduced by headlines, such as "Heat Wave Hits New York," or "Lonely-Heart Column." The lyrics are trenchant, and real, living people serve as the subjects. The butts of the play's satire include Presidents Hoover and Roosevelt, along with financier John D. Rockefeller. Even with its topicality, *As Thousands Cheer* ran for 400 performances, proving at least that sophisticated Broadway audiences could laugh at the troubled times, if only for a couple of hours in a theater.

The play included several musical numbers that have come down to the present as standards: Ethel Waters performed a show-stopping "Heat Wave," and both "Easter Parade" and "Suppertime" show Berlin at his best. "Easter Parade," incidentally, came from a previous 1917 effort of his entitled "Smile and Show Your Dimple." Even as prolific a composer as Irving Berlin can be excused for borrowing from himself now and then.

For the remainder of the 1930s, the siren song of Hollywood proved irresistible and Berlin would devote himself to creating some of his most memorable movie melodies. Not until 1940 and the opening of *Louisiana Purchase* would he return to Broadway. Out of that effort came "It's a Lovely Day Tomorrow," a lesser Berlin tune, but an enduring one.

Irving Berlin continued writing for both stage and screen long after the close of the 1930s. An all-around man of American music, he perhaps understood popular taste as well as anyone in the business.[2]

George and Ira Gershwin (1898–1937; 1896–1983)

These two talented brothers brought American music to new levels. George, the composer, started playing the piano early in life. By 1912, he was performing for money and had become what in the trade is called a song plugger. A job that originated on Tin Pan Alley, plugging involved taking the music and lyrics of a tune to different music publishers in hopes of getting the sheet music printed and distributed. Most pluggers did not write the music they promoted, yet they had to convince publishing firms that their songs were wonderful and stood the best chances of success. It did not take George long to realize he should be plugging his own music, not someone else's.

Gershwin had his first real success, "Swanee," in 1919 (lyrics by Irving Caesar). Al Jolson, a commanding star of stage, vaudeville, and recordings, heard it and made it one of the big hits of the era. Soon thereafter, Ira, George's lyricist brother, joined him and "Gershwin" became a name to be reckoned with in music circles by the early 1920s. Their collaborative musicals usually did well, and George enjoyed the added reputation of being a "serious" musician. In 1924, he had premiered *Rhapsody in Blue*, a concert piece commissioned by bandleader Paul Whiteman that received considerable acclaim. A number of preludes and other varied compositions followed, solidifying his position as a significant American composer. It is the brothers' film and theater music that most listeners know, however, and in that area the Gershwins are fully the equals of Berlin, Kern, Porter, or Rodgers and Hart.

In 1929, they wrote the music for a play called *Show Girl*. It starred Ruby Keeler, a talented young dancer, along with the popular vaudeville team of Clayton-Jackson-Durante (Lou Clayton, Eddie Jackson, and Jimmy Durante). The Gershwins had written a showpiece number entitled "Liza" for the male lead. With the song set to go on, Al Jolson, still very much a star and the husband of Keeler, sang it unexpectedly opening night—and several nights thereafter—from the aisles, upstaging the scheduled singer. Actually, it had all been planned, but audiences remained none the wiser, and "Liza" was henceforth associated with Jolson, just as the earlier "Swanee" had more or less become his personal property.

Strike Up the Band, the rewrite of a 1927 play that never got to Broadway, opened in 1930. The musical included such gems as "Soon" and "I've Got a Crush on You," as well as the title song. Although *Strike Up the Band* contains nothing topical, the orchestra personnel reflected the hard times descending on the country as a result of the Depression. The band had been organized by trumpeter Red Nichols, and he obtained the services of top-flight musicians like Benny Goodman, Gene Krupa, Glenn Miller, Jimmy Dorsey, and Jack Teagarden. Jobs were hard to find in 1930, and so these musicians gladly took the offer, anxious to get employment wherever they could find it. Many productions could claim such outstanding bands in those difficult days, a fact that provided audiences a superior level of musicianship during a show.

A 1930 portrait of George Gershwin (1898–1937), one of the major figures in American popular music. Individually, and in partnership with his brother Ira, Gershwin helped to define the idea of "standards," those songs that live on in the listener's mind, transcending time and popular musical trends. From "Swanee" (1919) to "Love Is Here to Stay" (1938), and with countless enduring compositions in between, he has survived as one of the dominant voices in American music during the 1920s and 1930s. [Library of Congress, Prints & Photographs Division]

Not until swing began to have an impact on popular taste would musicians of this caliber find consistent work more to their liking.

After the opening of *Strike Up the Band*, the year witnessed yet another production featuring Gershwin music. Called *Girl Crazy*, the musical cast two women who became stars during the 1930s, Ethel Merman and Ginger Rogers. It also featured a score that would become a star in its own right, including "Bidin' My Time," "Embraceable You," "But Not for Me," and the inimitable "I Got Rhythm," particularly as sung by Ethel Merman. Her rendition, certainly one of the most energetic performances of any song in any stage musical, overnight made her one of the all-time stars of Broadway theater. Another superlative band, put together by Red Nichols, backed her in style.

Perhaps no other Gershwin effort exhibited such a successful marriage of jazz, Broadway show tunes, and popular music. Virtually every notable jazz musician of that day or any other day would at one time or another play "I Got Rhythm," a staple of the jazz repertoire. George himself always held a special interest in the number, and in 1934 wrote a more serious work called *Variations on "I Got Rhythm."* The play went a long way in its own right, running for 272 performances in those dreary Depression days.

As conditions worsened around the country, the Gershwins collaborated on *Of Thee I Sing* in December of 1931. The show's book was written by George S. Kaufman and Morrie Ryskind, two important figures in Broadway history. Much of the plot revolves around presidents, politics, and the foibles of governments. The resulting story is satirical and topical, with music to match. Out of that mix came "Love Is Sweeping the Country," "Of Thee I Sing (Baby)," and "Who Cares?" Audiences responded, and the play ran for 441 performances, the longest-ever for a Gershwin show, and gained a Pulitzer Prize for Drama in the libretto and lyrics category.

Buoyed, the Gershwin brothers returned to Broadway in early 1933 with *Pardon My English*. It, however, failed to arouse much interest, despite having a melodious score, and closed after a disappointing forty-six performances. It contained such standards as "Lorelei" and "Isn't It a Pity?" and might have been expected to do better, but audiences clearly thought otherwise.

Despite the commercial failure of *Pardon My English*, the Gershwins opened *Let 'em Eat Cake* in the fall of 1933. Working again with writers George S. Kaufman and Morrie Ryskind, they proceeded to mount another topical play, one filled with Depression-era references in their lyrics. Numbers like "Down with Ev'rything That's Up," "Union Square," and the title song made for a kind of sequel to *Of Thee I Sing*, even to the point of bringing charac-

The popular editorial cartoonist Clifford K. Berryman (1869–1949) did this caricature of President Franklin D. Roosevelt in 1933, a bleak Depression year. The sheet music the president holds refers to a song penned by George and Ira Gershwin called "Of Thee I Sing (Baby)," and comes from their satirical musical of 1931–1932 entitled *Of Thee I Sing*. A dejected Al Smith, disenchanted with the New Deal, slumps behind him. Of course, the reference also can apply to the patriotic song "America" (1832), the original source of the Gershwins' witty title, but the political bite of the cartoon works best in its Broadway context. [Library of Congress, Prints & Photographs Division]

ters from the earlier production to the new one. Musically, however, about the only number of any real distinction in *Let 'em Eat Cake* was the romantic "Mine." One good song could not save the day.

Undiscouraged—their music, admittedly as bright and original as ever, could not overcome the plays—George and Ira Gershwin still had some ideas up their sleeves. In 1935, at New York's Alvin Theater, they unveiled *Porgy and Bess*, after an out-of-town run in Boston. They envisioned this work as an attempt to create a serious American play in an environment more used to frothy musical comedies. Based on the 1925 novel *Porgy* by DuBose Heyward, the prestigious Theatre Guild helped underwrite *Porgy and Bess*, and called the enterprise a "folk opera" in its billing. But the show opened—and thereafter usually played—in a traditional theater, not in opera houses or symphony halls.

Over the years, critics have debated whether or not *Porgy and Bess* should be seen as musical theater posing as opera, or opera that contains elements of popular musical theater. In an opera, the lyricist usually writes the words, or libretto, first; then the composer writes the music itself, fitting it to the libretto. In much musical theater, on the other hand, especially that of the 1920s and 1930s, the music precedes the lyrics. The composer creates a melody then the lyricist finds words appropriate to the music. In the case of *Porgy and Bess*, music and lyrics were done both ways, further muddying any clear definitions. Some of the lyric credits belong to DuBose Heyward, who wrote words to which George Gershwin then composed music. But credits also go jointly to both Heyward and Ira Gershwin. And finally, Ira Gershwin, as he usually did, wrote still more words to brother George's completed music. Such arguments, essentially academic in nature, ignore the fact that *Porgy and Bess* stands as unique in American musical and theatrical history. Regardless of who wrote what and in what order, its memorable score has made *Porgy and Bess* a favorite of both concert and theatergoers.

On stage, *Porgy and Bess* required an all-black cast. Ironically, the first major commercial recordings of music from the score featured Lawrence Tibbett and Helen Jepsen, two white artists. The archaic idea that somehow recordings by black artists—called "race records" in those days (see Chapter 1)—would not sell to white consumers still held sway in 1936. Eventually, such concepts fell by the wayside and the show has long since been recorded innumerable times by black and white performers, both in its entirety and most of the songs individually. *Porgy and Bess* has gone on tours, finally made it to film in 1959, and successfully straddled the difficult line between high art and popular entertainment.

Filled with some of the Gershwins' greatest music, much of the score has entered the standard repertoire. For audiences and listeners, it matters little who got the credit line; more important is how uniformly good the score remains. From "Summertime" to "My Man's Gone Now" to "It Ain't Necessarily So" to all the other numbers contained in the play/opera, *Porgy and Bess* remains a significant theatrical and musical achievement.

The brothers left New York and headed to Hollywood in the summer of 1936. Because of George's premature death in 1937, *Porgy and Bess* would be their last Broadway production. Ira lived until 1983 and worked with many

other composers, but his years with his brother remain unique ones, resulting in some of the best music Americans have ever enjoyed.[3]

Jerome Kern (1885–1945)

Like so many of his contemporaries, Jerome Kern at the beginning of his
musical career worked as a song plugger on Tin Pan Alley. He finally realized, as had George Gershwin, that he should be writing and plugging his
own music, and in 1903 had a minor hit with "Mister Chamberlain" (lyrics
by P. G. Wodehouse, who would become a frequent collaborator). The following year his name appeared on the playbill of a Broadway musical, *Mr.
Wix of Wickham*, and that headed him toward fame and success.

With major stage hits like *Sally* (1920; lyrics by Clifford Grey and Buddy
DeSylva), *Sunny* (1925; lyrics by Otto Harbach and Oscar Hammerstein II),
and *Show Boat* (1927; lyrics by Oscar Hammerstein II), Kern had become
well-established in theatrical circles by the late 1920s. For Broadway audiences hungry for some old-fashioned romanticism, Kern's theater work provides it. He completed the music for five shows over the period 1929–
1939, and that includes at least one enduring stage classic. Kern might have
found more lucrative outlets in Hollywood, and he did spend much of his
time composing for films, not the stage, but that hardly lessened his theatrical contributions.

Sweet Adeline (lyrics by Oscar Hammerstein II) opened in the fall of 1929,
just before the stock market collapse. A deliberate exercise in nostalgia (the
original "Sweet Adeline" had been composed in 1903, with music by Harry
Armstrong and lyrics by Richard H. Gerard), the play focused on the Gay
Nineties and tried to recreate a sense of innocence. Reality intruded with the
Crash, and the show closed. Although few remember *Sweet Adeline*, they may
recall a tune from the show, "Why Was I Born?"

In 1931, he collaborated with lyricist Otto Harbach for *The Cat and the Fid-
dle*. Subtitled "A Musical Love Story," Kern and Harbach provided two ro-
mantic standards: "She Didn't Say 'Yes' " and "The Night Was Made for Love."
The following year, Kern reunited with Hammerstein for *Music in the Air*.
Their joint work produced two more classics, "I've Told Ev'ry Little Star" and
"The Song Is You."

But all the foregoing may have seemed like dress rehearsals for 1933's
Roberta, one of the true masterpieces of the American musical stage. Work-

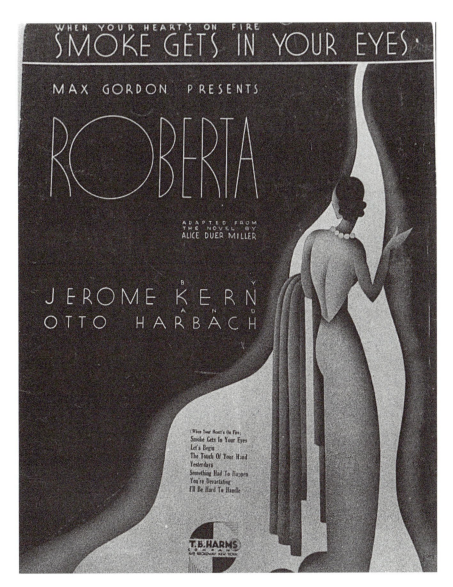

At times, the covers for sheet music could be quite stylized. This 1933 example for "Smoke Gets in Your Eyes" (music by Jerome Kern, lyrics by Otto Harbach; from the musical *Roberta*) captures the essence of 1930s high fashion: the permed hair, the long, slinky gown, and the Art Deco–influenced lettering. [Photograph by author; from the Al Harris Collection]

ing again with Otto Harbach, Kern created some of his loveliest melodies. Perhaps the best-known of the many standards to emerge from *Roberta* is "Smoke Gets in Your Eyes." Close behind would be "Yesterdays," and following that chestnut are "Let's Begin," "The Touch of Your Hand," and "I'll Be Hard to Handle" (lyrics by Bernard Dougall). With all the splendid songs, it might be understandable if the plot gets overlooked. Produced in the worst days of the Great Depression, the story concerns a fashion designer and a glamorous world far removed from everyday lives. On the other hand, such a romantic diversion may have served as a tonic for many in the audience, and certainly Jerome Kern had mastered serving up escapism in his music. *Roberta* played for a respectable 295 performances and enjoyed a film adaptation soon thereafter.

After the success of *Roberta*, Kern returned to Hollywood. Not until 1939 would he again compose for the theater. He and Oscar Hammerstein II joined forces for *Very Warm for May*. A box office failure, it closed out Kern's Broadway career, although he would continue to write for the movies. Despite its lack of success, *Very Warm for May* did yield "All the Things You Are," another standard that has stood the test of time.

If Jerome Kern's music were to be used as a guide to social history, the Depression never happened. Even his lyricists—and he worked with the best in the business—fell under his spell and wrote wonderfully romantic ballads, but topicality stayed far from their minds. A composer who created memorable melodies for both the stage and screen, Kern came from a school of writers who saw their profession as one of entertainment, not judgment or criticism. But none of that lessens his accomplishment as a composer, and many of his Broadway musicals must be ranked among the finest ever produced.[4]

Cole Porter (1891–1964)

Born into relative wealth in Peru, Indiana, Porter began to make his mark on Broadway in the later 1920s, although he had been actively writing music and lyrics throughout the decade. He finally enjoyed hits with "I'm in Love Again" (1925; from the revue, *Greenwich Village Follies of 1924*) and the suggestive "Let's Do It" (1928; from the play *Paris*). With those successes, he stood poised to take on the 1930s.

A constant presence in musical theater, Porter has the distinction of contributing some of the more adult—and certainly some of the most sophisticated—lyrics of the period. Like his contemporaries, especially Jerome Kern and Lorenz Hart, Porter's view of the world had little to do with economic crises or New Deals, but he was not above making topical references in his remarkable catalog of songs. Thanks once again to movies, radio, and recordings, he became widely known and his music has come down to the present as some of the best of the era.

In November of 1929, Porter premiered one of his many standards, "You Do Something to Me," for the musical *Fifty Million Frenchmen*. People took notice, and Porter's name next graced marquees in December with *Wake Up and Dream*, just a month after *Fifty Million Frenchmen*. Most songwriters rarely have two musicals going at once, but in Porter's case the reason can be easily explained. He had opened *Wake Up and Dream* in London that spring, and it made its New York debut at the end of the year. The play featured "What Is This Thing Called Love?" another Porter chestnut.

With two plays running on Broadway, it took only a short time before Hollywood came calling. For the remainder of the 1930s, Porter shuttled between the West Coast and the East, working comfortably within both theater and film.

The New Yorkers opened on Broadway during the 1930 Christmas season. A forgettable play, it nonetheless contained an unforgettable song, "Love for Sale." A controversial description of a prostitute, "Love for Sale" has entered the standard repertoire. Radio stations at the time found its risqué lyrics unsuitable for broadcasting, but it achieved hit status anyway, in large part thanks to a recording by Fred Waring and the Pennsylvanians. The record sold well, the public did not act offended, and so any restrictions on airplay have long since been dropped. Contemporary listeners might wonder about the concerns expressed "back then."

Almost two years passed before the opening of Porter's next play, *Gay Divorce* (1932). Starring Fred Astaire before he devoted most of his time to movies, the play has him performing "Night and Day." It also includes "Mister and Missus Fitch," a humorous play on words. When *Gay Divorce* was adapted for film in 1934, Astaire again got the lead male role and performed with Ginger Rogers, the second pairing for the two actors (the first had been in *Flying Down to Rio* in 1933). Speaking of words, Hollywood, nervous about the play's title, feared censor problems with the connotation of "happy divorce." Thus the movie version goes by *The Gay Divorcee*, a compromise that might raise serious doubts about why a "happy divorcee" should in any way be superior to a happy divorce.

Once more, two years went by before another Porter offering, but it proved worth the wait because the musical, *Anything Goes*, contains one of his most inspired scores. Standards like "I Get a Kick Out of You," "All Through the Night," "You're the Top," "Blow, Gabriel, Blow," and the title song, "Anything Goes," adorn the score. The stage version starred Ethel Merman, and she gave such a strong performance that the 1936 movie adaptation cast her in the same part, rather than a Hollywood star.

In 1935, Porter's *Jubilee* came to the stage. Another of those so-so plays with some memorable music, it features "Why Shouldn't I?" "Just One of Those Things," and a number most people initially dismissed, "Begin the Beguine." Fortunately, bandleader Artie Shaw learned about Porter's tune, and recorded it in 1938. It resulted in the biggest hit of Shaw's career, one that will always be associated with the clarinetist, and a song that helped epitomize the Swing Era.

Porter returned to New York with *Red Hot and Blue!* in 1936. The show contains one of those standards much beloved by cabaret singers, "Down in the Depths (on the Ninetieth Floor)." A painful recital about the problems of love, it has never been a big popular hit, but it has achieved a devoted following. On a more upbeat note, the show also features "It's De-Lovely" and "Ridin' High." Bob Hope, already an actor of some standing, sang "It's De-Lovely" with co-star Ethel Merman, by that time one of Broadway's leading lights.

You Never Know opened the 1938 Broadway season. As if to prove that not every musical can be a hit, it closed after just 78 performances, despite the presence of Cole Porter's name for music and lyrics. "What Shall I Do?" and "At Long Last Love" have endured far better than the play.

A month later, Porter's *Leave It to Me!* helped redeem the composer. It included his great "Get Out of Town" and a show-stopping "My Heart Belongs to Daddy." A young Mary Martin, just starting out, performed the latter number, and her rendition—all innocence and sophistication combined—instantly made her a performer to watch.

DuBarry Was a Lady (1939) proved to be Porter's final effort for the 1930s. Two standards emerged from the production, both humorous: "Friendship" and "Well, Did You Evah?" He then proceeded to enter the new decade with *Panama Hattie* (1940), a musical destined to run over 500 performances. A good show in many ways, but it lacked a distinctive Porter score. "Make It Another Old-Fashioned, Please" will not be remembered as one of his great songs. With those two plays behind him, Cole Porter would not return to Broadway until 1944 and *Mexican Hayride*.[5]

Richard Rodgers (1902–1979) and Lorenz Hart (1895–1943)

Composer Richard Rodgers met lyricist Lorenz Hart when both were still in their teens. Two personalities could not have been more different: Rodgers, steady and reliable, a highly organized person who possessed a strong work ethic; Hart, on the other hand, disorganized and erratic in his habits, bordered on being unstable. The two paired up anyway and by 1925 had written a number of songs, most of them forgotten. They then collaborated on a revue, *The Garrick Gaieties* (1925), which featured "Manhattan" and "Sentimental Me." Those songs have since become standards, but "Manhattan," as popularized by Paul Whiteman and his orchestra in a recording, soon put the composer and lyricist on their way to recognition as one of Broadway's premier songwriting teams. A string of hits followed, including "The Blue Room" (1926), "Mountain Greenery" (1926), "My Heart Stood Still" (1927), "Thou Swell" (1927), and "You Took Advantage of Me" (1928).

With a new production almost yearly (and often twice a year), Rodgers and Hart ranked among the most prolific of the many composers who found favor in the thirties. One song after another seemingly flowed from their collective imaginations, setting new expectations for the American musical theater. Thanks to movies, radio, and recordings, their music achieved two distinctions: much of it became popular in its own time and, more importantly, many of their songs have become "standards," those melodies and lyrics known by both the public and a variety of performers over a long period of time (for more on standards, see Chapter 2).

In 1929, Rodgers and Hart presented *Spring Is Here*. Not their greatest collaboration—those were yet to come—it nonetheless introduced audiences to "With a Song in My Heart." The number became associated with singer Jane Froman, and she performed it on stage as well as in the 1930 film adaptation of the play. A much later movie, *With a Song in My Heart* (1952), had Susan Hayward impersonating Froman, but Froman herself sang it on the soundtrack, thereby reaching an entirely new generation of listeners.

Heads Up also came to Broadway in 1929. A tuneful play about gangsters and Prohibition, it underwent considerable doctoring before its premiere. Fortunately, "A Ship without a Sail," another great Rodgers and Hart classic, survived the surgery.

Simple Simon opened in February of 1930, a time when people had begun sensing the realities of the economic calamity descending on the nation. A silly comedy starring vaudevillian Ed Wynn, the show featured a fine score by the songwriting duo. A standout was "Ten Cents a Dance," a soulful lament about the life of a taxi dancer, a woman employed by a commercial dance hall who will dance with any man willing to pay a dime. Sung by Ruth Etting, "Ten Cents a Dance" burnished her career, and reminded critics and audiences that Rodgers and Hart could handle just about any subject and make memorable music. Etting also had another star-defining number with "Love Me or Leave Me" (1928; music by Walter Donaldson, lyrics by Gus Kahn), a pulsating love song—but a non-Rodgers and Hart number—that had been interpolated into the show about two months after its opening. Etting had first performed it in *Whoopie*, a 1928 comedy featuring comedian Eddie Cantor. The producers wanted to strengthen what they perceived as a weak score and capitalize on Etting's association with the song.

As the Depression worsened, *America's Sweetheart* came to Broadway in early 1931. Although the play itself can best be described as superficial, it does contain an up-tempo response to hard times in "I've Got Five Dollars." This jaunty piece quickly became a hit, a musical antidote to unemployment, bread lines, and despair.

Rodgers and Hart headed west later in 1931, joining a number of their compatriots in Hollywood. They would not attempt another stage musical for four years, and instead focused their energies on movie scores, an area in which they also achieved success. In time, however, the pair tired of the West Coast and 1935 found them back in New York City scoring *Jumbo*, a Ben Hecht–Charles MacArthur offering produced by showman Billy Rose. A popular hit, *Jumbo* contained some of their greatest melodies, including "The Most Beautiful Girl in the World," "My Romance," and "Little Girl Blue."

Success apparently begets success, because 1936 found them writing yet another hit, *On Your Toes*. In this musical, Rodgers had the opportunity to compose an extended instrumental work, *Slaughter on Tenth Avenue*, a ballet. *Slaughter on Tenth Avenue* took on a life of its own, becoming a favorite of classical and "pops" orchestras everywhere. Of course, Hart contributed some fine lyrics for other songs in the show, notably "There's a Small Hotel" and "Glad to Be Unhappy."

Apparently, a burst of collective creative energy struck the two at this time, because Rodgers and Hart turned out new scores in what became almost a twice-a-year ritual. For example, their first play for 1937 was *Babes in Arms*, and the music included "Where or When," "I Wish I Were in Love Again," "My Funny Valentine," "Johnny One Note," "Imagine," and "The Lady Is a

Tramp," one of the greatest collections of American standards ever composed for a single play.

The music from *Babes in Arms* proved so rich that a song like "The Lady Is a Tramp" could later be used in the film version of *Pal Joey* (1957), a play they scored in 1940, but one in which that particular song does not appear. People knew "The Lady Is a Tramp," either from recordings or *Babes in Arms*, and perhaps its inclusion seemed appropriate in a Rodgers and Hart movie. On the other hand, "My Funny Valentine," a song widely recorded by both vocalists and instrumentalists in the last half of the twentieth century, languished during the 1930s. It seemed a forgotten, melancholy tune, until 1953, when Frank Sinatra "discovered" it and recorded it for his enormously popular *Songs for Young Lovers* album. After that, everyone wanted to record "My Funny Valentine" and it established itself as an enduring standard, although few might know its earlier origins.

In the fall of 1937, their second show, *I'd Rather Be Right*, opened on Broadway. Rodgers and Hart contributed "Have You Met Miss Jones?" and the humorous "We're Going to Balance the Budget," a subject of considerable concern in those post-Depression years. One of their few forays into topicality, the song stands as a trifle for the pair, but it does bear their most unusual title.

Maintaining their torrid pace, 1938's *I Married an Angel* gave audiences the title tune plus the haunting "Spring Is Here." In a bow to the success of Dale Carnegie's best-selling 1937 book, the show also included "How to Win Friends and Influence People," hardly their best-remembered effort.

Rodgers and Hart, along with author George Abbott, took Shakespeare's *The Comedy of Errors* and created *The Boys from Syracuse* for their second offering of the year. Another musical romp, the team created the delightful "Falling in Love with Love," "This Can't Be Love," and "Sing for Your Supper." The Bard would probably approve.

As the decade wound down, Rodgers and Hart enjoyed yet another Broadway hit, *Too Many Girls* (1939). The score includes the humorous "Give It Back to the Indians," a song about New York and its problems. Accompanying that was "I Didn't Know What Time It Was," one of their great love songs. They also penned "I Like to Recognize the Tune," a sly poke at contemporary musical arrangements that frequently buried the melody.

Higher and Higher went on stage in 1940; it contained "It Never Entered My Mind." Another great score followed with the opening of *Pal Joey* (1940).

Such standards as "Bewitched, Bothered and Bewildered" and "I Could Write a Book" came from that effort.

Lorenz Hart died in 1943, bringing to an end a remarkable pairing. Richard Rodgers would, of course, go on to team up with Oscar Hammerstein II, himself a most successful lyricist from the 1920s and 1930s. Together they would make stage history with *Oklahoma!* (1943) and a host of other great musicals. When looking back over the two careers of Rodgers and Hart and Rodgers and Hammerstein, a significant difference becomes clear: The first partnership will be remembered for its songs, some of the best standards ever written, most of which happened to be first performed on stage. The second pairing will be remembered more for its plays—*South Pacific, The King and I, The Sound of Music*, and so on. Some of the best musicals ever written, most of which had some great songs, but a case where the whole tends to be better than its individual parts.[6]

Stage Musicals by Others

Many other musicals came and went during the decade, and a significant number achieved great popularity during their runs. The listing below cannot be thought of as comprehensive or exhaustive; it merely mentions additional stage productions, year by year, that happened to contain some outstanding songs, thus contributing to the overall musical wealth of the 1930s.

The decade opened with one of a continuing series of all-black revues that had become a part of the New York theater scene for many years. Unlike some productions in that racially segregated era, *Blackbirds of 1930* not only had a black cast, but a black composer and a black lyricist in Eubie Blake and Andy Razaf. Out of the revue came two great standards, "Memories of You" and "You're Lucky to Me." The racial segregation that permeated Broadway, however, showed few signs of lessening, despite the show's success.

In 1931, *Billy Rose's Crazy Quilt* provided audiences a peppy score by Harry Warren, a songwriter who would make a considerable mark in Hollywood throughout the decade. For this show, he created "I Found a Million-Dollar Baby (in a Five-and-Ten-Cent Store)," with timely lyrics by Billy Rose and Mort Dixon.

Regardless of the nation's ongoing economic problems, 1932 proved a banner year for memorable show tunes. "I Gotta Right to Sing the Blues" (music by Harold Arlen, lyrics by Ted Koehler) made the 1932 production of *Earl Car-roll's Vanities* more than just another revue, and again provided singers with a number that allowed them a chance to display their talents.

Blackbirds of 1933 contributed "A Hundred Years from Today," another fine love song from composer Victor Young and lyricist Ned Washington. In this case the music came from a white writing team for an ostensibly all-black production. In no way whatsoever should that fact detract either from the revue or from the music itself. It does illustrate, however, the limited opportunities for black composers and lyricists during the 1930s.

In 1934, composer Vernon Duke enjoyed a good year with "What Is There to Say?" and "I Like the Likes of You," both written with lyricist E. Y. Harburg for the *Ziegfeld Follies of 1934*. He then went on to create both the words and music for "Autumn in New York." This wistful composition appeared in the 1935 musical *Thumbs Up!*

The *Earl Carroll Sketch Book* for 1935 contained "Let's Swing It" (words and music by Murray Mencher, Charles Newman, and Charles Tobias), one of the earliest references to swing on Broadway. Not the most memorable of songs, but it served as a hint of things to come.

Many of the enduring songs of the 1930s were written for revues that featured various artists in sketches, with music by a number of different composers and lyricists. In 1935's *Provincetown Follies*, "Red Sails in the Sunset" (music by Hugh Williams, lyrics by James Kennedy) proved no exception; it has remained a favorite over the years.

Continuing that trend, the perennial *Ziegfeld Follies (1936 Edition)* included the timeless "I Can't Get Started" (music by Vernon Duke, lyrics by Ira Gershwin). Filled with references about such things as President Roosevelt, the ongoing civil war in Spain, Greta Garbo, and polar exploration, on stage Bob Hope sang it to Eve Arden. It went over well then, and the topicality has dimmed the number not a bit for contemporary listeners.

In 1937's *Hooray for What!* the song "Down with Love" marked yet another successful effort by the team of Harold Arlen and E. Y. Harburg. The two would collaborate on a number of other projects, such as the play *Life Begins at 8:40* (1934) and the movies *Take a Chance* (1934) and *At the Circus* (1939).

Walter Huston, a distinguished actor who really could not sing, nevertheless talked-chanted-sang his way through "September Song" in a stunning performance for 1938's *Knickerbocker Holiday*. But he had good help: the music had been composed by Kurt Weill and the lyrics penned by playwright Maxwell Anderson.

Songwriters Dorothy Fields and Arthur Schwartz, undaunted by the high-caliber competition of the Gershwins, Rodgers and Hart, Porter, Berlin, and Kern, combined talents for 1939's *Stars in Your Eyes*. The show featured their numbers "This Is It" and "It's All Yours."

With 1940, the clouds of war had broken in Europe and increasingly threatened the United States. So Broadway turned, as it always does, to music and romance. The year saw *Keep Off the Grass*, a light-hearted romp that featured music by Jimmy McHugh, Al Dubin, and Howard Dietz, old pros all. The three collaborated on "Clear Out of This World," another love song destined to become a standard.[7]

Two Unusual Musicals

Not every musical of the 1930s concerned itself with matters of the heart or light comedy. In June of 1937, *The Cradle Will Rock* opened, but just barely. Featuring a book, music, and lyrics by composer Marc Blitzstein (1905–1964), the play had little in the way of memorable music but much in the way of controversy. A product of the Federal Theater Project (see Chapter 6) in New York City, it involved Orson Welles and John Houseman, two important figures in stage history, as director and producer. Its clearly leftist leanings stirred conservative congressional groups and they tried to block it. Deprived of a theater on opening night by government agents, the cast and crew searched for a new venue, and finally found the small Venice Theatre, which stood empty at the time. Cast and crew marched through the streets to the Venice, but then the musician's union forbade its members to perform after squabbling about pay. True to the traditions of show business, the show finally went on with Blitzstein himself playing a piano on stage and the actors scattered about in the theater seats speaking their lines as a single spot searched them out. Hardly traditional Broadway, but those in attendance loved it.

The Cradle Will Rock played two weeks at the Venice. After a break, it moved to the larger Windsor Theatre in early 1938, and eventually played for 108 performances. None of the music from the show had any impact, although audiences admired its sincerity. The score joins innumerable other protest songs from many eras, noble in their intent, but soon forgotten after their causes find resolution (see Chapter 5 for more on protest music). Blitzstein continued composing, mainly in the area of opera, but he remains little performed. Today Blitzstein is remembered not so much for that ground-breaking effort, but for his adaptation, in 1954, of Kurt Weill's *The Three-Penny Opera*, especially his English lyrics for "Mack the Knife," a song from the show that became a big hit for performers as disparate as Louis Armstrong and Bobby Darin. An eponymous 1999 movie that purports to tell about all the background escapades that accompanied the production briefly resurrected *The Cradle Will Rock* and its curious history.

Shortly after *The Cradle Will Rock* closed, another controversial play opened. The International Ladies Garment Workers' Union (ILGWU) sponsored a musical revue entitled *Pins and Needles*. Revolving around a loosely knit plot about labor unions versus "the Bosses," the play uses topical references ("Ford and Morgan swing it," "One big union for two," "Fifty million union members can't be wrong"), and clearly favors a union stand on contemporary work issues. Premiering in November of 1937, and with the smallest of budgets—no one in the largely unknown cast earned over $55 a week—it lacked the trappings of a big Broadway production. But somehow it struck a chord with usually jaded New York audiences, just as *The Cradle Will Rock* had done. Both the music and lyrics originated with composer Harold J. Rome (1908–1993), a young songwriter who today is best known for an innocuous pop tune called "Wish You Were Here" (1952). Marc Blitzstein of *The Cradle Will Rock* fame also gets listed in the credits for contributions to the book, although just what his contributions might have been remains open to question.

Initially performed at the small Labor Stage (formerly called the Princess Theatre), the success of *Pins and Needles* forced a January move to the Windsor Theatre, the same stage that had earlier taken in *The Cradle Will Rock*. A completely unanticipated hit, *Pins and Needles* ran into 1940; in the process, it set a record for musicals of the 1930s with 1,108 performances. Despite that long run, *Pins and Needles* went virtually unheard of by most of the nation. The play's "big number" was Harold Rome's "Sing Me a Song with Social Significance":

> I'm tired of moon-songs of star and June songs,
> They simply make me nap
> And ditties romantic drive me nearly frantic
> I think they're all full of pap.
>
> History's making, nations are quaking
> Why sing of stars above

For while we are waiting father time's creating
New things to be singing of.

Sing me a song with social significance
All other tunes are taboo
I want a ditty with heat in it,
Appealing with feeling and meat in it!

Sing me a song with social significance
Or you can sing 'til you're blue
Let meaning shine from ev'ry line
Or I won't love you.

Sing me of wars and sing me of breadlines
Tell me of front page news
Sing me of strikes and last minute headlines
Dress your observation in syncopation!

Possessor of what surely must be the most socially significant song title of the Depression, and featuring some timely references to breadlines and wars, "Sing Me a Song with Social Significance" may have been mass culture for dedicated Broadway fans, but for everyone else, it languished in obscurity.[8]

Broadway provided the nation an ample supply of timeless music. With enduring shows like *Roberta*, *Girl Crazy*, and *On Your Toes* lighting up marquees, and with more standards than anyone realized at the time coming from them, people everywhere knew their songs. Only a small percentage of the population ever saw these shows, but through movie adaptations, radio, records, and sheet music, millions everywhere got to know their tunes. Although the Depression curtailed some theatrical activity, by and large musicals continued to attract backers, delighting both audiences and listeners.

HOLLYWOOD

Sound pictures had become a fact of movie life by the late 1920s. When Al Jolson actually sang some of his biggest hits—"My Mammy" (1918; music by Walter Donaldson, lyrics by Sam M. Lewis and Joe Young), "Toot, Toot, Tootsie" (1922; words and music by Ted Fio Rito, Robert A. King, Gus Kahn,

and Ernie Erdman), "Blue Skies" (1911; words and music by Irving Berlin)—
in 1927's *The Jazz Singer*, the die was cast. People loved hearing Jolson's
voice, and the picture grossed over $3 million, an unheard-of sum. In that
landmark movie, Jolson had the benefit of sound only for his musical numbers. Aside from a few impromptu lines surrounding the songs, including
the memorable "You ain't heard nothin' yet, folks!" the film's dialogue remained silent and relied on cue cards to inform the audience of what the
players said.

Despite those deficiencies, the popularity of *The Jazz Singer* caused studio
heads to place an emphasis on movie musicals. Just like its counterparts on
Broadway, the sound musical promised big profits. In 1928 the veteran Al
Jolson returned in *The Singing Fool*, another part-talkie, part-silent picture,
and audiences again responded enthusiastically. Warner Brothers wisely
chose to hike ticket prices, charging an astronomical $3.00 for admission.
For that kind of money, people got to see and hear Jolson sing "It All Depends on You" (1927; music by Ray Henderson, lyrics by Buddy DeSylva and
Lew Brown), "Sonny Boy" (1928; music by Henderson, lyrics by DeSylva,
Brown, and Al Jolson), and "There's a Rainbow 'Round My Shoulder" (1928;
words and music by Dave Dreyer, Billy Rose, and Al Jolson). In another astute move, and something new at the time, the producers timed the release
of recordings featuring Jolson doing songs from the movie to coincide with
the release of the picture. Naturally, the advertisements promised "as heard
in the movie."

Clearly, it would be only a matter of months, not years, before "All Talking,
All Singing" became the norm. Seemingly overnight, the approximately
23,000 movie houses around the country had to accommodate this momen-
tous event, and change they did. In a remarkable display of catering to their
public, most theaters successfully made the switch from old equipment to
new. In the meantime, the studios busily rushed new musicals into production.

By 1929, *The Broadway Melody*, featuring songs by Nacio Herb Brown and
Arthur Freed, could advertise "100% Talking" and a score created just for the
film. Among the songs, "You Were Meant for Me" could be added to the growing list of standards being compiled by film musicals. *The Broadway Melody*
proved so successful that it garnered an Academy Award for Best Film and
any uncompleted silent pictures quickly converted to sound, as did any remaining theaters. Theaters failing to make the conversion soon found themselves out of business. Between 1929 and 1931, the number of movie theaters

actually declined, going from over 23,300 to just under 22,000. Economic forces, not technology, continued the slump; the numbers bottomed out in 1935, with about 15,200 theaters holding on. It would take years to return to anything close to the 1929 figures.

Despite the glum business picture, MGM's success with *The Broadway Melody* convinced the studio to contract Brown and Freed for another musical, a decision that resulted in *Hollywood Revue* (1929). This picture contained one of the team's best efforts, a song destined to be repeated many times: "Singin' in the Rain." Judy Garland reprised it in 1940's *Little Nellie Kelly*, and of course Gene Kelly in 1952 immortalized the tune for all time in the film of the same name.

When talking pictures swept over the movie market, the technology used to reproduce sound was similar to that utilized by the booming radio industry. Both media employed electrical sound reproduction, but radio had reached people first, thus establishing expectations. What audiences heard in those early talkies reinforced the "radio sound" concept. It might be an artificial, somewhat shrill sound coming from the theater's speakers, but it duplicated what people heard on the family radio. Overnight, electrically reproduced became the normal format for all modes of music, although the phonograph and record industries admittedly made the change from acoustic recording reluctantly. (For more on the development of "radio sound," see Chapter 1.)

The movies, however, enjoyed an added advantage over other media of the day: on recordings and radio, the audience *listens*; in a movie theater (or ballroom, nightclub, casino, or concert hall), the audience also *watches* the musicians. The movies therefore had the best of both worlds: sound and sight. The soundtrack might consist of background (aural only) music, but the screen could—and often did, during the 1930s—present larger-than-life images of the bands themselves, complete with the vocalists and the star instrumentalists. In fact, more and more bands and orchestras, when performing before a live audience, used electrical amplification while on stage so they would sound more like their recordings or broadcasts. It all came down to a neat blending of science and savvy marketing, one that would forever change musical reproduction.

In 1929, Hollywood studios released thirty-two musical films; since they made money, the total jumped to an astronomical seventy-two in 1930, an all-time record for the industry. What the audience heard in a theater could also be purchased in the form of recordings. And those profits would rise dramatically if the studios had more direct control of the music heard in films. The end of the 1920s and the beginning of the 1930s witnessed the major studios acquiring old, established music publishers. Tin Pan Alley, so intimately connected with New York City, became the target of West Coast movie entrepreneurs, anxious to have direct control over the all-important copyrights of published songs. That way, they would not have to pay an outside group for permission to use particular music in films. In addition, a host of composers and lyricists moved west, abandoning the old, but shaky, publishing strongholds for the security of employment in the booming film industry. This transition, a major one, further diminished the influence of once-mighty Tin Pan Alley.[9]

And yet, given the cyclical nature of cinema, musicals fell out of favor at the all-important box office the next year, 1931. From seventy-two musical productions in 1930, the number plummeted to a mere sixteen. Apparently, fickle moviegoers had had their fill; attention shifted to other film genres, and the studios displayed a reluctance to produce anything that would not show a profit. The earlier musicals had earned big money, led by pictures like the aforementioned *The Jazz Singer, Singing Fool,* and 1929's *The Broadway Melody*. In the meantime, audiences turned to pictures about crime (*Little Caesar*, 1930), more crime (*Public Enemy*, 1931), fantasy (both *Dracula* and *Frankenstein*, 1931), and drama (*Grand Hotel*, 1932). Once-mighty Warner Brothers, the studio that had brought Jolson to the screen, fell on hard financial times. In 1932, with losses in the industry running rampant, and an economic depression wracking the nation, only seven musicals reached movie screens.

With little to lose, in 1933 an almost-bankrupt Warner Brothers released *42nd Street*. Categorized as a "backstage musical" because it supposedly gives the audience an insider's view of the doings of the cast, it helped create the myth of the gutsy chorine, the young woman who fights overwhelming odds for her big chance. In the plot, Ruby Keeler, a dancer who would tap her feet to fame and many more major roles as a result of this movie, takes over at the last minute for the ailing star, played by Bebe Daniels. Featuring a memorable score by Harry Warren and Al Dubin, *42nd Street* soon recaptured the missing audience. Its release signaled the rebirth of the type, and its tough (but not hard) characters allow for some social commentary not often found in popular films.

Nineteen thirty-three turned out to be the bleakest year of the Depression; unemployment had reached its peak, affecting some 25 percent of the labor

The songwriting team of Harry Warren (standing; 1893–1981) and Al Dubin (seated; 1891–1945) struck movie gold during the 1930s. The two—Warren wrote the music, Dubin the lyrics—first came together in 1932 to work on the score for *42nd Street* (1933), the film that defined musicals for the decade. One hit after another followed that collaboration, and in 1935 they won a "Best Song" Academy Award for "Lullaby of Broadway," a number appearing in *Gold Diggers of 1935*. [Library of Congress, Prints & Photographs Division]

force. The worsening crisis had shaken the country's faith in hard work and deferred gratification, a situation that allowed directors and screenwriters an unusual forum. Movies like *42nd Street* affirm the old mythology of labor and its resultant rewards, that singing and dancing your heart out will bring about good things.

Flush with renewed success, Warner Brothers also released *Gold Diggers of 1933*, reinforcing the point about the value of hard work. Ginger Rogers, emerging as a star in her own right, sings a cheery number that challenges "Old Man Depression":

> "Gold Digger's Song (We're in the Money)"
> Music by Harry Warren; Lyrics by Al Dubin
>
> We're in the money, we're in the money;
> We've got a lot of what it takes to get along!
> We're in the money, the skies are sunny;
> Old man depression, you are through,
> You done us wrong!
> We never see a headline
> 'bout a breadline, today,
> And when we see the landlord,
> We can look that guy right in the eye.
> We're in the money, Come, on my honey,
> Let's spend it, lend it, send it rolling along.

A counter to all the grim statistics then gaining headlines, "We're in the Money" epitomizes the spunky attitudes espoused by many of the era's musicals. Rogers even voices some of the lyrics in Pig Latin—for what reason, no one seems to know—and for a brief moment the audience can believe that it is also "in the money." With all its upbeat messages and energetic hoofing, *Gold Diggers of 1933* ends on a surprisingly somber note. Joan Blondell, usually a wise-cracking comedian, gets to sing "Remember My Forgotten Man," a haunting number that features a circular geometric arrangement of silhouetted men, mostly forgotten veterans, marching in hopeless circles. This closing image serves as a grim, realistic reminder of the Depression lurking just outside the doors of the theater, along with the plight of veterans denied their benefits.

The studio completed its 1933 trilogy of feisty musicals with *Footlight Parade*, and cast none other than Jimmy Cagney as a hard-working, but broke, producer who refuses to admit that he might be down and out. In all three pictures, Ruby Keeler and Dick Powell sing and dance, establishing a partnership that would endure for much of the decade. Against a backdrop of gritty realism, the two personify youthful earnestness and innocence. Their appearances, both together and in separate pictures, captivated audiences. Powell could croon (passably) to Joan Blondell in *Broadway Gondolier*, a piece of fluff from 1935; Keeler could dance (quite well) on a giant human typewriter in 1937's *Ready, Willing, and Able*, an otherwise forgettable musical from 1937. But their popularity signaled a resurgence for the genre, one that had commenced with *42nd Street*.

One of the reasons people recall the music from these Warner Brothers pictures concerns their method of presentation. Choreographer Busby Berkeley became famous almost overnight because of the myriad ways he manipulated groups of actors and dancers on the screen. He created a visually bold and imaginative cinematic style; almost alone, he defined 1930s dance and the music accompanying it.

Like so many others, Berkeley had come to Hollywood from Broadway and went to work devising sequences of massed dancers that continue to amaze viewers. With military precision, his performers, accompanied by the tunes of the day, blossom into lush flowers, become complex geometric forms, shrink and expand. It enthralled audiences, their perspective often the "Berkeley top shot," an overhead camera that looks directly down on the dancers, allowing all the surreal shapes and patterns to evolve with the music. These films also treated moviegoers to much feminine pulchritude, despite the Code and its restrictions. Perhaps the Breen Office hesitated to censor frames the studio ostensibly presented as "art." Art or cheesecake, the Berkeley sequences are firmly grounded in Depression America. He makes it clear that his dancers, most of them members of the chorus, sweat and strain for minimal pay. They are not elitist members of a ballet troupe, and the working-class plots address the very real issues of unemployment and getting by as best as one can.[10]

As noted, the talents of Irving Berlin, the Gershwins, Jerome Kern, Cole Porter, and Rodgers and Hart dominated Broadway musicals during the 1930s; this same grouping of composers and lyricists also had a disproportionate impact on the movies of the period. The Hollywood studios saw what attracted audiences back in New York, and quickly began to line up the film rights to their work. In many cases, the dust had hardly settled on the stage before a movie adaptation of a particular musical went into production. At the close of the 1930s, over 450 musicals had poured forth from Hollywood, and a disproportionate number of them had been scored by the same group—Berlin, the Gershwins, Kern, Porter, and Rodgers and Hart.

Irving Berlin (1888–1989)

Most often associated with the Broadway stage and Tin Pan Alley, Irving Berlin also enjoyed strong connections with Hollywood and the movie industry. Since millions already knew his music, Berlin's name began to crop up in pictures from the first days of sound.

For example, in Al Jolson's landmark *The Jazz Singer* (1927), the popular entertainer sings "Blue Skies," one of the songwriter's great compositions. It had been written initially for a long-forgotten stage musical entitled *Betsy* (1911), and Berlin receives no credits in *The Jazz Singer* titles, but since so many people saw the film—far more than could ever see a stage play—it promptly enjoyed a new life, a song that enters collective memory.

In director King Vidor's *Hallelujah* (1929), a pioneering black musical, Berlin—uncredited again—contributed to the score. Vidor, a famous director of silent films, proclaimed *Hallelujah* to be an "all-black folk opera." Although it does feature a black cast, a rarity for the time, white songwriters, including Berlin, composed the score for the picture. Nothing of any musical note emerged from this effort, although Berlin penned "Waiting at the End of the Road" and "Swanee Shuffle." The latter number falls into the category of stereotypical "Mammy" tunes so popular then.

Irving Berlin provides much of the musical accompaniment to the film version of the Marx Brothers' 1925 stage play *The Cocoanuts*. Released in 1929 by Paramount Studios, this time the composer gets credited, just as he had in the successful Broadway show. *The Cocoanuts* did well as a movie, establishing the Marx Brothers as one of the best comedy teams of the day. "Florida by the Sea," "When My Dreams Come True," "Monkey-Doodle-Doo," and several others come from Berlin's pen, having originated in the theatrical version, and demonstrating that Broadway could be successfully transferred to Hollywood.

Those efforts, along with several other movie assignments, firmly established Berlin in the film community. In 1930, he worked on a picture called *Mammy*; no longer an anonymous contributor, the composer received full credit. Al Jolson, still riding on the publicity generated by *The Jazz Singer*, starred in the picture. Berlin and James Gleason had written a minstrel play entitled *Mr. Bones* in 1928, and *Mammy* served as its movie incarnation. Berlin's compositions include "Across the Breakfast Table," "Here We Are," and "To My Mammy." Uncomfortable as they might make people feel today, Berlin's variations on "Mammy" songs—stereotypical images and all—attracted listeners then, and must be understood in the context of their times.

Puttin' on the Ritz (1930), yet another movie musical featuring Berlin's tunes, contains one of his best-known compositions. At the time, Harry Richman, a popular song-and-dance man, sang "Puttin' on the Ritz" in the film and he considered it "his." But when Fred Astaire performed the same song some years later in the movie *Blue Skies* (1946), audiences promptly forgot Richman. "Puttin' on the Ritz" had a new owner, and Astaire has been associated with the number ever since. In addition to that classic, the movie also contains "With You" and "Alice in Wonderland."

In 1931, singer Bing Crosby had begun his march to fame, and *Reaching for the Moon*, a film featuring Berlin's music, helped him along. Crosby got to sing "When the Folks High-Up Do the Mean Low-Down," a jazzy little number that showcased Crosby's ability to lightly swing, as well as Berlin's ability to write just about any kind of tune. Throughout his long career, Crosby would be known primarily as a singer, but his engaging personality led to numerous movie appearances that gave him additional exposure. When not in a recording studio or at a radio station rehearsing for one of his shows, chances were good he could be found at a Hollywood back lot working on a new picture.

While Crosby's Hollywood star rose, Berlin's presence in the movies almost disappeared during the period 1932–1934. He had returned to New York and spent most of his time writing for Broadway and running his music publishing house. Occasional pieces by him can be found on various soundtracks; more likely than not uncredited and incidental to the pictures themselves. Such was the case with *Young Bride* (1932), *Only Yesterday* (1933), and *Kid Millions* (1934), the last a vehicle for entertainer Eddie Cantor. The comedian gets to reprise "Mandy," a 1919 Berlin signature song from the Ziegfeld Follies. But this hiatus did not mean a lessening of interest in film; it only gave Berlin pause before his triumphal return to the movies.

That return, which carried from 1935 to 1936, involved *Top Hat* (1935) and *Follow the Fleet* (1936), back-to-back musicals that catapulted him to the top of Hollywood songwriters: Both films featured Fred Astaire and Ginger Rogers, the reigning champions of movie musicals and dance. Berlin's lilt-

A typical movie poster from the 1930s, in this case *Follow the Fleet* (1936), a frothy musical featuring the inimitable Fred Astaire and Ginger Rogers. The producers realized the importance audiences gave particular songwriters, so instead of the director (Mark Sandrich) receiving billing, it is Irving Berlin and his song-packed score that gets credit, and in print the same size as that promoting the two stars. [Library of Congress, Prints & Photographs Division]

ing melodies for these pictures have long since become American standards, and they proved ideal for displaying the dancing prowess of the two stars. *Top Hat* showcased "Top Hat, White Tie, and Tails," a tune and lyric that neatly summed up the great movie musicals of the 1930s and the popular image of night life in big cities. But it also included "No Strings," "Isn't This a Lovely Day?" and another dance classic, "Cheek to Cheek."

Not to be outdone, *Follow the Fleet* offered "I'm Putting All My Eggs in One Basket," "Let's Face the Music and Dance," "Let Yourself Go," and "I'd Rather Lead a Band." With splendid music and lyrics, the dance team of Fred Astaire and Ginger Rogers, some of the best costuming and Art Deco sets ever seen, and cheerful, fast-moving plots, *Top Hat* and *Follow the Fleet* had it all. Small wonder they are still shown on television and continue to be looked on as almost-flawless models of the 1930s Hollywood musical.

Riding on the crest of popularity generated by those two films, Berlin stayed at the top with 1937's *On the Avenue*, a musical featuring Dick Powell and Alice Faye, two other popular favorites. "I've Got My Love to Keep Me Warm" and "This Year's Kisses" stand out in a sparkling score.

Carefree marked movie calendars in 1938 because it promised another Astaire/Rogers/Berlin outing, their third. The tunes tend toward the humorous, especially with "Since They Turned Loch Lomond into Swing" and "The Yam." But the film also includes such evergreens as "Change Partners" and "Carefree." Clearly, during the mid-1930s, Irving Berlin enjoyed a long-running career peak.

No such peaks can be maintained forever, and the songwriter coasted for the remainder of the decade, at least with his movie work. *Alexander's Ragtime Band* (1938) consists of a pastiche of older Berlin favorites, like "Blue Skies," "Easter Parade," and the title song. Great songs, all of them, but old wine in a new bottle. *Second Fiddle* (1939), on the other hand, serves as a vehicle to show off Sonja Henie's ice-skating skills, and the Berlin score lacks much inspiration. "Dancing Back to Back" (quite a departure from "Cheek to Cheek") and "When Winter Comes" do not rank among his most memorable compositions.

Other projects still beckoned this remarkable composer, and some of his greatest work still lay ahead. The 1940s would see *Annie Get Your Gun* (play, 1946), *Easter Parade* (movie, 1948), and "White Christmas" (1942; in the film *Holiday Inn*), reputedly the top-selling single of all time.[11]

George and Ira Gershwin (1898–1937; 1896–1983)

When the Gershwins arrived in Hollywood in 1936, they had by then established considerable renown in musical circles everywhere. *The King of Jazz*, a 1930 picture put together by bandleader Paul Whiteman, the so-called "King of Jazz," did in fact feature some of 1924's *Rhapsody in Blue* on its soundtrack. In 1926, George had collaborated with lyricist Herbert Stothart for *Song of the Flame*, a Broadway musical that involved other songwriters as well. Remade as a movie in 1930, it changed little, and Gershwin and Stothart's "Cossack Love Song" and the title tune played to movie audiences. *Girl Crazy*, the brothers' hit 1930 Broadway musical, also came to the screen, just two years after being on the stage, but in a lackluster adaptation. In 1943, it resurfaced as a Mickey Rooney–Judy Garland musical with the Tommy Dorsey band, and again in 1962, this time retitled *When the Boys Meet the Girls*, a film saved only by the presence of Louis Armstrong performing "I Got Rhythm."

Mention should also be made of 1931's *Delicious*. For that Twentieth Century–Fox movie, George wrote a piece variously called *Manhattan Rhapsody, New York Rhapsody*, and *Rhapsody in Rivets*. The first two titles refer to the movie's locale, the last to a section that suggests a riveter working on a construction project. These themes coalesced into the *Second Rhapsody for Piano and Orchestra* (1932), an expanded version of the music heard in the film. Not as well-known as his *Rhapsody in Blue*, the work nonetheless shows his continuing interest in blending popular themes with classical writing. *Delicious* also includes more typical joint George and Ira works, such as "Delishious," "Blah, Blah, Blah," and "Welcome to the Melting Pot."

As far as movies went, not until 1937 did the public feel the full force of the brothers' genius. Fred Astaire and Ginger Rogers, already two of the biggest Hollywood names of the decade, made their seventh picture together and their Gershwin debut with *Shall We Dance*. A fluffy concoction that features splendid dancing and an equally fine score, the movie ranges from the lovely "They Can't Take That Away from Me" to the happy "Slap That Bass," and sweetens the plot with songs like "Let's Call the Whole Thing Off" and "They All Laughed." *Shall We Dance* shows off Astaire, Rogers, and the Gershwins at their best. Virtually the entire musical accompaniment has entered the realm of standards, a prodigious feat.

RKO Pictures, the studio that had released *Shall We Dance*, doubtless wanted to cash in on the ongoing popularity of the two stars, but an additional pairing could not be arranged at that moment, and so *A Damsel in Distress* (1937) stars Fred Astaire and Joan Fontaine. Thanks to another bright Gershwin score, plus the comedy of George Burns and Gracie Allen, the film passes muster, but Joan Fontaine is no Ginger Rogers. Dancing aside, songs like "A Foggy Day," "Nice Work if You Can Get It," and "Things Are Looking Up" lift *A Damsel in Distress* above the general run of movie musicals and reinforce the shared genius of the brothers.

The Goldwyn Follies (1938), one of those "all-star" pictures that brings a number of personalities together, but not always successfully, sports another fine Gershwin medley. George had died in 1937, but *The Goldwyn Follies* had already gone into production at that time. Thus the numbers heard in the movie count among his last works. "Love Walked In," "I Was Doing All Right," and "Love Is Here to Stay" certainly survive the silly plot and make a fine legacy, plus the picture also boasts several additional songs co-written by Kurt Weill and Ira Gershwin, including "Spring Again."

With George gone, *Strike Up the Band* (1940) served as the final film of the era to claim a joint Gershwin score. Ostensibly a remake of the 1930 Broadway show of the same name, the movie version mysteriously drops virtually all the original music—"Soon," "I've Got a Crush on You"—for a rather flavorless score by composer Roger Edens and lyricist Arthur Freed. The title tune becomes the only piece from 1930 that survives such harsh editing. Yet another vehicle for the enormously popular Mickey Rooney and Judy Garland, along with the Paul Whiteman band, the movie shares little with its theatrical predecessor, but the chances are good that those who saw the movie never saw the play and vice versa. This same fate would occur to the Rodgers and Hart musical *On Your Toes* (play, 1936; movie, 1939), and that, too, involved Garland and Rooney (see below).

Over the years, George's unforgettable melodies, coupled with Ira's clever and sophisticated lyrics, have proved timeless, the kind of music that never goes out of date. Although their music pops up in numerous movies, the brothers actually spent little time writing directly for motion pictures. Drawn instead to New York and the theater, they apparently enjoyed the challenges of a Broadway show more than they did those found in a Hollywood musical.[12]

Jerome Kern (1885–1945)

Jerome Kern's association with Hollywood began early and lasted throughout most of his life. At first, he involved himself with revisions of his previous stage work as well as creating new Broadway productions. In time, however, his film career gained the upper hand and he finally abandoned Broadway altogether to focus on movie scores.

With the coming of sound, Universal Studios in 1929 rushed out a sound-and-silent mix of Kern's classic stage musical *Show Boat* (1927). Billing it as a "Super Talking Picture," the production left much to be desired. The studio abbreviated the original, substituting new, non-Kern material. With improving sound technology, *Show Boat* saw a second, more faithful movie adaptation in 1936 (see below), one that played on screens with much better results.

Sally, a film version of a 1920 Jerome Kern–Buddy DeSylva–Clifford Grey play, premiered in 1929. The producers unfortunately altered the score, and brought in a new number by Joe Burke and Al Dubin entitled "I'm Not Dreaming," but at least the Kern–Hammerstein classic, "Look for the Silver Lining" survived studio meddling.

Sunny, another Kern one-word production, first played on Broadway in 1925 and involved the talents of lyricists Otto Harbach and Oscar Hammerstein II. The screen adaptation was released in 1930. Although both the play and the film have long since been forgotten, "Who?" and "Sunny" live on from the score.

That same year, movie theaters also showed *The Three Sisters*, a musical not to be confused with Anton Chekov's 1899 drama of the same name. A little-known Twentieth Century–Fox film, it features a Jerome Kern–Oscar Hammerstein II score of equally little-known songs: "Lonely Feet," "Hand in Hand," "Keep Smiling," and "What Good Are Words?" Time has been unkind to both the movie and the score, since neither can be easily found today.

The memorable "She Didn't Say 'Yes'" comes from *The Cat and the Fiddle*, a 1931 Broadway musical developed by Kern and lyricist Otto Harbach. The two also wrote "The Night Was Made for Love" and "Try to Forget" for the play. With few changes, *The Cat and the Fiddle* adapted well to the screen in 1934, giving Jeanette MacDonald a good vehicle for her vocal skills.

As his fame grew, little time elapsed between Jerome Kern's stage presentations and their film adaptations. For example, *Music in the Air* first appeared on Broadway in 1932. Despite the severity of the Depression, it played for over 300 performances. Just two years later it appeared on movie screens across the land in a Twentieth Century–Fox production with Gloria Swanson. *Music in the Air* serves as a good example of the Kern–Hammerstein partnership. Not their greatest work, it nonetheless gave theater and film audiences the romantic "I've Told Ev'ry Little Star" and "The Song Is You."

I Dream Too Much (1935) features the rising opera star Lily Pons, which helps to explain its somewhat operatic presentation. The first film in which Kern teamed up with lyricist Dorothy Fields, the score seems designed around Pons's singing, no small task. Among the numbers fashioned for the contralto, "I'm the Echo (You're the Song that I Love)," "I Got Love," and the title song stand out. *I Dream Too Much* illustrates Kern's versatility as a composer, but it also demonstrates that he felt more at home writing popular melodies than trying to fit his style to a particular singer.

The movie *Reckless* (1935), a non-musical, does offer one Kern–Hammerstein collaboration, the title song. Performed by the underestimated Nina Mae

McKinney, "Reckless" gave McKinney, a black vocalist, some exposure to white audiences in a racially segregated time (see later in this chapter for more on McKinney).

The mid-1930s proved boom years for Kern and his collaborators, and in 1935 another of his Broadway plays made the transition from stage to screen. *Sweet Adeline*, written with Oscar Hammerstein II, had boasted a successful theatrical run in 1929. Not much tinkering occurred either with the story or the music, and audiences could enjoy Irene Dunne, along with "Why Was I Born" and "Here Am I," two lesser-known melodies from the original *Sweet Adeline*.

The third film to feature Fred Astaire and Ginger Rogers together was *Roberta* (1935); it also served as the first, but not the last, pairing of Jerome Kern with the two stars. Based on his 1933 Broadway smash hit, this popular picture employed the original score Kern had put together with Otto Harbach, plus two new numbers with lyrics by Dorothy Fields and Jimmy McHugh. The resultant score, one of the best ever for any Hollywood musical, offers such standards as "Let's Begin," "Smoke Gets in Your Eyes," and "Yesterdays" (all with lyrics by Harbach), plus "Lovely to Look At" and "I Won't Dance" (lyrics by Fields and McHugh). If anything, the film score improves on the stage version, plus the movie offers the nonpareil dancing of Astaire and Rogers.

Given his previous successes, Kern worked only with the most talented lyricists during the 1930s, and Dorothy Fields (1905–1974) has to be ranked in that elite group. One of the few women to experience success in the competitive business of song writing, Fields' career eventually covered some fifty years and produced more than 300 songs. Starting out on Tin Pan Alley in the 1920s, she teamed with Jimmy McHugh for a number of good tunes. In the early 1930s, she joined the exodus to Hollywood and wrote for movie musicals. Shortly thereafter she began working with Jerome Kern. Beginning with *Roberta* in 1935, they eventually collaborated on five movies, and her career moved constantly upward. Dorothy Fields returned to New York around 1941 to resume writing for the Broadway theater, a love she pursued until her death in 1974.

For their second film score, Kern and Fields created the music for *Swing Time* (1936), which also happened to be their second Fred Astaire–Ginger Rogers picture. Many fans maintain that *Swing Time* ranks as the best of the nine Astaire–Rogers pictures produced during the 1930s. If correct, the judgment comes in no small measure because of the superlative score that graces

Although seldom spoken of as a songwriting team (in the sense of Rodgers and Hart, Warren and Dubin, Razaf and Waller, George and Ira Gershwin, etc.), whenever composer Jerome Kern (1885–1945) and lyricist Dorothy Fields (1905–1974) worked together, outstanding music usually resulted. Both collaborated with others—Kern frequently wrote with Otto Harbach and Oscar Hammerstein II, and Fields and Jimmy McHugh penned some memorable songs—but in the 1930s the Kern–Fields partnership created such chestnuts as "A Fine Romance," "The Way You Look Tonight," and "Pick Yourself Up." In addition, Dorothy Fields stands out as one of the few women to find success in the male-dominated music world. [Library of Congress, Prints & Photographs Division]

the movie. "The Way You Look Tonight," the Academy Award winner for "Best Song" in 1936, highlights the picture. But *Swing Time* contains almost nothing but highlights: "A Fine Romance," "Pick Yourself Up," and the lilting "Waltz in Swing Time." All of these timeless songs became popular hits and embellished the careers of everyone involved.

By 1936, no movies mixed silent film with sound anymore; audiences took it for granted that all pictures had sound from beginning to end, and so the time had come to remake *Show Boat*, the great 1927 Kern–Hammerstein play that had been attempted as a silent-plus-sound movie in 1929 (see above). The resultant production, featuring Irene Dunne, Paul Robeson, Helen Morgan, and a host of other Hollywood stars, presents the original music, featuring standards like "Ol' Man River," "Make Believe," and "Can't Help Lovin' Dat Man." In addition, the film adds several new numbers—"Ah Still Suits Me," "I Have the Room Above Her," and "Gallivantin' Around"—and although hardly on a par with the 1927 score, neither do they take away from it. In all respects, this new *Show Boat* displays Kern at his best.

No more of Kern's earlier plays saw film adaptations until 1941. RKO Radio Pictures released *Sunny* at that time, a remake of his 1930 movie that had been fashioned from his original 1925 play, which illustrates just how complicated theatrical and cinematic lineages can be. In the meantime, the composer, successful in Hollywood, devoted his attention exclusively to movies, and did not participate in another stage production until 1939 and *Very Warm for May*.

Paramount Pictures came out with *High, Wide and Handsome* in 1937, a kind of history picture and musical rolled into one. It purports to tell the story about the quest for oil in nineteenth-century Pennsylvania. The words and music to accompany this tale came from Hammerstein and Kern. The fact that Paramount felt impelled to couch a historical event in musical terms perhaps suggests some timidity on the studio's part to focus on a little-known page from America's past. Although few recall the movie, "The Folks Who Live on the Hill," a romantic song that never refers to oil or American history, has become a standard, one beloved by many vocalists ever since.

When You're in Love (1937), another product of the Kern–Fields working relationship, stars Grace Moore, a prominent opera star. The movie resembles their earlier *I Dream Too Much* (1935), as a showpiece for contralto Lily Pons (see above). Not particularly memorable, the best number in *When You're in Love* is "Our Song," although Moore gamely takes a stab at Cab Calloway's signature "Minnie the Moocher" (1931; words and music by Calloway, Barney Bigard, and Irving Mills). By 1937, with everyone climbing onto the swing bandwagon, it may not have seemed too outlandish at the time for an opera star to tackle Cab Calloway and an up-tempo tune. Later generations might disagree.

Boasting both a story and lyrics by Dorothy Fields, Kern's *Joy of Living* (1938) comes across as a combination of screwball comedy and musical, with the capable Irene Dunne in the lead. The jump from musicals to comedy should not be thought a great one, since many film comedies utilized music as part of their plots, and vice versa. In fact, the term "musical comedy" effectively bridges any gap between the two genres. In addition to the humor, several standards like "You Couldn't Be Cuter" and "Just Let Me Look at You" emerged with the screenplay, a bright, cheery entry among the movies of the day.

For his final film score of the decade, Kern again worked with Dorothy Fields. *One Night in the Tropics* (1940) stars the rising comedy team of (Bud) Abbott and (Lou) Costello. This bit of fluff features "You and Your Kiss," "Back in My Shell," and "Simple Philosophy." Abbott and Costello might seem a far cry from the majesty of *Show Boat*, but Kern functioned as a popular—and commercial—composer. In retrospect, it is remarkable how much of his music, written for decidedly inferior movies, lives on, while the films themselves have been mercifully forgotten.

As the 1940s progressed, Jerome Kern continued to write for the movie medium. Only his untimely death in 1945 stopped his prolific pen, but he had been responsible for the scores of some twenty-four movie musicals. Of that total, some ten consisted of reworkings of his previous stage plays, but these often included new music. His compositions also could be heard incidentally and often uncredited in a number of other pictures. His lyricist collaborators—Dorothy Fields, Oscar Hammerstein II, Otto Harbach—have to be counted among the best of the best, and together they made a lasting impact on American popular song.[13]

Cole Porter (1891–1964)

Probably no one has achieved such sophistication in lyrics as Cole Porter. He first began to contribute to movie soundtracks in 1929, the year that saw the release of *The Gay Lady*, also called *The Battle of Paris*. The picture starred Gertrude Lawrence, a major star of the day, and she sang his "They All Fall in Love." It did not make Porter an overnight sensation, but it did boost his career.

In 1930, First National produced *Paris*, a film version of Porter's 1928 Broadway show of the same name. Apparently songwriter Harry Warren, soon to be an important composer of film scores in his own right, also contributed, uncredited, to this effort.

Several years elapsed before Porter's name again appeared on the screen. But this absence was probably his own doing; he busied himself in New York writing the music to a succession of Broadway musicals. Finally, in 1934, Porter's name once more adorned a film. *The Gay Divorcee*, the renamed movie version of Porter's 1932 play *Gay Divorce*, had its release. Incidentally, the aforementioned "Mister and Missus Fitch" did not make the cut. As with the title, the Code would not allow the language, and no one seemed able to reword it in such a way as to make it acceptable.

The second of nine Fred Astaire–Ginger Rogers musicals released during the 1930s, *The Gay Divorcee* stands as the only one with which Porter had any association. But the connection proved minimal because RKO had dropped most of his original score for new material. Only Porter's pulsating "Night and Day" survives. Con Conrad and Herb Magidson took on the remaining score; the two old pros contributed "A Needle in a Haystack" and the delightful "Continental." But the deletions from *The Gay Divorcee* had resulted in a new and different musical, and all the changes and negotiations perhaps soured Porter on Hollywood, thus explaining his greater devotion to musical theater.

In 1936, *Born to Dance* came to movie theaters. This picture marked Porter's return to film musicals. Not an adaptation of previous work, and featuring an intact score, *Born to Dance* boasted a topnotch cast including James Stewart and Eleanor Powell, two young and rising stars of the era. The music includes two classics, "Easy to Love" and "I've Got You Under My Skin."

In a curious turn, however, *Anything Goes* (1936) bears the same name as Porter's hit play of 1934, but once again much of the original music has disappeared, just as in *Gay Divorce/The Gay Divorcee*. Ethel Merman fortunately belts out "Anything Goes" and "I Get a Kick Out of You" in both the play and the movie, and she teams up with co-star Bing Crosby for a rendition of the sophisticated "You're the Top." But such classics as "All Through the Night" and "Blow, Gabriel, Blow" are obviously missing. Why the producers chose to cut these numbers from the movie remains a mystery, and the substituted songs, while adequate, do not do justice to this outstanding musical comedy.

Dancer Eleanor Powell appears in another Porter vehicle, *Rosalie* (1937). Although Sigmund Romberg and George Gershwin collaborated on a 1928 Broadway play of the same name, the two works share nothing other than identical titles. The movie *Rosalie* stars not just Powell, but also the popular Nelson Eddy doing the vocals. The movie resembles the frothy operettas then so much in vogue, which means that *Rosalie* lacks much of a plot. But that seemed to matter little to Porter; he managed to compose the memorable "In the Still of the Night" and "Who Knows?"

As the decade closed, MGM released *Broadway Melody of 1940*, a big-budget musical that featured the talents of both Fred Astaire and Eleanor Powell.

Porter responded to the challenge, composing "I've Got My Eyes on You" and "I Concentrate on You," and resurrecting his biggest hit of the 1930s, "Begin the Beguine." Made famous by numerous recordings, especially the 1938 version by Artie Shaw and his band, "Begin the Beguine" originally appeared in *Jubilee*, a 1935 Broadway show for which Porter wrote words and music.

Cole Porter would continue to contribute to movie scores and adapt his shows to the film medium for the rest of his life. But his connections to Hollywood remained tenuous. Producers apparently deemed much of his music too sophisticated or "too adult" for movie audiences, and Porter himself did not demonstrate that great a fondness for the film capital. New York, its clubs, its urbanity, seemed more suited to Porter's tastes. As a result, a good percentage of his most memorable music comes from stage productions, not movies.[14]

Richard Rodgers (1902–1979) and Lorenz Hart (1895–1943)

The unlikely pairing of the methodical Richard Rodgers and the mercurial Lorenz Hart created some of the finest music ever heard on the Broadway stage. Hollywood utilized their talents, since the popularity of sound created an unquenchable appetite for movies containing music. With their unparalleled history of stage hits, they were natural choices to write songs for a variety of films.

In 1930, First National Pictures released *Spring Is Here*, the film version of Rodgers and Hart's 1929 play of the same name. A remarkably quick turnaround from stage to screen, the show offered audiences the memorable "With a Song in My Heart," a tune that almost immediately entered the ranks of standards.

Leathernecking, the title given to the screen adaptation of *Present Arms*, a 1928 musical by the team, had its screen release in 1930. In both versions, "You Took Advantage of Me" proved the hit number, although "A Kiss for Cinderella" also became popular.

Another Rodgers and Hart musical, *Heads Up*, likewise saw a quick transfer to film. It had played on Broadway in 1929, and appeared on the screen in 1930, just as had occurred with *Spring Is Here*. Both versions of *Heads Up* boasted "A Ship without a Sail," an enduring standard, along with several other lesser-known tunes.

Despite its deceptive use of a song title written by the team, *Ten Cents a*

Dance (1931) cannot be thought either a musical or a Rodgers and Hart creation. Instead, the movie serves as a turgid melodrama for actress Barbara Stanwyck. The plot recounts the dreary life of a taxi dancer. The song, a doleful lament taken from their 1930 musical, *Simple Simon*, does get played in the film and fits the movie's story, but that marks the limit of their involvement.

The two collaborated on *The Hot Heiress* in 1931. Hardly their most inspired score, the screenplay forced them to create such songs as "Nobody Loves a Riveter" and "You're the Cats." But they worked as artists for hire, as did most composers and lyricists, both on Broadway and in Hollywood; their job called for providing music appropriate to the project, and sometimes that meant some rather forgettable tunes.

In the depths of the Depression, the pair did create *Love Me Tonight* (1932), a light-hearted vehicle for the popular French entertainer Maurice Chevalier, along with Jeanette MacDonald. One of the best Rodgers and Hart scores ever, it featured "Mimi," "Isn't It Romantic?" "Lover," and the title song. If anyone needed proof that the movies could provide escapism, *Love Me Tonight* should do that job well.

The Phantom President (1932) featured an all-star cast consisting of George M. Cohan, Jimmy Durante, and Claudette Colbert. Given a line-up like that, this musical should have been more. Even the Rodgers and Hart score lacks anything memorable, although "Give Her a Kiss" comes close.

The two got back on track with *Hallelujah, I'm a Bum!* (1933), a musical comedy featuring Al Jolson. The film captures some of the essence of the Depression in Ben Hecht's and S. N. Behrman's literate script, much of which the authors wrote in rhyme. Unemployment and money worries drive the story, and Rodgers and Hart responded with songs like "You Are Too Beautiful" and "I'll Do It Again," plus a good Depression number, "What Do You Want with Money?" They even appear in uncredited cameos in the picture.

With the success of such movies as *42nd Street* and *Gold Diggers of 1933*, the industry began to look more favorably on musicals. In an attempt to attract larger audiences to that format, the studios would every so often trot out their most popular stars in films that harked back to the revues of Broadway. Such was the case with *Dancing Lady* (1933) and *Hollywood Party* (1934), both produced by MGM. The first picture stars Joan Crawford, Clark Gable, Nelson Eddy, and provided Fred Astaire his film debut. It also gave musical teams like Harold Adamson and Burton Lane, Jimmy McHugh and Dorothy Fields, Nacio Herb Brown and Arthur Freed, as well as Richard Rodgers and Lorenz

Hart, an opportunity to create a musical backdrop. Much of the Rodgers and Hart score remains forgettable—they contributed "That's the Rhythm of the Day"—allowing Adamson and Lane to garner top honors with "Everything I Have Is Yours" and "Heigh Ho, the Gang's All Here," the latter taken from a 1931 edition of *Earl Carroll's Vanities*.

In the second film, *Hollywood Party*, (Stan) Laurel and (Oliver) Hardy star, along with most of the MGM stable. Rodgers and Hart, Brown and Freed, Walter Donaldson and Gus Kahn, and Donaldson and Howard Dietz composed the songs. Perhaps the Donaldson–Kahn number, "I've Had My Moments," outshines the others; certainly Rodgers and Hart's "Reincarnation," "Hello," and the title tune have been forgotten. But their inclusion did indicate a renewed interest in musicals, good news for songwriters everywhere.

That interest spread beyond American shores; *Evergreen* (1934), a Rodgers and Hart original, appeared in a British production that was also released to theaters in the United States. The somewhat unbelievable story of a young woman masquerading as her mother, the movie contains several outstanding numbers, including "Dancing on the Ceiling" (a tune dropped from Broadway's *Simple Simon* in 1930), "Dear, Dear," and "If I Give In to You."

Bing Crosby and the two songwriters found themselves teamed in a light musical called *Mississippi* (1935). It proved a good pairing for both, although the major parties did not get along well on the set. Despite much bickering over the music, Rodgers and Hart created several memorable numbers— "Soon" (not to be confused with a 1930 song of the same title from the Gershwins), "It's Easy to Remember," and "Down by the River." Crosby enjoyed a hit with "It's Easy to Remember," but he would not record anything else by Rodgers and Hart for several years thereafter.

Dancing Pirate, another movie trifle for which Rodgers and Hart contributed the music, played on the nation's screens in 1936. The lilting "When You're Dancing the Waltz" originated with this little-known film, as did "Are You My Love?" but the film's greatest claim to fame comes from its being the first musical in which the cameras filmed the dance sequences in Technicolor.

Fools for Scandal (1938), a comedy designed to feature the talents of Carole Lombard, did not do well critically. The accompanying Rodgers and Hart score, about as light as the movie, included one standout number, "How Can You Forget?"

The songwriting partnership had opened *Babes in Arms* on Broadway in 1937. A big hit for them on stage, MGM adapted it to film in a lavish 1939 production, but one that does violence to the sparkling original score. Two of the hottest players in MGM's fold at the time were Judy Garland and Mickey Rooney. The studio cast them for *Babes in Arms*, but at the cost of much of the stage music. Favorites like "I Wish I Were in Love Again," "My Funny Valentine," "Johnny One Note," "Imagine," and "The Lady Is a Tramp" inexplicably disappeared, leaving the title tune and "Where or When" as the Rodgers and Hart survivors. But the cinematic *Babes in Arms* does not lack for music; the movie includes such writers as Stephen Foster ("Camptown Races," others), John Philip Sousa ("Stars and Stripes Forever"), George M. Cohan ("Give My Regards to Broadway"), and the veteran team of Nacio Herb Brown and Arthur Freed ("Good Morning," "You Are My Lucky Star"). Incidentally, much the same thing happened to George and Ira Gershwin's *Strike Up the Band* the following year; the play went to Hollywood to be shot as a Judy Garland/Mickey Rooney movie, and it lost most of the original score in the process (see the Gershwins, above).

The big studios, although capable of releasing the most mediocre movies, recognized quality scoring. With a sympathetic director and producer, everything came together and a fine picture resulted. Other times, too many hands and too many interests muddied up what might have been an outstanding film. *Babes in Arms* serves as a case in point. When MGM obtained the rights to the Rodgers and Hart musical, they clearly wanted to promote the team of Judy Garland and Mickey Rooney in order to capitalize on the young actors' popularity. Perhaps with a view that much of the score would be seen as "too adult" for the two young actors, the studio hired songsmiths Brown and Freed to create substitutions. Thus the excisions, thus the additions. Actually, a hit from the movie version was Brown and Freed's "Good Morning," a perfect vehicle for the youthful energies of Garland and Rooney. Thirteen years later, in *Singin' in the Rain*, another MGM opus, Debbie Reynolds, Donald O'Conner, and Gene Kelly gave "Good Morning" a rousing rendition. History repeats itself, and standards live on. With such a change in credits and music, the theatrical *Babes in Arms* and the screen adaptation become two different vehicles. Both provide audiences good musical comedy, each displays its own merits, but any attempts to compare them can be equated with the old apples-and-oranges conundrum.

Nineteen thirty-nine also saw the release of *On Your Toes*, another film adaptation of a Rodgers and Hart musical, this one dating from 1936. Just as with much of *Babes in Arms*, the memorable original score almost disappears. But not entirely. Most of the songs remain, but are relegated to background music instead of production numbers. Nonetheless, "There's a Small Hotel" gets its due, and Rodgers' foray into ballet, *Slaughter on Tenth Avenue*, receives the Hollywood works of lighting, camera angles, and all the rest. As with *Babes in Arms*, however, the film and the play remain poles apart.

On the other hand, *The Boys from Syracuse* (1940), taken from their 1938 Broadway success, stays reasonably close to the stage version. Author George Abbott based his book on Shakespeare's *The Comedy of Errors*, but Rodgers and Hart made their score very much a part of the twentieth century. "Sing for Your Supper," "This Can't Be Love," "Falling in Love with Love," and "He and She" emerged as standards to be added to the two songwriters' growing list.

Too Many Girls (1940) served as the last movie collaboration of the decade for the pair. Originally on stage in 1939, its move to the screen did little damage. The score includes "You're Nearer," "I Didn't Know What Time It Was," and the tongue-twisting "Potawatomine." Film and television buffs might find the casting for the movie of particular interest. On the stage, Marcy Westcott had the lead, but on the screen Lucille Ball took top honors. Also Lucy's husband-to-be, Desi Arnaz, landed a role in the movie. Despite her prominent part in a Rodgers and Hart musical, Ball's rise to stardom had to wait until television and *I Love Lucy* in 1951.

With Lorenz Hart's death in 1943, Richard Rodgers had to seek a new lyricist. He of course found a splendid match in Oscar Hammerstein II. The new team of Rodgers and Hammerstein would write theatrical history with their great hits like *Oklahoma!* (play, 1943; film, 1955), *Carousel* (play, 1945; film, 1956), *South Pacific* (play, 1949; film, 1958), and many others. For the 1930s, however, the pairing of Richard Rodgers and Lorenz Hart also made history, with the two contributing a body of unforgettable songs to American music.[15]

Additional Movie Musicals

With so many musicals being churned out by Hollywood, obviously other songwriters had hits in addition to all those piled up by Irving Berlin et al. The brief chronological listing that follows mentions some of the significant songs that appeared in movies and then, through radio, records, and sheet music, attained a kind of immortality of their own. In short, these songs also became standards. Since hundreds of new compositions came out almost yearly, any listing should be considered somewhat arbitrary and not be thought a complete survey of the genre.

In 1929, *The Broadway Melody*, a film that echoed its obvious debt to the Great White Way, featured Nacio Herb Brown and Arthur Freed's "You Were Meant for Me." It has the distinction of being the first movie musical to win a "Best Picture" Academy Award, a rare honor for this kind of film.

Mabel Wayne and Billy Rose combined their talents for words and music and came up with "It Happened in Monterey" for 1930's *King of Jazz*. The "King" of the title refers to Paul Whiteman, a popular bandleader who attempted to integrate jazz elements into his music.

Palmy Days (1931) contains "There's Nothing Too Good for My Baby" (Con Conrad, composer; words by Ballard MacDonald and Dave Silverstein). The song remains memorable for an energetic performance by Eddie Cantor, and the movie itself displays some examples of early Busby Berkeley choreography.

A real classic came along in 1932, one of the hardest years of the Great Depression. *Crooner*, a movie about a young musician trying for success as a singer, features a song entitled "In a Shanty in Old Shanty Town" (music by Little Jack Little and John Siras, lyrics by Joe Young). The film reflects reality; some people, particularly hard-hit by the crisis, had been reduced to living in shanty towns. Consisting of collections of decrepit shacks and makeshift dwellings, many had sprung up in urban centers across the country. A popular term for them was "Hooverville," a sardonic reference to President Hoover. The song, outwardly light-hearted, takes on a certain poignance that later generations of listeners might miss (see Chapter 1 for more on this movie and its connections to crooning).

Fred Astaire and Ginger Rogers' dancing could make almost any song seem magical. "The Carioca" (music by Vincent Youmans, lyrics by Gus Kahn and Edward Eliscu) proved no exception. Their interpretation of it steals the show in the first Astaire–Rogers pairing, *Flying Down to Rio* (1933).

Although mentioned previously, any survey of 1933's music must include virtually the entire scores for *42nd Street* and *Gold Diggers of 1933*. These two movies revitalized the Hollywood musical, and thanks must go to composer Harry Warren and lyricist Al Dubin; they put the spark into so many songs—"Shuffle Off to Buffalo," "You're Getting to Be a Habit with Me," "Pettin' in the Park," and "The Gold Digger's Song (We're in the Money)"—to name but a few. Surely Irving Berlin, Jerome Kern, and the others nodded their heads in admiration.

"My Old Flame" (1934), yet another unforgettable movie song from the 1930s, came from composer Arthur Johnston and lyricist Sam Coslow. Its host picture, *Belle of the Nineties*, stars Mae West, who performs the song in her inimitable style.

With musicals again drawing audiences and making money for Hollywood, the major studios held the form in high esteem by 1935. Harry Warren and Al Dubin, the aforementioned writing duo that had helped accomplish this feat, came back for an encore by scoring a sequel, *Gold Diggers of 1935*. This edition included a big hit, "Lullaby of Broadway," another tip of the hat to the Broadway tradition.

Composer Arthur Johnston worked with lyricist Johnny Burke to create "Pennies from Heaven" (1936), a standard first heard in the film of the same name. Bing Crosby, by then a major star, did the vocal honors with the tune.

Although the operetta form has never been terribly popular in the United States, for a few brief years during the 1930s, Jeanette MacDonald and Nelson Eddy made it their personal property. Starting with a surprisingly successful adaptation of Victor Herbert's *Naughty Marietta* (1935), the two teamed up again for a Hollywood version of Rudolph Friml's *Rose Marie* (1936). They went on to make a total of six of these frothy concoctions between 1935 and 1940. *Rose Marie* stands as probably their most successful pairing; the film includes "Indian Love Call" (1924; music by Rudolf Friml, lyrics by Oscar Hammerstein II), the number forever associated with the "singing sweethearts." *Bitter Sweet* (1940) and *Sweethearts* (1940) concluded their efforts for the decade, and the magic had admittedly worn thin. MacDonald was much the stronger performer of the two. Eddy, an adequate singer, came across as wooden playing his roles. Nevertheless, the fanciful costuming and Graustarkian sets, coupled with fairy-tale plots and some exuberant vocalizing, won an affectionate place in the hearts of millions of 1930s moviegoers. The operetta fad gave people a welcome dose of escapism as the country continued to fight the economic woes brought on by the Depression.

In 1938, Harry Warren teamed up with lyricist Johnny Mercer for "Jeepers Creepers." This bouncy little tune became part of a Dick Powell vehicle entitled *Going Places*, but Powell does not perform the song; Louis Armstrong takes the vocal part, and he sings the lyrics to a horse. What worked then might seem embarrassing and stereotypical today, but audiences probably found it hysterical at the time.

As the decade wound down, the hits kept coming. Harold Arlen, usually remembered as the composer of rather serious romantic melodies, and E. Y.

Harburg, the noted lyricist, wrote "Lydia, the Tattooed Lady" (1939), a hilarious spoof of anything in the least romantic. The song tells of the amorous adventures of Lydia through her many tattoos. This came from the same team that wrote the spirited score for *The Wizard of Oz* (1939). None other than Groucho Marx sang "Lydia" in *At the Circus*, so that might explain its silly lyrics. Goofy as it may be, "Lydia, the Tattooed Lady" actually possesses a good melody, along with some admittedly clever lyrics. Over time, it has entertained generations of listeners and established a little niche for itself in the annals of American music.

Swing reigned as king by 1940, and the movies obediently bowed to its popularity (see Chapter 4 for a listing of films featuring popular swing orchestras). One of the hits of that year had the title "Rhumboogie" (also called "Rhumbaboogie"; music by Don Raye; lyrics by Hugh Prince), a number that capitalized on both Latin music (the rhumba) and the growing interest in boogie-woogie, a lively form of piano blues that emphasizes a constantly repeated bass line. The tune appears in a boisterous Ritz Brothers comedy called *Argentine Nights*. "Rhumboogie" may not be the greatest song of all time, but it reflected popular trends. As an added plus, the film also features the Andrews Sisters, an energetic trio that captured the Swing Era in much of their music and would go on to have many hits throughout the 1940s.

Studios big and small also produced many other purely musical films during the 1930s, virtually all of them brief, running anywhere from three minutes to fifteen minutes. Variously called "shorts," "soundies," "featurettes," and the like, they usually focused on a particular band or singer. Since the typical bill at a theater might consist of two regular feature-length films, or a "double feature," plus "assorted short subjects," theater managers had to find appropriate films to accompany the newsreels, previews, and cartoons then commonplace. Producers specializing in the genre cranked out countless band shorts to satisfy this need. In an era when movie imagery tended to be as segregated as anything in society, these brief fillers gave black performers a much-needed outlet, a chance to be seen and heard on screen by large audiences. Bandleaders like Louis Armstrong, Duke Ellington, Cab Calloway, Fats Waller, and many others often headlined these short features.

A case in point would be the career of the aforementioned Nina Mae McKinney (1913–1967). She was working on the chorus line of *Lew Leslie's Blackbirds of 1928* when a talent scout spotted her. Soon thereafter McKinney landed a role in King Vidor's *Hallelujah* (1929), a musical spectacle that boasted an all-black cast. From that impressive beginning, she moved to an

MGM contract, but little work, because producers could not find sufficient roles for the vocalist. She finally spent much of the decade playing in cheap productions geared for black audiences. Despite the potential of being one of the leading actresses of the 1930s, she found herself reduced to playing in movies such as *Safe in Hell* (1931), *Kentucky Minstrels* (1934), *St. Louis Gal* (1938), *The Devil's Daughter* (1939), and *Pocomania* (1939), usually as a seductress or a woman with a questionable reputation who also gets the opportunity to sing somewhere in the movie.

Diverse small studios, with names like Million Dollar Productions or Creative Cinema Corporation, produced McKinney's films. A few larger organizations, such as Republic Pictures and Vitaphone, also utilized her talents. Despite the inequities, McKinney starred in at least fourteen films during the decade, most of which went unseen by white moviegoers. She continued her career into the 1940s, still playing stereotyped black roles.[16]

The Rise of Swing and the Triumph of the Big Bands

At the onset of the Great Depression—the end of the 1920s, the beginning of the 1930s—bands and orchestras, accompanied by lots of dancing, comprised a major part of the American entertainment scene. Popular dances, such as the Black Bottom, the Charleston, and the Varsity Drag, evolved into new steps, with names like the Shag, the Lindy Hop, the Suzy Q, the Big Apple, Truckin', and the Little Peach. With radios in many homes, people listened to jazz-influenced arrangements, and orchestras led by Ben Bernie, Isham Jones, Vincent Lopez, Paul Whiteman, and many others provided music for dancing. No one knew it at the time, but the stage had been set for the rise of big-band swing that would sweep the nation in the mid-1930s. In retrospect, it might seem a bit strange that it took half of the decade before swing emerged as the nation's primary musical format.

THE JAZZ HERITAGE

The 1920s have been called "The Jazz Age," a misleading title, because up-tempo dance music featuring an array of brass instruments does not necessarily equate to jazz. Such music usually exists as pop music with some jazz-like overtones. Until 1930 or so, jazz existed on the margins, a musical format produced and consumed principally by American blacks. For the larger white audience, traditionally written and arranged songs dominated the 1920s, just as they did in every decade of the twentieth century.[1]

From its rough beginnings in New Orleans during the 1890s and 1900s, jazz has relied on collective, polyphonic improvisation. In fact, improvisation—the ability of players to depart from a strictly ordered score—gives jazz its uniqueness. Other popular music depends on a prearranged structure, arrangements that do not allow for such freedom on the part of instrumentalists. A song may sound "jazzy," but more often than not the players are merely reading from an arrangement.

Although jazz has always played a role in the swing phenomenon, jazz itself has never been a major component of popular culture. It directs its appeal to innumerable subgroups, avid followers of particular forms who often disdain other kinds of musical expression. The swing of the thirties certainly grew out of jazz, but those who embraced swing might genuinely profess an ignorance about the larger subject of jazz itself. Swing, a facet of popular culture, grew on its own, not because of its links to jazz. Inflections taken from jazz certainly appeared in the music, but swing represented a much larger cultural, historical, and musical event that swept aside virtually everything before it. To paraphrase Duke Ellington, it really didn't mean a thing if it didn't swing, at least for a while; by the mid-1940s, however, the craze had run its course.

Music scholars have long proclaimed jazz as "America's music." Many of its historical roots may lie outside the country, especially certain rhythmic qualities and vocal nuances, but the music termed "jazz" grew up in the United States, a melding of influences as diverse as the nation itself. Despite such a rich heritage, only occasional compositions have attracted a broad, mass audience. By and large, that audience has traditionally shunned any jazz in its purer, unadulterated forms, accepting instead watered-down arrangements that tend toward the simplistic and repetitive, or novelty items that rely on gimmicks.[2]

With the advent of swing in the 1930s, jazz came the closest it has ever come to widespread popularity, that brief period called the Swing Era, roughly 1935 to the early 1940s. But swing itself cannot be defined as jazz, at least not jazz in any academic definition of the term. It, too, exists as an amalgam, a mix of jazz, dance music, popular songs, and standards that receive a rhythmic emphasis that causes them to "swing."

In swing, the blending of these various components, along with tight instrumental arranging, results in a form of popular music that relies on ensemble playing, not individual improvisation. The end result might contain considerable jazz-like phrasing, even at times including brilliant, improvised passages, but such contributions go to the collective whole. The music remains swing, not jazz, and the two get intermixed with enough structure to be palatable for the general public. Although the roots of much swing might therefore come from the jazz side of things, the new hybrid forswears a certain portion of its parentage for commercial success.[3]

THE BIG BANDS

In the 1920s, bandleader Paul Whiteman had crowned himself "The King of Jazz." Uneasy lies the crown; within a few short years, an entirely new musical royalty was enthroned: *Count* Basie, *Duke* Ellington, and a new king, the *King* of Swing, Benny Goodman. Other high ranks included tenor saxophonist Lester Young as "The President," or "Prez"; the peers of alto saxist Earle Warren dubbed him "The Earl"; and vocalist Billie Holiday became "Lady Day." But before the usurpers—along with all their many loyalists—could begin their reigns, a revolution had to be fought over the type of music being played.

The Crash of 1929 hit the music business hard. Two-thirds of the nation's unionized musicians found themselves out of work in 1933. Paul Whiteman, the king of a shaky empire, had to release ten members of his thirty-piece band. The solution to the problem lay somewhere out there, but it took several years for struggling bands, record companies, and radio producers to discover it.

Sweet Bands and Swing Bands

Despite the Depression, a few orchestras grimly hung on, and a handful of new ones even came on the scene. Most of these groups could be categorized as "sweet bands," a somewhat condescending phrase that designated aggregations that played in the tradition of "country club music," or "potted palm music." These terms translated as a sedate and restrained approach to performance. Arrangements tended to be uncomplicated and soothing, the perfect background for polite social dancing, with innocuous, bouncy rhythms that would never get in the way of conversation and dinner. Their singers crooned syrupy lyrics that reassured listeners that love would ultimately conquer all.

In the early thirties, the sweet bands—Larry Clinton, Eddie Duchin, Shep Fields and His Rippling Rhythm, Sammy Kaye ("Swing and Sway with Sammy Kaye"), Hal Kemp, Wayne King ("The Waltz King"), Guy Lombardo and His Royal Canadians, Fred Waring and His Pennsylvanians, to name just a few—drew increasingly large crowds and sold a respectable number of recordings.[4]

At the same time as the sweet bands entertained dancers and diners, another kind of orchestra attempted to establish a foothold among listeners and critics. At first, no term existed to identify these bands, but they distinguished themselves by playing many up-tempo numbers, emphasizing rhythm, soloists, and hard-driving arrangements that revealed the jazz roots anchoring the music. They encouraged listeners to get up and dance, but not necessarily to a waltz or a fox trot. These bands—groups like Cab Calloway, the Casa Loma Orchestra, Duke Ellington, Fletcher Henderson, McKinney's Cotton Pickers, Chick Webb, and others—stood on the forefront of a musical revolution.

What they played involved a synthesis of two strands of American music, popular dance numbers and jazz. Paul Whiteman, the deposed king, had searched for this synthesis, but seldom achieved it. But this new wave of orchestra leaders—mostly black and thus unknown to much of the public—had discovered an approach that found receptive audiences who were tired of the blandness of so many of the sweet bands. The phrasemakers called them "swing bands," and they lived up to the name. As more people became aware of these bands, interest grew and other musicians came aboard. Soon, a quiet shift became a stampede: Charlie Barnet, Count Basie, the Dorsey brothers, Benny Goodman, Harry James, Jimmie Lunceford, Artie Shaw, and a host of other bands, orchestras, and combos demanded America's attention. The Swing Era had begun.[5]

Black Bands

A number of trailblazing black orchestras, active during the twenties and early thirties, experimented with new directions in music. Most recording executives thought an insufficient audience existed for these bands, and tended to ignore their efforts. A few of the more daring companies, looking to niche

A black entertainer who appealed to all audiences at a time of intense racial segregation, Cab Calloway (1907–1994) proved successful leading a band, playing night clubs, recording, and performing on radio and in movies. He scored a big hit in 1931 with his own "Minnie the Moocher" (words and music by Cab Calloway, Barney Bigard, and Irving Mills); its refrain of "Heigh-de-ho" endeared him to millions. Irrepressible on stage, his energy and solid swing music opened avenues previously closed to black artists. [Library of Congress, Prints & Photographs Division]

audiences, did issue what they called "race records." These usually consisted of recordings of blues and jazz, almost always by black performers and aimed at black consumers. The industry finally discovered, when record sales had plunged with the impacts of the Depression, that a significant number of white listeners also displayed an interest in this music (see Chapter 1 for more on the recording industry and "race records").

The dawn of the thirties therefore saw a sizable audience already familiar with many different bands, both black and white. Unfortunately, the bulk of black musicians labored under the tyranny of segregation. The white public might know about them through the medium of recording, since most clubs and other outlets observed strict racial separation, and the majority of radio stations refused to play black artists. The opportunities to perform live before white audiences were therefore limited, and integrated bands remained unheard of until the later 1930s.

For example, the all-black Fletcher Henderson Orchestra could reasonably be called the hottest band in the land at the beginning of the thirties, but the restrictions applied to black musicians kept his genius concealed from a potentially huge audience. Although Henderson (1898–1952) finally recorded for Victor in 1932, the company failed to effectively promote him. Limited distribution kept his music from spreading, and it would not be until 1935, when Henderson began selling charts to Benny Goodman, that recognition came, and then it arrived in terms of a successful white band.

Despite the setbacks and the segregation, rumors spread in musical circles about a new kind of dance music, and this word filtered down to a growing public. Sometimes the news got out through swing bands ensconced in large cities at clubs or dancehalls; more often people heard about it from groups large and small that crisscrossed the country, playing wherever and whenever they could. Called territory bands, hundreds of such groups, black and white, dotted the musical landscape, setting up for endless one-night stands, packing up, and moving on to the next town, the next venue. But they carried the message, and public awareness grew.

In the Midwest, Walter Page's Blue Devils, along with Bennie Moten's Kansas City Orchestra, experimented with blues-based tunes that possessed an infectious rhythm. In New York City, Duke Ellington, Fletcher Henderson, and Chick Webb formed adventuresome orchestras that featured mostly new compositions and arrangements. Many of the young black musicians then on their way up played with these bands at one time or another, and the impacts of that exposure would be felt throughout the 1930s.

Duke Ellington (1899–1974), always an individualist, early on established his own distinctive sound and by the late 1920s his pen had contributed such classics as "East St. Louis Toodle-oo" (1926), "Creole Love Call" (1927), and "The Mooche" (1928) to his rapidly growing repertoire. But Ellington also had to cater to preconceptions about jazz. His recordings from the 1920s frequently consist of "jungle music," the old stereotype of African origins and primitive rhythms. That he could both create so-called "jungle music" and transcend it at the same time serves as a testament to Ellington's genius. By the 1930s, that phase of his career lay behind him, and his compositions, increasingly urbane and refined, no longer carried any rhythmic racial connotations. "Mood Indigo" (1930), "Sophisticated Lady" (1933), and "I Let a Song Go Out of My Heart" (1938) can hardly be categorized as either white or black, but instead live on as part of the canon of American popular music.[6]

Fats Waller (1904–1943), with hits like "Ain't Misbehavin'" (1929; music by Fats Waller and Harry Brooks, lyrics by Andy Razaf) and "Honeysuckle Rose" (1929; music by Fats Waller, lyrics by Andy Razaf), likewise received popular acclaim, as did McKinney's Cotton Pickers, a hard-swinging outfit that featured arrangements by Don Redman, a forward-thinking musician who eventually took over leadership of the band and then led one under his own name during the 1930s.

As has been the case numerous times in American life, a seemingly invisible subculture—in this case, black—laid the groundwork for what would later become a dominant part of the majority, or white, culture. Lacking the attractive recording contracts with the major companies, and forced often to play in substandard clubs and dancehalls, these bands soldiered on, with little expectation of the profits and celebrity that more often accompanied their white counterparts.

The Count Basie band can serve as an example of this spirit. This aggregation, born in the Midwest, grew out of two competing Kansas City groups, Walter Page's Blue Devils and Bennie Moten's Orchestra. Everybody in both bands knew one another, including the leaders, and a friendly but highly competitive rivalry existed. Page could rightfully accuse Moten of stealing musicians, and Moten could cheerfully accept the blame. In the free and easy atmosphere of Kansas City in the late 1920s, the two coexisted until 1931, when Page caved in and joined Moten's crew. Then Moten got ill and William "Count" Basie (1904–1984; an admiring radio announcer granted the royal title) took over nominal leadership of the group in 1935. He then formed a new band, the Barons of Rhythm, a name that did not stick, but he carried

A typical shot of Thomas "Fats" Waller (1904–1943), an enormously popular pianist-vocalist-songwriter who reached his widest audiences during the 1930s. Often teamed with lyricist Andy Razaf (1895–1973), the duo turned out such enduring numbers as "Black and Blue," "Honey-suckle Rose," "Ain't Misbehavin'," and a host of others. A consummate entertainer, Waller's infectious grin and boisterous singing style endeared him to millions. [Library of Congress, Prints & Photographs Division]

on, playing every club and dancehall he could find, and finally got a long-term contract with The Reno, a Kansas City nightclub.[7]

The Basie aggregation did late-night broadcasts from The Reno on a powerful Midwestern radio station, and John Hammond, a young jazz critic who also doubled as a talent scout, heard them on his car radio one night. He liked what he heard and immediately decided to find out more about this swinging group; in early 1936 he urged them to come East for better exposure. Such is the stuff of legends. After a period of adjustment, the Count Basie Orchestra left The Reno, went to New York (via Chicago) to become a significant part of the swing scene there, and even landed a recording contract with Decca Records.

With a rhythm section that consisted of Basie on piano, Walter Page on bass, Jo Jones on drums, and Freddie Green on guitar, Basie could boast the best timekeeping machine in the business. The light, airy, but insistent beat kept dancers on the floor and listeners happy. The band additionally featured three strong vocalists during this period, Billie Holiday, Helen Humes, and Jimmy Rushing. With instrumental hits like "One O'Clock Jump" (1937; music by William "Count" Basie) and "Jumpin' at the Woodside" (1938; music by Count Basie), and blues like "Sent for You Yesterday" (1938; music and lyrics by Eddie Durham and Jimmy Rushing), the Basie orchestra quickly climbed to the top in popularity.

John Hammond (1910–1987), the man behind the discovery of the Count Basie Orchestra, merits attention. Born into a wealthy family, Hammond enjoyed the luxury of being able to fund and pursue projects that interested him. At an early age, he realized his love for jazz, and determined he would make his career in this field. He became a promoter of little-known artists, he strove to expand the audience for jazz, and he worked for greater racial equality among musicians.

With his financial independence and outspoken views, Hammond attained prominence in jazz circles by the mid-1930s and associated with the leading names in the music business. He wrote about racial and social injustice in newspapers and magazines, and often found himself a lonely voice at a time that still condoned segregation. Some of his debates with other critics ran on for months, and he at times scored major victories. In the mid-thirties he struck a rapport with bandleader Benny Goodman, the "King of Swing," and he urged Goodman to integrate his orchestra, a suggestion that eventually led to the inclusion of black musicians such as vibraphonist Lionel Hampton and pianist Teddy Wilson in the previously all-white band. The battle progressed slowly, but John Hammond could usually be found on the front lines.

In 1935, he paired singer Billie Holiday with pianist Teddy Wilson for a series of recordings on the Columbia label. Considered classics of their kind, the records went far in establishing the careers of the two, as well as that of tenor saxophonist Lester Young, who backed them on most of the tracks. Holiday's singing so impressed Count Basie that he signed her as vocalist with his band in 1937.

Columbia Records hired Hammond as a producer on a permanent basis in 1937, a time when Columbia had made the decision to build a library of big-band swing, and the relationship resulted in a number of classic recordings. He would continue to work with Columbia off and on for many years, and eventually had a hand in establishing the careers of Aretha Franklin, Bob Dylan, and Bruce Springsteen, among many others, long after the 1930s faded into memory.

Hammond's concern about the continuing racial divide in jazz and swing led him to organize a large-scale concert built around these musical formats. Called *From Spirituals to Swing*, his idea came to fruition in New York's staid Carnegie Hall in December of 1938, just eleven months after Benny Goodman's precedent-breaking appearance there in January of that same year. With a sell-out crowd in attendance, the festival integrated jazz, swing, blues, Dixieland, Gospel, and even some folk music.

Most traditional sponsors felt reluctant to associate themselves with such a racially inclusive event, and so Hammond convinced *The New Masses*, the cultural journal of the American Communist Party, to help underwrite the concert. This controversial move tainted Hammond's reputation in the eyes of some critics, who painted him as a Communist sympathizer, but their accusations only further convinced him of the rightness of his cause.

Divided into seven sections, the music ranged from traditional spirituals performed by Sister Rosetta Tharpe, to big-band swing, in this case the popular Count Basie orchestra. In between, there were jam sessions, boogie-woogie, and a healthy dose of the blues, the latter featuring Jimmy Rushing, Basie's star vocalist.

From Spirituals to Swing served as a celebration of black American music, particularly jazz, and also as an introduction for any remaining white audiences still unaware of the many black contributions to popular music. Fortunately, the concerts have been preserved on recordings, an important social document that pointed to the growing acceptance of black music by white listeners. Audiences loved *From Spirituals to Swing* and Hammond engineered a second edition for Christmas Eve of 1939. Even with a war raging in Europe and the likelihood of U.S. involvement, the concert heightened everyone's holiday spirits. This time around, Hammond got the Theater Arts Committee, an avowed leftist theatrical group, to sponsor it. Although the novelty of the first *From Spirituals to Swing* had worn off, the second concert also proved a success, both for Hammond and for jazz and swing.[8]

White Bands

Despite a prevailing public ignorance about black bandleaders, a handful of white orchestras recognized the musical advances they advocated and attempted to incorporate elements of this new music into their own arrangements. Even some of the sweet bands, such as Gus Arnheim, Clyde McCoy, and Ozzie Nelson, carefully mixed some jazz-like phrasing into otherwise traditional dance numbers, although it must be said they did so cautiously.

One of the first white groups to achieve some success with swing was the so-called Orange Blossoms band out of Detroit, Michigan. One of many bands managed by entrepreneur Gene Goldkette and his National Amusement Corporation in the 1920s, the Orange Blossoms broke from his organization in 1929 and became a collective, with the nominal leader being an alto saxist named Glen Gray. The group also changed its name to the Casa Loma Orchestra, after a posh Toronto club they had played.

Gray (1906–1963) continued to lead the Casa Lomans into the 1930s; on the basis of their popularity, they had the honor of being the first band to head up the new *Camel Caravan* show, a CBS network production that debuted in 1933 and featured dance music along with a bit of swing. Thanks to this radio exposure, the Casa Loma Orchestra achieved great popularity, especially on the college circuit. More in the style of Paul Whiteman than Fletcher Henderson, Gray and his Casa Lomans nonetheless played some tightly arranged, up-tempo numbers that got people listening to new trends in popular music. Bridging the gap between sweetness and swing, they could play the smooth ballads and standards, but they could occasionally let loose with an up-tempo "killer-diller" number. Many of these charts came from the band's chief arranger, Gene Gifford, pieces like "Casa Loma Stomp" (1930) and "Maniac's Ball" (1933). The band swung as no white band had before it, opening the way for other leaders and arrangers. In 1937, Gray took over lead-

In 1933, RCA Victor introduced its Bluebird label. Designed to sell for 35 cents, instead of the 75 cents (and even $1.00) then charged for Victor recordings, these economical discs helped slumping sales. They also proved a boon for popular artists. In this illustration, bandleader Ozzie Nelson, later remembered for the radio and television series *The Adventures of Ozzie and Harriet*, provides a bit of swing with "Stompin' at the Stadium" (1938; music by Bickley Reichner and Clay Boland). [Photograph by author; from the Bryan Wright Collection]

ership completely, and henceforth the group would be known as Glen Gray and the Casa Loma Orchestra.[9]

Although the Casa Lomans led the way for subsequent white bands, no story tells the rise of swing better than the odyssey of Benny Goodman (1909–1986). From late 1934 until May of 1935, the clarinetist and his orchestra participated in *Let's Dance*, a three-hour Saturday night show broadcast on NBC. He split airtime with Xavier Cugat, a colorful Latin bandleader, and Ken Murray, maestro for a decidedly sweet group. Transmitted coast-to-coast, *Let's Dance* happened to share its name with the title of Goodman's theme song. The program originated in New York City, and ran from 10:30 P.M. to 1:30 A.M. Goodman's slot filled the final hour, which meant people on the West Coast listened to him much earlier, thereby ensuring a larger audience and greater exposure. The show introduced Goodman—and big-band swing—to millions of listeners, and they liked what they heard.[10]

In the spring of 1935 he parted company with *Let's Dance* and embarked on a nationwide East-to-West road tour with his band. Contrary to much musical mythology that has grown up about that trip, it did not prove an unmitigated disaster. People had been listening to their radios, and so Goodman and his band had some prior fame. Locations like Pittsburgh, Salt Lake City, and Oakland gave the group reasonably warm welcomes. On the other hand, Denver rejected his new music. Management and dancers there wanted current hits or old standards. Some even requested that he play "more slowly" or that he skip the up-tempo numbers. Frustrated, the band pulled into the Palomar Ballroom in Los Angeles in August. But the Angelenos were ready; his *Let's Dance* segment had come on their radios at 9:30 P.M., they had been listening, and wanted more of the same. The concert, a rousing success, lifted the spirits of Goodman and his sidemen, but the tour still had many miles to go.

Heading back east, the band played to a warm welcome in Chicago's Congress Hotel. The Windy City labeled the new music "swing"; the name stuck, getting the Swing Era officially underway. By the time of his return to New York, Benny Goodman had gained some celebrity, and he and his band possessed known, successful qualities. In June of 1936, *The Camel Caravan*, which had debuted on CBS Radio in 1933 and featured the aforementioned Casa Loma band, changed its format slightly. Gray departed, CBS hired the Goodman aggregation, and used *Benny Goodman's Swing School* as part of its new title. Broadcast on Tuesday evenings, the refurbished show would last for three years and then move to rival NBC for an additional year. Ballrooms and dancehalls bid for open dates; the band toured New England and played the Steel Pier in Atlantic City. The Madhattan Room, located in New York's Hotel Pennsylvania, signed the clarinetist and his orchestra to a long-term contract that commenced at the end of the year.

Since his work at the Madhattan Room involved evenings, Goodman agreed to play a matinee at the Paramount Theater on Times Square in New York City. The orchestra arrived early at the theater for rehearsal on March 3, 1937. Although it was a cold, wintry morning, people had been waiting outside the building since before dawn; the crowd, youthful and skipping school, grew as opening time approached, the line snaking around the theater. Worried police gathered, and finally ordered the management to open the Paramount's doors at 8:00 A.M. Over 3,000 fans rushed inside, and 2,000 disappointed ones milled around on the street.

The Goodman band ran through a brief rehearsal in the theater's basement, then assembled on its ascending stage and rose to the cheers of thousands of enthusiasts. As the orchestra went into its numbers, the fans, warmed by the music, got up and began to jitterbug in the aisles. Ushers had no luck in getting them back into their seats, and the morning concert continued, with dancers surging down to the bandstand itself, the more daring actually getting on the stage and jitterbugging next to the musicians. Everyone seemed to take it all in stride, and the band played five shows that day. Estimates place overall attendance at 21,000 people, far more than would ever hear him in a hotel setting. Goodman even made a return visit to the Paramount in 1938. It all happened again—the audience out in the aisles, the dancing—giving birth to a swing tradition. For the first time, mainly working-class adolescents took a musical event and turned it into a national fad. This was popular culture at the grassroots level.

In January of 1938, Benny Goodman and His Orchestra stormed one of the citadels of high culture, Carnegie Hall. The event had been arranged by impresario Sol Hurok, a man usually connected to the classical world of symphony orchestras and chamber groups. But the remarkable attention Goodman had been receiving in concerts, hotel appearances, and on radio had convinced many that he deserved a more "respectable" hearing, that perhaps swing had qualities unappreciated by the musical elite.[11]

That winter evening, Carnegie Hall billed his appearance as a "Jazz Concert," although "Swing Concert" would probably be a more accurate description. Either way, Goodman and his entourage legitimatized contemporary popular music for the broadest possible audience. Reportedly, no one danced in the aisles, but the black-tie audience clearly tapped its feet and relished the exposure to this new phenomenon.

Goodman himself, replete in cutaway and tails and clearly the main attraction, led his big band and also his trio and quartet, all of whom came properly attired in tuxedos. Guest musicians included such black stars as Teddy Wilson, Count Basie and members of his orchestra, Lionel Hampton, and some Duke Ellington alumni (Ellington himself refrained from playing, but had a front row box seat)—performing side-by-side with their white counterparts. That Carnegie Hall audience witnessed how, in a segregated society, swing could act as a bridge, bringing blacks and whites together. Not only that, the music also assimilated popular and high culture in ways seldom attempted before. And what happened at the concert was repeated across the land: any resistance to swing soon evaporated in the face of its sheer popularity. Thanks largely to concerts and radio, but also to records, jukeboxes, and the movies, swing amassed the largest, most diverse audience any musical form had ever enjoyed.

After an impressive opening with "Don't Be That Way" (1934; music by Edgar Sampson and Benny Goodman, lyrics by Mitchell Parish), a smooth up-tempo dance tune that epitomized popular swing of the day, the concert gained momentum. *Twenty Years of Jazz*, a historical pastiche of styles, provided a capsule history, from ragtime to "Blue Reverie" (1936; music by Duke Ellington and Harry Carney), a recent Duke Ellington composition.

The concert moved to smaller, more intimate groupings, with the popular Benny Goodman trio (Goodman, clarinet; Teddy Wilson, piano; Gene Krupa, drums) and quartet (adding Lionel Hampton on vibraphone). But finally, the moment many people had been waiting for arrived: the Goodman band's extended version of "Sing, Sing, Sing" (1936; music by Louis Prima; arrangement by Jimmy Mundy). Previously recorded, this twelve-minute opus had become standard fare for Goodman by then, but most recorded versions of it lack the excitement generated at Carnegie Hall. After a series of spirited solos by various band members, pianist Jess Stacy took the spotlight. He reciprocated by producing a memorable piano interlude, one of those special moments that could only happen in a live performance. Fortunately, the concert was recorded, and the moment has been preserved.

As the well-dressed audience filed out of Carnegie Hall, they might not have been aware they had just witnessed a historic event. Not only had Benny Goodman brought swing and a healthy serving of jazz to a venue previously closed to those musical formats, he had also stepped on many of society's restrictive practices. His trio and his quartet included black artists (pianist Teddy Wilson and vibraphonist Lionel Hampton), and most of the guest musicians also were black. Goodman helped to open the doors to integrated bands and, given his popularity, he had no hesitation in using the best musicians, black or white, he could find. No one seemed to mind in the least, a telling comment on the fallacy of segregation.

The Glenn Miller Orchestra turned out to be another popular aggregation of the later 1930s. He illustrates both the differences and the similarities between the sweet and swing categories. Miller's band could play the slow, syrupy ballads, often accompanied by a singer who made no attempt to "swing" the lyric. But the orchestra could also perform jazz-tinged arrangements of up-tempo tunes that any swing band could envy. Miller straddled both camps, but he also pleased both.[12]

Pitfalls lined the road to stardom for Miller, and he labored in near-anonymity during much of the decade. He tried some recordings with Brunswick in the mid-thirties, but they went nowhere and did nothing. With so many bands competing for the listener's attention, it behooved leaders and arrangers to create a distinctive sound for a group. Just having a couple of good sidemen was not enough; the ensemble playing also had to attract notice. Without that extra something, the band blurred off into mediocrity, joining dozens—or hundreds—of other aggregations plagued with the same problem. With all the orchestras on the road and recording, it now seems remarkable that so many achieved a distinctive "sound" during the 1930s.

At first, Miller free-lanced, playing trombone and writing arrangements for various bands; he joined the Dorsey Brothers Orchestra in the mid-1930s, and there he experimented with riffs and fadeouts, techniques that would later become the signature of his own band. He also began employing the device of having a clarinet playing an octave over the other reeds; it sounded different, and he liked its potential. After the stint with the Dorseys, Miller continued freelancing, polishing his skills as an arranger. He tried additional recording contracts with Decca and Brunswick records, but nothing of any great distinction ever got cut.

In 1937, he took the plunge and formed a fresh orchestra under his name. A nondescript aggregation, it failed within a year. By early 1938, however, Miller tried again. He obtained a new contract with RCA Victor's Bluebird label, a move that encouraged him to go on. It proved a wise decision; in the spring of 1939, one of his first discs for Victor/Bluebird contained two new songs: "Sunrise Serenade" (music by Frankie Carle, lyrics by Jack Lawrence) and "Moonlight Serenade" (music by Glenn Miller, lyrics by Mitchell Parish). Both attracted attention—"Moonlight Serenade" would shortly become the band's theme—and landed the orchestra a summer job at Glen Island Casino, a lovely restaurant and ballroom overlooking New York's Long Island Sound. Once ensconced there, the Miller band attracted still more attention doing radio spots, plus the records kept coming—hits like "Little Brown Jug" (1939, arranged by Bill Finegan), a remake of an old 1869 tune, "In the Mood" (1939; music by Joe Garland, lyrics by Andy Razaf), "Tuxedo Junction" (1940; music by William Johnson, Julian Dash, Erskine Hawkins, and Buddy Feyne), and "Pennsylvania 6-5000" (1940; music by Jerry Gray, lyrics by Carl Sigman) could be heard everywhere on the air, and people crowded record shops trying to obtain copies. By early 1940, the newcomer had displaced the king; Glenn Miller's orchestra enjoyed greater popularity than Benny Goodman's, and no letup appeared in sight.

DANCING AND SWING

Swing benefited everyone: millions purchased recordings by their favorite bands, bought tickets to hear them in person, and an impressive number of fans took to the dance floor. Swing could be up-tempo, but it also emphasized melody; it could be hummed, whistled, sung, and, for a whole generation of devotees, danced to. Much popular music in the early 1930s was designed for dancing, and for most people this meant the fox trot, a traditional combination of slow and quick steps. But dance crazes came and went, just as they do in all decades. In addition to the relatively staid fox trot, the 1930s witnessed the rise of many dances that involved the partners putting on a performance, or to "cut a rug," as the slang of the day would have it (i.e., the couple's dance steps are so good—so "sharp"—that they destroy the rug or carpeting beneath their feet). The 1920s may have had the Charleston, but the 1930s had an entire collection of dances summed up by one word: jitterbug.

The term probably derives from the jerky, or "jittery" motions that can occur in the dance, plus in slang a "jitterbug" defined a person—possibly inebriated or similarly impaired—who had the "shakes," the "jitters." In some circles, instead of "jitterbug," people preferred the simpler "bug," and some even proclaimed themselves "ickies," the roots of which shall go unexplored.

The jitterbug identified a number of distinctive exhibition-style dances, several of which provided onlookers as much pleasure as the dancers themselves. For example, the Lindy (or Lindy Hop) served as a kind of jitterbug. Some believe the name derived from Charles Lindbergh (or "Lindy," as he was fondly called), the man who in 1927 became the first person to fly solo across the Atlantic. In this acrobatic step, "taking off" and "landing" while dancing suggested flight. Another popular dance, called the Big Apple, combined square dancing and swing jitterbugging. A group dance, it placed people in a circle who obeyed a caller. The caller might instruct individuals or couples to move to the center of the circle and "shine" or "peel," or other silly terms associated with apples; a fad, but a popular one.

Other dances associated with the swing craze included the Shag, Truckin', and the Lambeth Walk, all popular in the later years of the decade. In the

If any dance is associated with the later 1930s, it would be the jitterbug. Usually up-tempo and vigorous, the steps could be stylized or improvised. The perfect response to big-band swing, dancers flocked to the floor to try out the latest fads, and orchestras and combos everywhere kept them happy playing a mix of hits and standards. [Library of Congress, Prints & Photographs Division]

first, small hops and kicks served as the order of the day; Truckin' involved shrugging the shoulders rhythmically, plus raising an arm and pointing a forefinger upward. The Lambeth Walk, an import from England, had couples walking forward and then backward with their arms linked. At the proper moment, they would thrust their thumbs into the air and say "Oy!" Another fad, but it had its moment of fame.

Nothing, however, equaled the jitterbug itself. Danced to medium or up-tempo numbers—the more up-tempo the better, for many—the jitterbug involved many steps and constant motion. Whatever their choices, Americans turned out on dance floors in record numbers, all in response to the swing craze that embraced the entire nation. They were "Stompin'," "Scattin'," "Jumpin'," and even "Beguining." Translation: the four terms refer to popular dance tunes of the 1930s: (1) "Stompin' at the Savoy" (1936; music by

A 1937 photograph showing a group performing the Big Apple, a popular dance of the Swing Era. Although the word "jitterbug" has come to identify collectively most of the dance fads that swept the country then, each had its own distinctive steps and rituals. The Big Apple supposedly resembled picking and peeling apples, although onlookers might be hard put to see the connections. The name, by the way, came from a Columbia, South Carolina, night club where the dance first evolved—it had nothing to do with New York City. [Library of Congress, Prints & Photographs Division]

Benny Goodman, Edgar Sampson, and Chick Webb, lyrics by Andy Razaf), (2) "Scattin' at the Kit Kat" (1936; music by Duke Ellington), (3) "Jumpin' at the Woodside" (1938; music by Count Basie), and (4) "Begin the Beguine" (1935; words and music by Cole Porter).

Harlem's Savoy Ballroom, "The Home of Happy Feet," became the mecca for devoted jitterbugs. In fact, throughout the swinging thirties the Savoy's management had to replace the club's hardwood dance floor every three years. "Stompin' at the Savoy" (1936; music by Benny Goodman, Edgar Sampson, and Chick Webb, lyrics by Andy Razaf), an up-tempo dance classic that shares its lineage with both Benny Goodman's orchestra and Chick Webb's Savoy house band, served as an appropriate anthem of the era.[13]

Fast, furious, improvised, or practiced, the era's attitude toward dancing can be found in the title of a hit tune associated with the Jimmie Lunceford band: "Tain't What'cha Do, It's the Way That'cha Do It" (1939; music by Sy Oliver, lyrics by Trummy Young).

RADIO PROGRAMMING AND SWING

Radio figured prominently in the popularization of swing, since it provided the means by which most Americans received music in the thirties. What got programmed—and what did not—also illustrates how commercial interests, once they decided that swing could be profitable, attempted to keep the music "white." Seldom did black bands enjoy significant air time; the choice shows went to white bands, and major record labels continued to push their white stars. As in the larger society, black artists found themselves relegated to second-class citizenship. But swing's appeal transcended race; its audience, young and liberal, represented mass values, not traditional class ones. By the end of the decade, more and more black musicians, buttressed by a huge, youthful following, finally began receiving their due.

As chronicled above, Benny Goodman had been on the air with *Let's Dance* in 1935. By the end of 1937, Goodman and his band had long since moved to CBS for Camels and recorded for Columbia, Tommy Dorsey's orchestra performed on NBC for Raleigh-Kools and cut their records with Victor's Blue-bird label, Kay Kyser and his band could be found on the Mutual network, and even veteran Paul Whiteman had inaugurated a new swing show on CBS for Chesterfields (he would be replaced by Glenn Miller in 1939). The biggest of the new crop of radio shows turned out to be a CBS venture, *The Saturday Night Swing Club* (1936–1939). Virtually every major swing aggregation played this popular show, although the studio orchestra, led by Leith Stevens and made up of top sidemen, could easily hold its own. But anywhere one turned the dial, swing was king. By 1940, estimates had over 200 dance bands of one kind and another traveling the landscape, playing concerts, dances, radio shows, and making recordings.

The networks, sensing the appeal of the big bands, made them the spotlight orchestras for numerous popular shows. For example, *The Fitch Bandwagon* (1938–1948), *Kay Kyser's Kollege of Musical Knowledge* (1937–1949), *The Chesterfield Quarter-Hour* (1931–1933), *The Old Gold Show* (1934), *The Camel*

Combining a crowd-pleasing mix of music and comedy, Kay Kyser (1906–1985) carved himself a niche in the entertainment field that lasted well beyond the 1930s. The leader of his own band since the 1920s, he blossomed with network radio, creating *Kay Kyser's Kollege of Musical Knowledge*, a musical quiz show that ran from 1937 to 1949. As the "Old Professor," complete with mortarboard, he amused audiences with his easygoing humor. With him, above, is Penny Wise, one of his "faculty assistants" on the popular show. [Library of Congress, Prints & Photographs Division]

Caravan (1933–1954), and *Let's Dance* (1934–1935) serve as but a sampling of the many shows that revolved around orchestras and popular tunes.

In contrast to contemporary American radio, many of the musical performances heard in the 1930s came in the form of live broadcasts. Stations certainly used recordings in their programming, but in the Big Band Era many aggregations traveled directly to the studio to perform. Conversely, the networks and their affiliates sometimes sent crews to clubs or concert halls to capture the live sound of an orchestra. These broadcasts, called "remotes," meant a station possessed the necessary portable equipment that allowed live coverage of an event. As a result, many bands relied on radio for exposure, a time when they could play selected numbers from their "book" (a collection of scores a particular band might perform) and allow the unseen audience an opportunity to sample more than a single song.

Radio stations found band remotes a cheap way to present music over the air. Wherever a band might play—a dance hall, a pavilion, an auditorium— the station could then transmit the performance to a network (NBC or CBS) for national distribution. In addition, any station could make a transcription, usually on a disc, but sometimes on wire recorders, thereby preserving the performance. Recordings could then be made from these transcriptions. Out of all this electronic wizardry any kind of music could be captured, a fact that led to the revitalization of the record business. Swing and the big bands, in fact, served as a catalyst for the sagging record business, a catalyst that first began to have its effects through the widespread availability of radio.

In addition to their remote capabilities, larger stations often retained studio bands. These groups did yeoman service and could have lineups that included some of the best instrumentalists in the business. Their job consisted of playing for live commercials, background music for dramatic shows, backing singers and vocal groups, and generally being available whenever someone called for live music. More often than not, what they played could be categorized as mundane; no one considered the studio band the star, who or what they accompanied received the attention. Nonetheless, studio orchestras provided stable employment for countless musicians.[14]

THE MOVIES AND SWING

When Hollywood realized that swing had all the trappings of a new national craze, the studios wasted no time in capitalizing on it. Bands big and small, black and white, band leaders known and unknown, along with vocalists and singing groups, were snatched up and thrust into movies. The quality of the films mattered little in the haste to have a swing number or two in the course of the story. That translated as a lot of flops (*Check and Double Check*, 1930), some mediocrities (*Second Chorus*, 1940), and a small group of pictures that accurately captured the flavor of this new phenomenon (*Hollywood Hotel*, 1937). These movies also gave visual representation to a number of black artists previously invisible to their audiences and heard only on radio and recordings.

The list of feature-length films in Table 2 (alphabetical by performer) serves merely to suggest the intense movie interest that surrounded swing. Most of the roles consist of bit parts or extended cameos; Hollywood's regular roster of non-musical stars took the leads, and the musicians provided the latest hits and some occasional dialogue. But their presence signified a growing awareness of swing and those who played it. Dating from the end of the 1920s to the beginning of the 1940s, this list illustrates what an important part musical popularity played in determining studio choices for production. In the interest of brevity, the innumerable band shorts—five- and ten-minute films featuring a particular group or song—have not been included unless otherwise noted.

YOUTH AND SWING

Any study of the 1930s and music must address the importance of youth culture. The 1920s may have had "flaming youth," but the thirties had young music connoisseurs, particularly in the area of swing. Thanks to fan magazines, radio shows, and the movies, they possessed an incredible amount of knowledge about the musical changes occurring during the decade. These self-styled swing experts effectively challenged the elitist authoritarianism that had traditionally dictated taste in the arts; for their part, they brought about a refreshing openness to music. Plus, they bought millions of records, giving them the all-important commercial clout to accompany their aesthetic preferences. The old wisdom that "experts" dictated standards for art, literature, and music came tumbling down in the Depression.

The decade witnessed a democratization of the arts, propelled particularly in popular music by those young people who emerged as the new *cognoscenti*. They understood that even jazz and swing practiced a kind of exclusivity: you

Table 2
Movies and Swing in the 1930s[15]

Artist	Movie and Date
Ivie Anderson (vocalist)	*A Day at the Races* (1937)
Louis Armstrong (trumpet and band leader)	*Mixed Doubles* (1930), *Pennies from Heaven* (1936), *Artists and Models* (1937), *Every Day's a Holiday* (1938), *Going Places* (1938)
Ray Bauduc (drummer)	*Let's Make Music* (1940)
Sidney Bechet (saxophonist)	*Moon Over Harlem* (1939)
Cab Calloway (band leader)	*The Big Broadcast* (1932), *International House* (1933), *The Singing Kid* (1936), *Manhattan Merry-Go-Round* (1938)
Bob Crosby (band leader)	*Let's Make Music* (1940)
Jimmy Dorsey (band leader)	*That Girl from Paris* (1936)
Duke Ellington (band leader)	*Black and Tan* (1929; short), *Check and Double Check* (1930), *Dancers in the Dark* (1932), *Murder at the Vanities* (1934), *Many Happy Returns* (1934), *Symphony in Black* (1934; short), *Belle of the Nineties* (1934), *Hit Parade of 1937* (1936)
Nick Fatool (drummer)	*Second Chorus* (1940)
Nat Gonella (trumpet)	*Sing as You Swing* (1937)
Benny Goodman (band leader)	*The Big Broadcast of 1937* (1936), *Hollywood Hotel* (1937)
Bob Haggart (bassist)	*Let's Make Music* (1940)
Lionel Hampton (vibraphonist)	*Sing Sinner Sing* (1933), *Pennies from Heaven* (1936), *Hollywood Hotel* (1937)
Billie Holiday (vocalist)	*Symphony in Black* (1934; short)
Claude Hopkins (band leader)	*Dance Team* (1931), *Wayward* (1932)
Ina Ray Hutton (band leader)	*The Big Broadcast of 1936* (1935)
Gene Krupa (drummer)	*Hollywood Hotel* (1937), *Some Like It Hot* (1939)
Eddie Lang (guitarist)	*The Big Broadcast* (1932)
Ted Lewis (band leader)	*Is Everybody Happy?* (1929), *The Show of Shows* (1929), *Here Comes the Band* (1935), *Manhattan Merry-Go-Round* (1937)

(continued)

Table 2 (Continued)

Artist	Movie and Date
Guy Lombardo (band leader)	*Many Happy Returns* (1934)
Wingy Manone (trumpeter)	*Rhythm on the River* (1940)
Lucky Millinder (band leader)	*Paradise in Harlem* (1939)
Ray Noble (band leader)	*The Big Broadcast of 1936* (1935)
Louis Prima (band leader)	*Rhythm on the Range* (1936), *Manhattan Merry-Go-Round* (1937), *Start Cheering* (1937), *You Can't Have Everything* (1937), *Rose of Washington Square* (1939)
Raymond Scott (band leader)	*Ali Baba Goes to Town* (1937), *Love and Hisses* (1937), *Nothing Sacred* (1937), *Happy Landing* (1938), *Rebecca of Sunnybrook Farm* (1938)
Artie Shaw (band leader)	*Dancing Co-Ed* (1939), *Second Chorus* (1940)
Stuff Smith (violinist)	*52nd Street* (1937)
Maxine Sullivan (vocalist)	*Going Places* (1938), *St. Louis Blues* (1939)
Joe Venuti (violinist)	*The King of Jazz* (1930), *Garden of the Moon* (1938)
Fats Waller (pianist)	*Hooray for Love!* (1935), *King of Burlesque* (1935)
Ethel Waters (vocalist)	*On with the Show* (1929), *Gift of Gab* (1934)
Paul Whiteman (band leader)	*King of Jazz* (1930), *Thanks a Million* (1935), *Strike Up the Band* (1940)
Teddy Wilson (pianist)	*Hollywood Hotel* (1937)

had to be a fan, know the bands and sidemen, and collect the records. But they also saw in swing a new expression of independence. Even the jitterbug, so lamented by many in the older generation, represented a form of sexual equality and freedom. Certainly the Swing Era marked the emergence of a mass youth culture, a culture that even hinted at racial harmony, although it would be a long time coming. Swing's victory over entrenched interests revolutionized the industry, opening once-closed doors to musicians and leading to the ascendancy of rhythm 'n' blues and rock 'n' roll in the 1940s and 1950s.[16]

THE TRIUMPH OF SWING

By 1938, swing could be found just about anywhere. That summer, a Swing Festival on Randall's Island drew 24,000 people. The mammoth event featured twenty-five bands and lasted some six hours. That same year, bandleader Tommy Dorsey cut "Boogie Woogie," a big-band instrumental version of a piano composition written and recorded by Clarence "Pinetop" Smith in 1928 as "Pinetop's Boogie Woogie." Up to that time, most white listeners viewed boogie-woogie, an instrumental approach to rhythm that stresses a repeated bass figure, as a kind of low-class black music, and paid it little heed. Although collectors sought Smith's record over the years, it had little impact on the mass audience. Dorsey's version, however, quickly changed all that. The Dorsey record sold a million copies and made boogie-woogie a part of the expanding world of swing and a prominent part of white popular culture. Within the next couple of years, bands and pianists of every description performed boogie-woogie tunes to enthusiastic applause, and white groups scored most of the hits.

This appropriation of an essentially black musical format by white performers had occurred before in American culture. Ragtime, New Orleans jazz (but called "Dixieland"), even swing itself saw the same thing happening. Count Basie's theme, the up-tempo "One O'Clock Jump" (1937; music by William "Count" Basie), had first been recorded by the band in 1937, but a majority of record buyers ignored it. Benny Goodman cut the tune in 1938, and his version enjoyed modest success. Then Harry James and his band released a 1938 single that included "One O'Clock Jump"; the number took on hit status, climbed the charts, and proved so successful that the trumpeter even garnered a second big success with "Two O'Clock Jump" (1942; music by Harry James, Count Basie, and Benny Goodman), a not-too-subtle variation on the original.

Big bands and small groups, instrumentals and vocalists, originals and variations—it mattered little to swing enthusiasts. Record sales kept pace with all the live performances, reaching $26 million in 1938. Singles sold at the rate of 700,000 discs a month, their highest rate ever. In 1939, Columbia Records, a perennial third against Decca and RCA Victor, introduced a new, laminated disc that advertised much better sound quality and longer life than the shellac records of the competition. It retailed for 50 cents, but no one seemed to mind. By that time, eager buyers were snatching up 140 million recordings a year. Said Duke Ellington, "Jazz is music; swing is *business*."[17]

Two national magazines closely followed the swing phenomenon, chronicling its meteoric rise and eventual fall. Chicago-based *Down Beat* (founded 1934) and New York-based *Metronome* (founded 1932; an outgrowth of two previous publications of the same name that dated back to the 1880s) quickly established large circulations and their readership showed no hesitancy about voicing opinions. Other magazines, among them *Swing*, *Tempo*, and *Jazz Hot*, also had their followers, but they lacked the large circulations enjoyed by *Down Beat* and *Metronome*. Regardless, all these journals remained fiercely combative about jazz and swing, taking to task anyone who voiced opposition to either. Trade journals like *Variety* and *Billboard* also covered swing, but more objectively, tracking record sales, song rankings, and business matters connected with the music industry.

In 1936, *Down Beat* inaugurated its annual readers' poll; a short time later, *Metronome* followed suit. Hardly scientific, these polls served primarily as popularity contests instead of indicators of true merit, but they did provide indications about readers' tastes at the time. Cries of dishonesty and racism sometimes accompanied these votes, since the magazines included the ballots within their pages and zealous fans could send in multiple copies by buying extra issues. No accurate statistics exist on the racial breakdown of the two periodicals' readership, but some people felt white musicians received favoritism at the expense of their black counterparts. On the other hand, a few black publications ran polls of their own, and then critics voiced the reverse charge. Despite the scattered complaints, readers eagerly anticipated the yearly polls, and they doubtless had an effect on resultant record sales.[18]

As the decade closed, countless musicians and hundreds of bands crisscrossed the nation, providing swing to an insatiable public. Thousands more musicians played in stay-at-home bands; every community had at least a few dance bands or combos that provided nightly or weekend music. Department stores and specialty shops reveled in skyrocketing record sales, and everyone talked about his or her favorites. A heady time, the Swing Era gave Americans a shared music unlike anything before or since.

[*Note*: A number of bandleaders have been mentioned in this chapter; the reader is directed to Chapter 7 for additional information about them, along with their sidemen, vocalists, and arrangers.]

Roots Music

The 1930s, an era of musical innovation, also marked a time of crippling national economics. It might then be reasonably expected that at least some of
the period's music would reflect the crisis. For the most part, however, songwriters either ignored economic hardships or they approached them
obliquely, not head-on. Works that attempted to comment on the times tended
to be dismissed—or not heard at all—by a mass audience. Still, writers turned
out union songs, protest songs, laments about miners and farmers and mi-
grants, but no big hit topical tunes captured the public's fancy.

What follows consists of an overview of some of the secondary musical
movements that arose during the 1930s. Although the popular song, along
with standards, continued to dominate American music, different groups and
regions often had certain musical forms that also enjoyed popularity. In the
western sections of the country, cowboy tunes had their fans. Cajun music,
practically unheard outside Louisiana, had its core of devotees. Labor unrest,
an outgrowth of the Depression, continued a tradition of protest songs that
goes back to the nineteenth century. Long ignored by white audiences, black
blues and Gospel music flourished despite the overwhelming popularity of
the big bands and dance music.

With radios in many homes, and phonograph recordings readily available,
virtually any musical taste could find fulfillment. Small rural stations broadcast country songs and regional folk music; their urban counterparts might

reach out for black listeners, ethnic groups, laborers, or other minority audiences largely ignored by the major networks. Via these modern electronic media, the demassification of American music began in earnest, a process that would accelerate through the rest of the twentieth century. Today, "rock"—in the broadest of terms—serves as the leading form of American popular music, but no single style completely dominates what people hear. Soft rock, hard rock, easy listening, Top 40, country, golden oldies, traditional, avant garde—each has its fans, and what strikes people's fancy one place may be ignored in another. *Your Hit Parade* (discussed in Chapter 1), on the other hand, spoke for an overwhelming majority in the later 1930s, whereas no such voice of inclusiveness would be possible today. The seeds of musical diversity had germinated during the Depression. They might not bloom until some years later, but already the first shoots were poking through the surface.

COUNTRY AND WESTERN MUSIC

It may seem hard to believe that most Americans had little acquaintance with country/Western music during the 1930s. True, the style possessed a base of fervent fans, but they constituted a distinct demographic minority, a "niche audience" in media parlance, one that had little voice in most popular music of the time. As such, it enjoyed little national airplay (but with the exceptions noted in the paragraphs below), and individual record sales seldom approached the figures attained by swing bands and big-name vocalists. *Your Hit Parade*, for example, almost never featured a "country" song in its weekly countdowns.

In spite of these obstacles, country music began to make its first appearances on radio stations in the mid- to late 1920s. WLS, a Chicago-based station, first broadcast *The Barn Dance* in 1924. The creation of George D. Hay, one of the early promoters of country music for radio, it proved a commercial success. The show would run on WLS until 1933, at which time NBC picked it up for network transmission. NBC changed the name to *The National Barn Dance* and retained the show until 1942. WLS continued carrying it until 1960; after a station format change, rival WGN took it over and ran it until 1969. During the Depression years, Alka-Seltzer, a pain remedy, provided continuous sponsorship, a fact that suggests a sizable listenership and continuing sales.

With a strong signal and a location in the essentially rural Midwest, WLS proved an ideal venue for such a show. A fixture on Saturday evenings, *The National Barn Dance* competed directly with a similar show, *Grand Ole Opry* (see below). WLS, which had been launched by merchandising giant Sears, Roebuck (the call letters stand for "World's Largest Store"), reflected in its programming the large rural audience that also bought many items from the famous Sears catalog.

The music played on *The National Barn Dance* came from many sources: primarily country tunes, but also swing, pop numbers, and plenty of silliness. Regulars on the show included, among many others, the vocal duet of Lulu Belle (b. Myrtle Cooper) and Scotty (Scott Wiseman, her husband); Henry Burr, a crooner; and the Hoosier Hot Shots, a comedy quartet that enjoyed considerable regional popularity. Originally in vaudeville, the Hot Shots came to prominence in 1933 after their exposure on *The National Barn Dance*, and soon ranked as one of the top musical novelty acts of the day. In addition to vocalizing and on-stage antics, they employed a slide whistle and clarinet as their lead instruments, added a washboard for rhythm, with a result that might be classified as hillbilly hokum. Their repertoire included such numbers as "From the Indies to the Andes in His Undies," "I Like Bananas Because They Have No Bones," and "The Coat and the Pants Do All the Work." Audiences loved it all, making them the precursors of groups like Spike Jones and His City Slickers.

Since it billed itself as a "Barn Dance," callers provided instructions to actual on-stage square dancers, a radio concept perhaps difficult to conceive for those raised in a visual television age. In addition to the musical acts and the dancing, various comedians did their routines, and everyone performed in costume for the studio audience. The show soon outgrew WLS's studio facilities and had to move to a large Chicago theater, but it continued to be associated with the radio station. Whereas movie tickets cost only a dime, it took ninety cents to gain entrance to *The National Barn Dance*, making it one of the few radio shows that charged admission. Even in the dark days of the Depression, it took months of waiting to obtain a reservation to the show.

In 1925, WSM, a Nashville, Tennessee, station, commenced broadcasting *WSM Barn Dance*, a direct competitor to *The National Barn Dance*. Also developed by George D. Hay, he had no hesitation in making a reference to his popular WLS creation. In 1927, the show changed its name to *Grand Ole Opry*. The "Grand" and "Opry" portion came about because of a preceding network music show, Walter Damrosch's *Music Appreciation Hour* (see Chapter 6). Listeners to that show occasionally heard grand opera, and so the humorous play on words. Thanks to WSM's strong signal and its location in the southern Appalachians, *Grand Ole Opry* soon attracted a wide audience on Saturday nights, its regular time. NBC, already leading the country field with *The National Barn Dance*, picked up the show for network audiences in 1939, keeping it in the schedule until 1957. Throughout the 1930s, listeners could therefore hear both *The National Barn Dance* and *Grand Ole Opry* in back-to-back time slots. Even after NBC dropped the show, WSM has continued its *Opry* radio broadcasts into the present.

Often called a "hillbilly show," *Grand Ole Opry* made no effort to alter that perception. It relied on rustic humor, costumes, and numerous amateur musicians, many from the surrounding hills. In time, the show grew more polished, but it never forsook its rural roots. Like its Chicago counterpart, *Grand Ole Opry* quickly outgrew its WSM studios and began to perform in a series of Nashville theaters and auditoriums. Audiences traveled for miles to be present for Dr. Humphrey Bate and His Possum Hunters, Uncle Dave Macon, the Crook Brothers, and Roy Acuff and His Smoky Mountain Boys.

These two shows, plus the ubiquity and popularity of radio, helped raise at least some public consciousness about country music. With the exception of Chicago, however, neither show had much play in major urban markets, and went instead to the smaller stations broadcasting to more rural audiences. Estimates range from 5 to 10 million for their Saturday evening programs, but those geographically scattered listeners did not have a significant impact on national radio ratings. Given the localized success of *The National Barn Dance* and *Grand Ole Opry*, other country radio shows proliferated, but none could match the audience for these originals.[1]

The National Barn Dance and *Grand Ole Opry* pioneered the popularization of country music on radio, but numerous country performers established careers through recordings. Chief among them would be Jimmie Rodgers (1897–1933). A guitarist and vocalist, or yodeler, Rodgers had worked on regional railroads, thus acquiring the name "The Singing Brakeman." In order to capitalize on his workingman status and create a shared identity with his audiences, he frequently appeared in railroader's gear, especially the traditional peaked cap. These homely touches helped establish his career, particularly in the rural South during the Depression. More recently, critics and fans alike have dubbed him "The Father of Country Music."

Whether or not he deserves such a sweeping appellation will have to be left to future generations, but he did significantly influence the direction American country music would take. In 1927, Rodgers signed a recording contract with Victor Records. At that time, Ralph Peer, one of the first artists-and-repertoire (or A & R) men in the business, had set up a portable recording studio in Bristol, Tennessee. An important figure in the spread of country music through the South, Peer had an ear for new talent. He guided Rodgers through the process of cutting records, and these early efforts did well enough that Peer and Victor encouraged Rodgers to do more.

In subsequent recordings, Rodgers branched out, incorporating his trademark yodels into the music. His "Blue Yodel" (1927–1928) series consisted of thirteen songs incorporating yodels into their structure. "Blue Yodel #1 (T for Texas)" became one of his early hits, establishing him as an innovative musician. Others—"Blue Yodel #4 (California Blues)" and "Blue Yodel #8 (Muleskinner Blues)"—also enjoyed some celebrity.

By incorporating generous elements of black blues and jazz into his music, Rodgers earned the respect of both blues and jazz players. His compositions became an amalgam of varied styles, and all the while it attracted diverse admirers. A true entertainer, he could incorporate the steel guitars of Hawaii in "Everybody Does It in Hawaii" (ca. 1930), and traditional pop elements in "My Blue-Eyed Jane" (1933). Rodgers died prematurely from tuberculosis in 1933, but not before recording "Whipping that Old T.B. Blues" and "T.B. Blues" (both 1933). In 1929, a short film came out that showed Rodgers performing. Called *The Singing Brakeman*, it has the distinction of being the first movie that starred a country artist.

During his brief recording career, Rodgers cut over 100 songs, and his estimated total sales exceeded 12 million records over a span of just seven years. Most of those sales went to rural and small-town buyers, although he undoubtedly had some urban fans. Despite his impressive output and sales, Rodgers cannot be thought of as a mainstream performer. He seldom appeared on radio—neither *The National Barn Dance* nor *Grand Ole Opry* took advantage of his talents—his movie work consisted of the above short, and so he remained on the periphery of national show business. His greatest recognition came after his death, not during his lifetime.[2]

At the same 1927 Bristol session where Rodgers first recorded, a soon-to-be famous family also made its recording debut under the direction of Ralph Peer. Led by A.P. Carter (1891–1960), and including his wife Sara (1898–1979) and sister-in-law Maybelle (1909–1978), the Carter Family cut several sides for Victor. The discs did well enough that a year later they recorded "Keep on the Sunny Side," their signature song.

Innumerable small labels proliferated during the 1930s. Romeo Records, initially a part of the larger Cameo Records group, could be found in S. H. Kress variety stores. The American Record Company (ARC) acquired Romeo in 1931 and continued selling the 25-cent discs until 1939. The Carter Family, led by A. P. Carter, accompanied by his wife Sara and sister-in-law Maybelle, could be counted among the many varied performers who cut sides for these struggling labels. With a background in Southern rural churches, the Carters emerged as one of the first country music groups to be recorded. [Photograph by author; from the Bryan Wright Collection]

Other early recordings like "Wabash Cannonball," "I'm Thinking Tonight of My Blue Eyes," and "Will You Miss Me when I'm Gone?" gradually circulated throughout the South and Southwest, establishing the Carter Family's name. One particular Victor recording, "Wildwood Flower" (1928; re-recorded in 1935), attained considerable stature in country music, selling over 100,000 copies by the early 1930s. The story of a jilted woman, it featured Sara's singing and Maybelle's guitar. When Peer left Victor and moved to the ARC label (see Chapter 1), the Carter Family followed. In 1936 they signed with the new Decca enterprise. More family members joined the group, and the Carters became a force in country music. Like Jimmy Rodgers, they were prolific in their output, releasing over 250 sides between 1927 and 1943, the year the original trio broke up with Sara's departure.

During the 1930s, Sara played autoharp and sang in a distinctive alto, and A. P. (as most knew him) sang bass. Maybelle, capable as a soprano, distinguished herself on guitar, employing a new, innovative melodic style that put the instrument in a lead role instead of just rhythm. Her technique found many appreciative listeners and would come to be a part of country music. The trio's utilization of vocal harmony, along with Maybelle's strong guitar work, shaped both country and bluegrass music for years to come.

A. P. Carter liked to travel through the isolated regions of the mountainous Southeast, collecting old Appalachian songs, hymns, and lyrics from the people who lived there. The trio would then transcribe his findings into arrangements they could perform. Despite their emphasis on traditional music, the group would on occasion delve into topicality. In 1936, A. P. wrote "No Depression (in Heaven)," a tune that acknowledged the world beyond their immediate region.

In the late 1930s, the Carter Family traveled to Del Rio, Texas. There, they crossed the border into Mexico to perform on radio station XERA in Ciudad Acuna. A powerful—500,000 watts—AM operation, unemcumbered by FCC regulations, XERA traded in questionable advertising, medical fraud, right-wing politics, and fundamentalist religion. The Carters, however, seemed blissfully ignorant of those aspects of the station's broadcasting, or maybe they just needed the money paid them. At any rate, they did two shows a day, aiming their music at unseen audiences hundreds of miles away. This widespread exposure allowed the Carters to be heard and known by more people than they could imagine.

Maybelle's daughter, June Carter (1929–2003), joined the group in 1939. In time, June Carter would marry (her third marriage) in 1968 none other than a rising country singer named Johnny Cash (1932–2003). Henceforth, she carried the name June Carter Cash and emerged as a popular country entertainer. Rosanne Cash (b. 1956), Johnny's daughter from a previous marriage, became June Carter's stepdaughter, and thus continued a musical dynasty.[3]

Because of the Depression, musicians of every stripe, urban and rural, found concerts and even small club dates difficult to procure. No one had the ready cash to pay them for performing. In order for listeners to know about them, it became essential to have recording contracts and radio exposure. In addition, jukeboxes contributed to the expansion and popularity of country music. Found everywhere, especially in the rural South at bars and cafes, their selections varied by region and demographics. As might be expected, those in many roadside eateries included some country and hillbilly music. Performers not likely to be heard on most radio stations could therefore at times be found on jukebox menus, and this availability stimulated record sales (see Chapter 1 for more on the jukebox phenomenon).[4]

Sound movies similarly influenced who listened to what. For example, Westerns have long been a popular genre in film. A number of cowboy actors achieved stardom when they sang in their own pictures. Examples from the 1930s would include Bob Baker, Dick Foran, Ken Maynard, and Tex Ritter, but Gene Autry (1907–1998) and Roy Rogers (1911–1998) emerged as the most successful of "the Singing Cowboys," virtually defining the type.

In movie after movie, the two vocalized and strummed their guitars, often while astride their own prize horses, Champion and Trigger. Their success prompted "The World's Only Singing Cowgirl" in the person of Dorothy Page, although it seems she survived only two films. Collectively, the violence was low and the humor corny in the bulk of these pictures, but for several generations of moviegoers, Autry and Rogers epitomized the straight-talkin', fair-dealin', sharp-shootin' cowboy.

In terms of popularity, fame, or even lifespans, the two closely matched one another. Autry began his movie career in 1934 with *In Old Santa Fe*; he played a square dance caller. He had earlier recorded a sentimental tune that rose to be a minor hit in 1931: "That Silver-Haired Daddy of Mine" (words and music by Jimmy Long and Gene Autry). All of this led to a starring role in a twelve-part serial, *The Phantom Empire* (1934). Given his association with "That Silver-Haired Daddy of Mine," he sang the song in no less than eight separate episodes of *The Phantom Empire*.

Autry again appeared on record charts with "Tumbling Tumbleweeds" (1934; words and music by Bob Nolan), a song featured in a 1935 movie of the same name. And, in case anyone missed episodes of *The Phantom Empire*, he also reprised "That Silver-Haired Daddy of Mine" yet again. With these successes, Autry became a marketable property, starring in dozens of low-grade Westerns. Most of them featured not just horses and six-guns, but plenty of country (or cowboy) music. Often accompanied by his humorous sidekick, Smiley Burnette, Autry went on to make such pictures as *Red River Valley* (1936), *Rootin' Tootin' Rhythm* (1937), *Prairie Moon* (1938), *Rhythm of the Saddle* (1938), and countless others. Out of these efforts would come songs like "Red River Sweetheart" (1936; words and music by Smiley Burnette), "Mother Nature's Lullaby" (1938; words and music by Gene Autry, Johnny Marvin, and Fred Rose), and "Melody Ranch" (1940; words and music by

The advent of sound films brought about the birth of the "singing cowboy," a staple of Western movies throughout the 1930s. Chief among this new, musical breed of hero were Gene Autry (1907–1998; above) and Roy Rogers (1911–1998). As apt to draw a guitar as a six-gun, they starred in dozens of low-budget pictures that often emphasized music and comedy over the more traditional shoot-outs. [Library of Congress, Prints & Photographs Division]

Gene Autry and Fred Rose). A measure of Autry's success: by the mid-thirties, merchandising giant Sears, Roebuck offered a "Gene Autry" guitar in its catalog for any aspiring singing cowboy.

Roy Rogers' film career did not blossom quite as early as Gene Autry's, but it also took off during the 1930s. Born Leonard Slye in Ohio, he, along with Tim Spencer and Bob Nolan, formed a musical group called the International Cowboys in 1934. That somewhat highbrow title shortly gave way to the more folksy Sons of the Pioneers, and the group began to appear in movies, especially Gene Autry's early Westerns. Slye—originally billed as "Dick Weston"— also played some solo roles in these pictures. By 1938, he had been christened "Roy Rogers" in *Under Western Stars*.

Maintaining a furious pace, Rogers made twenty-one Westerns between 1938 and 1940, and emerged as the only cowboy rival to Autry. His pictures

Country music attracted a broad audience. In this 1937 photograph, a homesteader from south central Pennsylvania enjoys a moment away from his labors while he fiddles a Western tune. In rural areas, sheet music might prove the primary source of new and traditional songs, although sweeping electrification rapidly brought in radio and recordings. [Library of Congress, Prints & Photographs Division]

all serve up generous amounts of singing, and the titles range from *Shine On, Harvest Moon* (1938) to *The Ranger and the Lady* (1940). Three years after Autry had recorded it, Rogers performed "Tumbling Tumbleweeds" with the Sons of the Pioneers in *Old Wyoming Trail* (1937). It seemed only fitting, since Bob Nolan, one of the original Sons of the Pioneers, had composed it in 1934.

No big hits came from Roy Rogers, just a steady stream of Western-tinged songs. "The Man in the Moon Is a Cowhand" (1938; words and music by Roy Rogers and Tim Spencer), "I've Sold My Saddle for an Old Guitar" (1938; words and music by Fleming Allan), and "Ridin' Down the Trail" (1939; words and music by Roy Rogers, Eddie Cherkose, and Cy Fever) never made any major hit lists, but they did acquaint millions with a popularized form of country music.

Slightly outside what most people listened to or heard on radio or records, the music in movie Westerns lacked the glitter and sophistication of the stage music of a Gershwin or Porter. It seldom provided the rich melodies associated with standards, but it featured a simplicity and honesty people found attractive. A mainstream entertainer like Bing Crosby, recognizing the latent popularity in such tunes, made a movie entitled *Rhythm on the Range* (1936). In it, he sang "I'm an Old Cowhand" (1936; words and music by Johnny Mercer) and "Empty Saddles" (1936; words and music by Billy Hill and J. Kiern Brennan). The latter number briefly made the listings on radio's *Your Hit Parade*, suggesting public receptiveness to Western tunes. Successes like this helped pave the way for the rise of country music following World War II.[5]

WESTERN SWING

Western Swing, a kind of spin-off from country music, evolved with the swing craze that so characterized the national musical mood in the later 1930s. The term more often than not refers to one group, Bob Wills and His Texas Playboys, although many different bands in the southern and western states, especially Oklahoma and Texas, attempted to play in the style. Wills (1905–1975) set most of the patterns for the music; competing groups like The High Flyers, The Tune Wranglers, The Oklahoma Playboys, and The Cowboy Ramblers imitated him. At times called "Hilllbilly Swing," "Okie Jazz," "Country Swing," "Southwestern Swing," and "Texas Swing," the music possessed a blend of big-band Dixieland and jazz, some blues, and a healthy dose of traditional country guitars and violins (or "fiddles"), along with some singing. At first, the term "swing" still had not entered the popular vocabulary, and so people called these groups "hot string bands," but somehow it all came together in an infectious mix that proved irresistible for dancing. Regardless of its name, Western Swing remained a regional phenomenon; few people outside the lower Great Plains knew much about it, and Wills and his numerous counterparts labored in relative obscurity.

Prior to Wills and the Playboys, many string bands—groups consisting of guitars, fiddles, and their variants—traveled the region. Often called "territory bands," because they covered a designated area, or territory, these groups played endless one-night stands in small towns and dancehalls. Since recording companies viewed their music as local or regional, with limited appeal, these bands seldom landed record contracts. Or, if they did, the companies promoted them to what they saw as narrow niche audiences, just as they did with "race records" for black performers and listeners. In marketing terms, "Western Swing" and all its variations designated a type of music that would not receive national promotion or distribution.

The Light Crust Doughboys (so named by their radio sponsor, the Burris Flour Company) can be seen as a seminal band in this movement, one that would influence others in the early years of the decade. Playing out of Fort Worth, Texas, the personnel included Bob Wills on violin and Milton Brown on vocals. The group's blend of Texas two-steps and fox trots proved popular, and led others to try the same.

After a falling-out with management, Brown and Wills quit the Doughboys and formed bands of their own. In 1932, Milton Brown and His Brownies began to compete directly with the Light Crust Doughboys in different radio shows from two Fort Worth stations. Brown (1903–1936), an innovator, added electrified steel guitars, an upright bass, and a piano to his ensemble, instruments that became commonplace in subsequent Western swing bands. He continued to do the vocals, but the music contained increasingly strong elements of swing.

For his part, Wills left Texas and moved to Oklahoma where he established Bob Wills and His Playboys (the "Texas" would come later to avoid confusion with the Oklahoma Playboys). Although he saw to it that his band had guitars and fiddles, he also borrowed a page from the big swing bands back East by including horns and drums. Tommy Duncan handled the vocal chores, and Wills himself added some fiddle playing, along with "hollers" and occasional comments. He eventually landed some recording contracts, cutting sides like "Take Me Back to Tulsa" (1941; words and music by Bob Wills and Tommy Duncan), "Milk Cow Blues" (1934; words and music by K. Arnold), and his biggest hit, 1940's "San Antonio Rose" (words and music by Bob Wills).

During the latter half of the 1930s, the Wills band filled dancehalls and roadhouses every night it took to the road. The group played blues, rags, stomps, and syrupy ballads, but they could also play real jazz and swing numbers. They performed hillbilly songs and novelties, but sounded best when they stuck to swing with a Western touch. Yet Wills and the Playboys had no real following outside Texas and some neighboring states. Within their territory, however, they capitalized on radio broadcasts and record purchases to create a hybrid that utilized both country music and swing.[6]

WOODY GUTHRIE (1912–1967)

Occupying a curious middle ground between country music and protest songs, and with a generous helping of folk, blues, and popular tunes thrown in the mix, balladeer Woody Guthrie has come down to the present as a major voice in the left-wing movements of the thirties. Something of a generalization, and part of the contemporary nostalgia about the decade, Guthrie's reputation did grow during the 1930s, but he enjoyed at best a limited following. His "So Long, It's Been Good to Know Ya" (1935; originally titled "Dusty Old Dust") came from music used in a traditional work by Carson Robison called "Ballad of Billy the Kid" (1930); Guthrie reworked it and added his own words. Among his best-known compositions, it has entered music annals as a "Dust Bowl ballad" and represents his style well. It reflects the hard times of the Depression, especially the harsh weather and drought conditions experienced by farmers in the western half of the nation. Ironically, the song gained its greatest popularity not in 1935, but in 1951 when a folk group called the Weavers recorded it, a time far removed from Depressions and Dust Bowls.

As a teenager, Guthrie learned to play the guitar and the harmonica. He wandered throughout Texas and Oklahoma, absorbing the flavor of the region and compiling knowledge about country music. Eventually he would compose more than one thousand songs, many of which relied on the music of others for their melodies. After the limited success of "Dusty Old Dust," Guthrie journeyed to Los Angeles and in 1937 landed a radio program. He co-starred with singer Maxine Crissman—who billed herself as "Lefty Lou"—and the two talked and sang for two years as *Woody and Lefty Lou*, developing a dedicated audience in the process.

A tireless songwriter, Guthrie continued to compose while on the West Coast. He celebrated outlaws ("Pretty Boy Floyd," 1939), the dispossessed ("I Ain't Got No Home," "Dust Bowl Refugees," both 1938), and the poor ("If You Ain't Got the Do Re Mi," 1937). As the 1930s wound down, much of his music took on more of a political edge, and by the 1940s he had moved to compositions about the labor movement and social inequities and injustices. But, contrary to much popular belief, that segment of Guthrie's career took place after the 1930s.

In 1938, he also wrote a newspaper column for *The People's World*, a Communist periodical based in Los Angeles. Called "Woody Sez," the column presented Guthrie as something of a homespun, populist philosopher. In it, he espoused the causes of working people and farmers, a thread that he would amplify in his music. Since *The People's World* had Communist Party connections, his association with the paper tainted his reputation in the eyes of many and would haunt him during the 1940s and 1950s, a time of rabid anti-communism.

Guthrie left Los Angeles and went to New York City in 1939 to pursue commercial recording. Here he would write "This Land Is Your Land," a kind of alternative national anthem for many during the turbulent 1960s and 1970s. The melody came from a country blues called "Rock of Ages" by Blind Willie Davis. The Carter Family (see above) had recorded this song as "When the World's on Fire," and it featured Maybelle Carter in her distinctive guitar style. Guthrie, who had few qualms about "borrowing" the music of others, incorporated the Carter version into his own composition. He himself did not record "This Land Is Your Land" until 1944 in a series of sessions for Folkways Records. Made immensely more famous in later recordings by such widely popular artists as Bob Dylan (1961), Pete Seeger (1962), and Peter, Paul, and Mary (1962), "This Land Is Your Land" displays Guthrie's yearning for social equality among all Americans, and serves as a fitting summation of his career (see also the next section).[7]

LABOR AND PROTEST MUSIC

The Great Depression affected everyone, particularly those in the lower economic echelons such as laborers and farmers. Often ignored in popular culture, these groups occasionally found a small voice through music. Although the audience tended to be limited to those involved in a particular struggle or victims of an injustice, protest music flowered during the 1930s as people tried to articulate their woes and anger through song.

Woody Guthrie, possibly the best-known author of protest music, has been identified as a spokesman for the dispossessed and downtrodden. He also wrote a number of pro-labor, anti-business songs that endeared him to workers and enraged "the bosses," "the fat cats," "the Big Crooks," "the Greedy Rich Folks"—those whom he perceived as manipulating and controlling the fate of ordinary working-class people. Most of these songs, such as "Union Maid" (1940), "Boomtown Bill" (1942), and "Ludlow Massacre" (1944), came out after the 1930s had drawn to a close and fall outside the limits of this study.

Sarah Ogan Gunning (1910–1983), a name not so familiar as Guthrie's, often sang alongside him. They even co-wrote several labor songs. She composed her music from personal experience and tended to be direct in her quest for solutions, usually opting for union membership as the way to survive oppressive conditions. Among her pro-union songs are "Come All Ye

Coal Miners" (1931) and "Dreadful Memories" (1932), laments about the fate of miners and their impoverished families in Harlan County, Kentucky.

Not all the music of the period concerned itself with coal mining. Textile workers likewise attempted to organize and a number of 1930s songs commemorate their battles. Dave McCarn (1905–1964) recorded "Cotton Mill Colic" in 1930, a significant contribution to the movement. He also wrote "Poor Man, Rich Man (Cotton Mill Colic No. 2)" (1930) and "Serves Them Fine (Cotton Mill Colic No. 3)" (1931). Bob Miller (1895–1955) displayed sympathy for farmers and textile workers with "Eleven Cent Cotton, Forty Cent Meat" (1932) and "The Poor Forgotten Man" (1932). Finally, a man named Dorsey Dixon had important compositions in this area with his "Weave Room Blues" (1932) and "Babies in the Mill" (ca. 1933).

In 1935, Sarah Ogan Gunning moved to New York City, making friends with folk singers, radicals, Communists, and others active in the labor movement and musical protests. During her stay, she broadened her palette and penned "I Hate the Capitalist System" (ca. 1937) and "I'm Going to Organize" (ca. 1938). She appeared in concerts and recorded her music, some of which has survived the passage of time.

Similarly, Florence Reese (1900–1986) wrote "Which Side Are You On?" in 1931. It celebrated the United Mine Workers of America and the National Miners Union, labor organizations that represented those working the mines, and urged people to join. The song would be recorded in 1941 and become a union organizing favorite. Aunt Molly Jackson (1880–1960; a half-sister to Sarah Ogan Gunning) also composed many titles; in the hard-hit mining towns, "Miner's Hungry Ragged Blues" and "Poor Miner's Farewell" (both 1933) did well. She also had the lyrics to some of her songs printed in *The Little Red Song Book*, a collection of labor songs that the Workers Library, a left-wing, radical publisher allied with the Industrial Workers of the World, or IWW, issued in 1933.

Many other singers—Tillman Cadle, Jim Garland, Maurice Sugar, plus a host of anonymous performers—protested on the side of labor throughout the 1930s. Seldom recorded by any major labels—if recorded at all—their voices and names have largely been lost, although a number of their songs were assimilated into laborers' causes beyond the confines of Kentucky.

Working together, Pete Seeger, Woody Guthrie, and folklorist Alan Lomax in 1940 compiled a book of labor-oriented protest songs. Given the times, the collected lyrics were considered too radical, and no publisher could be found. Eventually, however, attitudes mellowed and *Hard Hitting Songs for Hard-Hit*

People came out in 1967, a time of renewed interest in folk music. The book contains a varied selection of songs, and serves as a good introduction to this kind of music.[8]

Finally, mention must be made of composer Earl Robinson (1910–1991). Robinson had enjoyed an academic musical background, but chose to involve himself in various left-wing causes during the 1930s, such as the Young Communist League. Out of this exposure came socially significant songs like "Joe Hill" (1936) and "Abe Lincoln" (1938). They had a cult following, but failed to attract a large, diversified audience. Undoubtedly, Robinson's most popular composition was "Ballad for Americans" (1938; lyrics by John Latouche), a frankly pro-American song that came to fame through a CBS radio broadcast. The network had on its schedule a show called *Pursuit of Happiness* that ran from 1939 to 1940. In one segment during November of 1939, baritone Paul Robeson performed "Ballad for Americans," and those listening found it a strong narrative piece (see Chapter 7, "Vocalists," for more on Robeson).

Following its radio success, "Ballad for Americans" emerged as a fixture at the ongoing 1939–1940 New York World's Fair. By 1939, everyone sensed World War II was in the offing; it had become a question of when. For many, the times demanded patriotism, and the RCA Pavilion on the Flushing Meadow fairground featured the frankly propagandistic song three times a day. This occasion marked the height of Earl Robinson's public renown.[9]

FOLK MUSIC, ETHNIC MUSIC, AND THE LOMAXES

The early years of the twentieth century embraced many musical formats. With the rise of recording technology, the voices and styles of many older musicians, fortunately, were saved. Much of the music of this era fell into an oral, nonwritten tradition, a tradition that might have been lost had not recordings preserved the work of these untrained musicians. Music historians refer to many of their efforts as "folk music," a general reference that covers various levels of performance and style. For example, the preceding comments on country music, especially the compositions played by the Carter Family, could easily be placed in the broad contexts of folk music.

Burl Ives (1909–1995), himself a rising figure in the folk music scene of the late 1930s, hosted a fifteen-minute radio show (1940–1941) that gave many in the audience their first exposure to this kind of music. Broadcast on

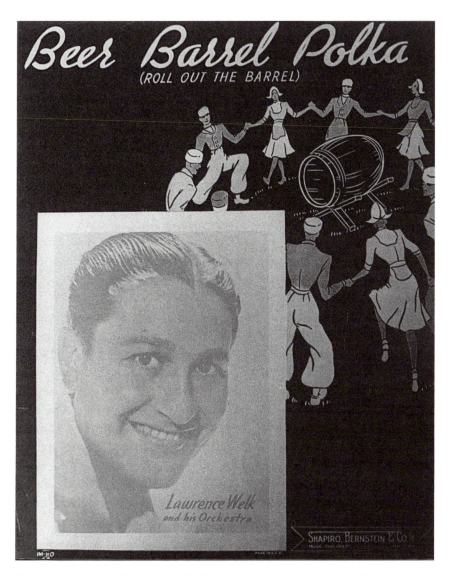

The sheet music cover for "Beer Barrel Polka" (1939; music by Jaramir Vejvoda, lyrics by Lew Brown and Wladimir A. Timm). This tune, an unexpected hit from a little-known Broadway play entitled *Yokel Boy*, helped to establish the Lawrence Welk orchestra. The music's popularity did not, however, lead to a rash of polkas; it stands instead as an illustration of the isolated number that momentarily catches the public's fancy and then disappears. [Photograph by author; from the Al Harris Collection]

both NBC and CBS at various times, it served as some of the first media recognition of a largely ignored branch of American song.

Little in the way of ethnic music achieved great popularity during the 1930s. Cajun songs seldom found audiences much beyond Louisiana's borders. A few regional bands struggled for recognition, but with little success. The Hackberry Ramblers, Leo Soileau, and Harry Choates issued recordings of Cajun tunes, but distribution faltered in surrounding states. Those groups that enjoyed any commercial success tended to Americanize their repertoires, usually adding Western Swing and country touches, plus virtually eliminating the trademark accordion, in their quest for acceptance. Any nationwide awareness of Cajun music would have to wait until after World War II.[10]

"Beer Barrel Polka" (1939; music by Jaramir Vejvoda, lyrics by Lew Brown and Wladimir A. Timm) proved an unexpected hit from a Broadway play entitled *Yokel Boy.* For whatever reasons, the public took to the tune, but that did not precipitate a sudden showering of polkas or other Polish music. "Beer Barrel Polka" represented one of those musical shots in the dark, a surprise hit, but little else.

Were it not for John Lomax (1867–1948) and his son Alan (1915–2002), knowledge of this rich musical heritage of rural America, especially as occurred in the southern half of the country, would be severely limited today. A Texan fascinated by all forms of folk music, John Lomax had spent much of his life in academia. In 1932, the Macmillan Publishing Company accepted his proposal for a wide-ranging anthology of American folksongs and ballads. He then worked out an agreement with the Library of Congress's Archive of American Folk Song for recording equipment so he could capture this music in the field instead of at a studio. Although he did not know it at the time, the next ten years of his life would be occupied with this project. The entire Lomax family became partners in the endeavor, and youngest son Alan eventually became a paid employee of the Library of Congress with the title of Director of the Archive of American Folk Song.

The Lomaxes traveled the back roads and small towns of the country, recording the songs of everyday people. Generous funding allowed them to upgrade their recording apparatus. They soon acquired an acetate disc recorder that they lugged around in the trunk of their car. Its high quality of reproduction meant that future generations of musicologists would be able to hear accurate recordings, and written notations meant to accompany them proved unnecessary.

ALAN LOMAX

 Authority on American Folk-Lore . . . Archivist to the Library of Congress . . . Commentator and Artist on "Columbia's School of the Air"

An undated picture of a young Alan Lomax (1915–2002), a man who, along with his father, musicologist John Lomax (1867–1948), did much to make Americans aware of their folk heritage. Covering the country's byways and back roads, the two collected hundreds of examples of true folk music from its original sources, those largely untrained musicians and singers who had preserved and created a body of music ignored by much of the nation. [Library of Congress, Prints & Photographs Division]

Additional funding allowed the Lomaxes to extend and broaden their quest, taking them ever farther afield. During this time, they made many acquaintances, people who would then lead them to obscure artists they might otherwise have overlooked. In 1939, Alan recorded jazz pianist Jelly Roll Morton, and in 1940 he captured the music of Woody Guthrie and bluesman Leadbelly (Huddie Ledbetter).

Considering the enormity of their task, John and Alan Lomax preserved a remarkable amount of music, over 10,000 songs, ranging from folk, blues, labor, protest, to ethnic. The war ended the project in 1942, but out of their efforts the Archive of American Folk Song emerged as the finest collection of American folk music available anywhere.[11]

BLUES

Blues, the blues, blues music—the terms may vary, but they all refer to a rich body of music that originated in the United States sometime in the late nineteenth century. With widespread roots in African chants and rhythms, slave field hollers and work songs, popular narrative melodies, spirituals and European-American hymns, the blues grew up across the southern tier of states. New Orleans served as one melting pot, but rural communities in Alabama, Mississippi, and Texas, along with the track of the Mississippi River itself, also made contributions. By the 1930s, the blues had become firmly established as an important part of American musical tradition, existing as both a form and a feeling. Many important performers could be found singing and playing the blues, formally and informally, in clubs, roadhouses, joints and dives, preserving and expanding this uniquely American idiom.

Impossible to define with any precision, the blues told—and continue to tell—the stories of jilted lovers, lost hopes, and the yearning for a better life. But all was not sadness and despair; often the blues also spoke of faith and hope, that the sun would "shine in my back door someday." In many ways a history of the black experience in America, most of the early blues practitioners were themselves black, recounting their own lives. Not until the 1940s and thereafter would white musicians in any numbers begin to explore the blues. By and large, however, the blues have remained a primarily black form of expression.

The popularity of the blues coincides with the rise of the recording industry. Most radio stations refrained from playing blues records, citing fear of listener (i.e., white) backlash, and so the marketing of so-called "race records" in black communities gave most artists their only public exposure beyond their own regional areas of influence (see Chapter 1 for more on "race records"). The Great Migration of black workers from the rural South to northern urban centers also brought with it a heightened awareness of the blues, especially in Chicago. In time, the blues moved from an emphasis on the individual performer to a greater reliance on group expression, going from the vocalist accompanying himself on guitar to a small band playing behind the singer, and with the piano often displacing the guitar. What had been in essence a kind of folk expression became a much more polished, commercialized style of music. These forces, coupled with the rise of swing and its almost universal acceptance, allowed a majority of important blues musicians to finally get heard by large audiences.

Among the more notable blues artists of the 1930s, such performers as Big Bill Broonzy (1893–1958), Lonnie Johnson (1894–1970), Robert Johnson (1911–1938), Leadbelly (1888–1946), Memphis Minnie (1897–1973), Bessie Smith (1894–1937), and Josh White (1908–1969) must be counted. But many others also played the blues. Often, in the tradition of wandering minstrels, their names have been lost. But in the hard times of the Great Depression, the blues flourished, even if much of the population never knew the performers and never heard their songs.

Big Bill Broonzy (born William Lee Conley Broonzy) came to prominence as a country blues singer and guitarist. He sang of the sharecroppers and rural life of Mississippi, although he could also delve into the timeless subject of love and its consequences. By the late 1930s, he had established himself in Chicago, the new center for many blues musicians, and moved increasingly to the urban topics so many of his contemporaries featured. An excellent guitarist, he recorded frequently during the 1930s for small labels, and reached the height of his popularity during the decade. In 1938 he played a significant role in John Hammond's *From Spirituals to Swing* concert (see Chapter 4 for information about this concert).

Among Broonzy's compositions and recordings are "Southern Flood Blues" (1937); "Just a Dream" (1939), a song about racial inequities; and "Looking Up at Down" (1940), a protest about black poverty. Despite his popularity among blues fans, Broonzy's audience remained limited, and so did his relative freedom to deal with themes that would have been unacceptable for a more mainstream performer at that time.

With one foot planted in the blues tradition and the other in the evolving jazz of the day, Lonnie Johnson performed equally well in either area. His blues, most of them originals, attracted listeners. In 1925, he won a blues contest sponsored by Okeh Records in St. Louis, and soon thereafter had a contract with the label. On his way with personal appearances and recordings, Johnson soon met trumpeter Louis Armstrong and the two struck up a friendship. From that relationship came recording dates with Armstrong and his Hot Fives and Johnson's acceptance in the jazz community. This led to appearances with Duke Ellington and his orchestra and blueswoman Bessie Smith. Despite his versatility, Johnson occasionally had to seek employment outside of music. His is a familiar story: a talented musician who can never quite achieve that level of recognition that brings with it financial freedom.

The Mississippi delta region served as the center for much blues activity. Considered one of the great practitioners of this regional style, Robert Johnson brought an intensity to his singing and playing that moved anyone fortunate enough to hear him. A master of the slide guitar, he accompanied himself and sang of his harsh life and experiences. During a series of sessions in 1936 and 1937, Johnson recorded forty-one songs (including alternate takes) for the American Record Company and its Vocalion label. These sides constituted his entire recorded output, since he died in 1938. During his brief life, only a handful of the total saw release; not until 1990 did Columbia Records package all forty-one, a time when interest in the blues surpassed anything he had experienced a half-century earlier.

Many of those forty-one sides have had a great influence on subsequent artists like the Rolling Stones and Eric Clapton. "Terraplane Blues," possibly Johnson's best-known song, became something of a blues hit in 1937. The "Terraplane" of the title refers to a sedan manufactured by the Hudson Motor Company during the thirties. As such, "Terraplane Blues" joins a select company of songs about automobiles that reflect much about the car culture of the country. In addition, his anguished "Hellhound on My Trail" (1937) is considered by many to be one of his best efforts.

Leadbelly (b. Huddie Ledbetter) came to some fame during the 1920s, especially among blues fans. A difficult individual, he moved between violence and performing his music for whomever would listen. In jail for murder between 1918 and 1925, he turned to composition and mastering the twelve-string guitar. Imprisoned again in 1930, his release did not occur until 1934, and that with the considerable help of folklorist John Lomax (see above). Leadbelly celebrated his freedom with a series of concerts, broadcasts, and recordings that often featured numbers like "Good Night, Irene" (1939), "Midnight Special" (traditional), "Easy Rider" (ca. 1935) and "Rock Island Line" (1937), performances that assured his place among the masters of the blues idiom, and songs that would go on to become big hits for other artists.

The association with John Lomax meant that Leadbelly often performed before white audiences, something denied most black blues artists in those segregated times. Despite this exposure, however, he remained outside the mainstreams of American music. For most white listeners, the blues represented black culture, an interesting foray into the primitive and unknown, but something to be approached with caution. Throughout the 1930s, despite the well-meaning efforts of people like the Lomaxes, neither Leadbelly nor the blues in general could ever break through the wall of reserve that separated this kind of music from other, more popular, formats.

One of the few women to make a name for herself in the blues idiom, Memphis Minnie (b. Lizzie Douglas) emerged as a big star on the blues circuit during the 1930s. She wrote and recorded hundreds of songs, many—if not most—of which have been lost over the years. She moved from singing in the streets of Memphis to performing in the nightclubs of Chicago. Her risqué "Bumble Bee Blues" (1929) served as her first hit and established her credibility as a performer among her male counterparts.

Minnie sang about the standard blues subjects—love, money, hardship. Always a stylish dresser on stage, she played while standing, a break with the tradition of sitting and playing. She linked the country traditions of the South with the urban blues of Memphis and Chicago. From the beginning, Minnie displayed great facility with the guitar and could outplay most of her male counterparts. By 1940, she had taken up the electric guitar, one of the first musicians to do so.

A big star in the 1920s, Bessie Smith gained the title "Empress of the Blues" early in her career. Blessed with a strong voice that required no electric amplification, Smith could belt out songs over the din of crowds and still be heard. In her heyday, Smith commanded upwards of $2,000 a week to perform, making her the highest-paid black entertainer in the country. Yet by 1931, Columbia Records had dropped Smith, citing her "dated style" and claiming declining sales. Smith tried for a comeback in 1933 with a new burst of activity and a more contemporary approach to the music. Accurately foretelling the rise of swing, her 1933 records lack much of the emotional intensity that had colored her blues performances just a few years earlier.

A new generation of listeners nonetheless came to appreciate Smith and her selection of popular ballads, and her sidemen in one instance included Benny Goodman, the later King of Swing. It appeared that a new career had opened for Smith, but a tragic automobile accident in 1937 stopped this revival of interest and today she is usually remembered more as a figure from the 1920s.

Another skillful guitarist, and one with a unique voice, Josh White enjoyed considerable popularity during the 1930s. He signed with ARC's Banner label in 1932, and recorded a number of sides with them over the next several years. He worked in a variety of styles, including the blues, gospel, protest songs, and even some folk and cabaret singing in the 1940s and 1950s.

During the 1930s, he found success with "St. James Infirmary Blues" (1930; words and music by Joe Primrose), a popular blues; he would continue to play and record it throughout his career. White also had some association, both knowingly and unknowingly, with left-wing and radical groups. Although this would get him into trouble during the anti-Communist 1950s, it also allowed him to compose some harsh protest blues during the 1930s. An example would be his 1936 "Chain Gang Boun'," an indictment of a justice system that sometimes placed innocent people, usually black, in the hands of wardens that made them endure the tortures of a forced-labor chain gang.[12]

GOSPEL MUSIC

In many ways a kind of ecclesiastical offshoot of the blues, Gospel music flowered in the 1930s. Credit for this rise in interest and popularity needs to be directed to the Reverend Thomas A. Dorsey (1899–1993; he should not be confused with Tommy Dorsey, the popular trombonist and bandleader of the 1930s), a man often considered the father of modern Gospel music. Dorsey had earlier distinguished himself as a blues pianist. During the 1920s and until his conversion to the Gospel format, he had teamed with Tampa Red (1900–1981; b. Hudson Whittaker), a popular blues vocalist and guitarist. At the time, people knew Dorsey as "Georgia Tom," and he and Tampa Red recorded often. Their best-known recording was "It's Tight Like That" (1928), a raucous blues that soon entered the repertoire of many musicians and groups.

But Dorsey sought more from his music, and looked to religion as a place to find it. He fused the traditional blues with spirituals, Baptist hymns, and other musical formats he found in black churches; the mix worked well, effectively blurring the lines between the sacred and the secular. His new form of Gospel music quickly gained acceptance among black congregations, blending as it did jazz, blues, and improvisation with the strong foundation of religious prosody. By 1932, Dorsey had founded a Gospel publishing house, giving himself and his supporters a ready outlet for their innovative approach to music. In addition, radio stations, often hesitant to play straight blues, found no problems broadcasting this uplifting religious music, thus further increasing the potential audience.

The deaths of his wife and daughter led Dorsey to write "Precious Lord, Take My Hand" in 1932. Since recorded by many different performers, "Precious Lord, Take My Hand" has become the best-known Gospel song of all time. Although it contains blues elements, it also demonstrates a primary difference between Gospel and most blues music: the blues tend to focus on trials and tribulations, but Gospel music casts an affirmative light on any situation. The tone remains hopeful; good news—the implicit message of much evangelical religion—will win out. In keeping with this view, Dorsey also wrote "There Will Be Peace in the Valley" in 1937, another classic in the genre.

A noted performer in the Gospel idiom during the 1930s was Sister Rosetta Tharpe (1915–1973). A skilled guitarist, she made several Decca recordings in 1938 that carried the Gospel message. One side included a Dorsey composition, "Hide Me in Thy Bosom." Retitled "Rock Me" for the recording session, it became a hit. Impresario John Hammond (see Chapter 4), after hearing these sides, got Tharpe to appear in his 1938 *From Spirituals to Swing*, a concert that attracted thousands of appreciative listeners. With her strong voice and stylish guitar playing, Tharpe embarked on the road to stardom. She followed this success with another recording, "This Train" (1938), that helped to put Gospel permanently on the musical map.[13]

6

The Classical Tradition and the Federal Music Project

Americans have long embraced a love–hate relationship with classical music. In a culture that espouses self-improvement, people see serious music as intrinsically superior to more popular forms. At the same time, these same individuals favor the more accessible, "easier" popular formats for their own listening. This disingenuous situation prevailed throughout the 1930s, a time when a number of groups, both private and governmental, actively attempted to raise the level of American musical literacy. Despite the best of intentions, the efforts failed. Most people continued to buy and listen to pop songs, and then swing overwhelmed all other music in the latter half of the decade.

AMERICAN CLASSICAL MUSIC DURING THE 1930s

Few serious compositions attracted strong public attention during the period, and the classical tradition suffered from both the competition of other musical formats and continuing economic constraints. For classical recordings, that situation translated as disastrous: by 1931, 500 copies constituted the average sales total for a classical disc, although that figure did begin a slow upward climb after 1933.

Despite the apparent lack of public interest, many people in broadcasting and the recording industry felt an obligation to provide American listeners access to classical music. Both local stations and the networks presented shows that focused on educating listeners about, and exposing them to, what critics and musicologists considered the best in serious composition. These experts believed that with education and exposure, the public's taste in music could and would be uplifted.

Radio programming, especially on NBC and CBS, the two primary networks, included shows that not only played classical recordings or employed studio orchestras, but also discussions of so-called "serious music" led by leaders in the field. Far more classical programming could be found on American radio than can be heard today.

Several factors accounted for this emphasis on cultural programming. The Federal Communications Commission (FCC), an outgrowth of the Federal Radio Commission (FRC; 1927–1934), had been formed in 1934 to regulate the rapid, rambunctious growth of the medium. Among its many mandates, the commission possesses the power to approve new stations by granting them permission to broadcast and to shut down those already on the air by revoking their licenses. Without proper FCC sanction, a station can be banned from the air. Since the commission operates under the principle that the airwaves belong to the people and not to commercial interests, it therefore professes an interest in the content of a station's programs, although it holds no overt censorship powers and stresses self-regulation. It can forbid certain obscenities from the air, monitor fraudulent advertising, ban religious and racial bigotry, along with slanderous or defaming commentary, all in the name of the "public interest."[1]

In the years preceding World War II, many broadcasters interpreted this interest as a not-so-subtle urging on the part of the FCC to maintain high standards of programming. Such tacit government encouragement reassured the industry that everyone benefited from classical broadcasting, that these offerings reflected the required high standards. In addition, some members of Congress at that time talked openly about "educational radio," and suggested setting aside frequencies to accommodate nonprofit broadcasting. Whether the FCC's mandates and Congress's threats included classical music probably depended on a station manager's perception of what constituted high standards, but certainly radio stations across the country strove to provide a mix of selections designed to appeal to the widest range of listeners.

Another reason stations featured "serious" music in their schedules involved prestige. Variety and lively competition characterized the early days of radio, and the contemporary concept of "niche stations," like "Middle of the

Road," "Adult Contemporary," or "Golden Oldies" that appeal to a particular group or class of listeners had not yet evolved. In the thirties, variety ruled the radio day: A mystery show could be followed by a comedy program which, in turn, might be followed by something like the *NBC Music Appreciation Hour*, *The Firestone Hour*, or the *Radio City Music Hall of the Air*, all of which typically offered classical compositions. The more distinguished the orchestra, the greater the fame of the conductor, the better stations and sponsors liked it, since they saw having the biggest names in classical music as direct reflections of the excellence of both the station and its underwriters.

This linking of prestige with classical music illustrates the continuing dichotomy between elite and popular culture. Although no nation consumes more popular culture—mass-market movies, best-selling fiction, comic strips, and pop songs—than the United States, well-meaning critics, artists, and academics at times step forward and try to raise the country's "standards," implying in their criticism that popular culture somehow does not measure up to the elitist variety.

It should therefore come as no surprise that American broadcasting suffered this kind of examination, both from within and without the industry. In response, networks and individual stations offered serious drama ranging from Shakespeare to the latest avant-garde playwrights, intellectual discussions on many different topics, and classical music—lots of it. Whether or not increasing on-air classical selections raised anyone's musical standards can not be answered with any accuracy, but certainly radio in the 1930s offered unparalleled opportunities for listeners to hear the era's finest artists in performance. In addition, stations viewed the broadcasting of high culture as good public relations. As radio grew ever more commercialized during the decade, evidence of cultural programming enhanced a station's (or network's) reputation.

NBC and CBS, the two primary radio networks, had in-house symphony orchestras almost from their inceptions, and they vied to land other major aggregations. Live broadcasts of important orchestras could be heard with some frequency. Since both networks had connections to the recording industry, it behooved them to acquaint listeners with the classics, on the theory that such an acquaintance would lead to increased purchases of classical records, or so the thinking went. Any accurate cause-and-effect data are, however, impossible to cite. Still, the feeling persisted throughout the 1930s that classical music programming benefited stations, networks, record companies, and of course listeners.[2]

Radio Shows Featuring Classical Music

Among the leading "serious music" network radio shows of the decade, the following deserve mention (listed alphabetically):

The American Album of Familiar Music (NBC, 1931–1950). Not really a classical program, *The American Album* delivered just what its name promised; familiar music. Neither the pop tunes of the day nor the symphonies of great composers received air time. Instead, the show mixed "light classics" like Stephen Foster or John Philip Sousa, adding in a potpourri of older songs from earlier decades. This meant some of the well-known melodies and themes from the classics, but seldom the entire work.

The Atwater-Kent Hour (NBC, 1926–1931; CBS, 1934). Sponsored by one of the best-known radio manufacturers of the day, this pioneering show attracted some of the leading names in classical music and opera to radio for the first time. It also brought to light the negative attitude many performers had toward radio, a medium they felt lowered their art to mass entertainment. Some stars refused to perform on any broadcasts; others only agreed to perform anonymously at first; but good money, and the realization that the medium of radio itself neither raised nor lowered artistic standards, changed their attitudes. The success of this show opened the gates to many similar productions. Josef Pasternack ably led the Atwater-Kent Orchestra.

The Bell Telephone Hour (NBC, 1940–1958). A latecomer among serious music productions, the show featured Donald Voorhees conducting the Telephone Orchestra. It mixed light pops, semiclassical, and the better-known classics, and followed the format of maximum music and minimal talk, one established by the *Telephone Hour*'s many predecessors.

The Boston Symphony Orchestra (NBC, 1932–1936). Led by Serge Koussevitzky, the esteemed Boston ensemble also appeared sporadically at other times throughout the decade. The orchestra and Koussevitzky share the distinction of being the first to perform a concert live for radio broadcast, an event that took place on NBC in 1926. An estimated 1 million listeners tuned in, thus catching the attention of radio executives everywhere and paving the way for the many classical music shows that would follow.

The Carborundum Hour (CBS, 1929–1938). Instead of a permanent conductor, guest artists filled in most of the time slots of this long-running series. The producers, however, placed an emphasis on obtaining the services of prominent classical musicians.

The Cities Service Concerts (NBC, 1927–1956). The Cities Service Orchestra had only two conductors during the decade: Rosario Bourdon (1927–1938) and Frank Black (1938–1944). Under their tenures, the show took on a format resembling a musical mix. Soprano Jessica Dragonette headlined the show; her voice, not strong enough for the concert stage, proved ideal for the radio microphone. Already a star of the airwaves when she joined *The Cities Service Concerts* in 1930, she had made her name with *The Philco Hour* (NBC, 1927–1929), a show that served up light operettas. She remained with her new venue until 1937, giving *The Cities Service Concerts* consistently high ratings, and offered listeners who might not tune into just a symphony orchestra some variety. Dragonette herself emerged as an early celebrity whose career the technology of radio made possible.

The Cleveland Symphony Orchestra (NBC, 1932–1934; CBS, 1935–1936; NBC, 1936–1938). From 1933 to 1943, Artur Rodzinski held the baton in Cleveland. During his stay, the orchestra drew an impressive network radio audience.

The Columbia Symphony Orchestra (CBS, 1929–1930). The house orchestra for the fledgling Columbia broadcast network, conductor Howard Barlow formed and led the group. After 1930, the Columbia orchestra played only occasionally until the creation of *Everybody's Music* in 1936 (see below).

The Curtis Institute Musicale (CBS, 1933–1941). The Curtis Institute, based in Philadelphia, boasted a ninety-piece orchestra under the direction of Fritz Reiner for this classical offering. Since most of the broadcasts took place in the late afternoon, it might be presumed that the network saw the show as an educational venture that would be heard by a school-age audience. Contemporary statistics indicated, however, that most children and adolescents preferred the afternoon adventure serials like *Dick Tracy* (1934–1939, 1943–1948), *Jack Armstrong, the All-American Boy* (1933–1951), *Little Orphan Annie* (1930–1942), and many others then proliferating across the radio dial.

The Eastman School of Music Symphony (NBC, 1932–1942). Howard Hanson (see below), a respected American composer and conductor, also served as the director of the Eastman School based at the University of Rochester in New York State. Like the broadcasts emanating from the Curtis Institute, the Eastman program came on in the late afternoon, possibly establishing some competition between the two schools and the rival networks. For his part, Hanson saw to it that most of the works performed on the broadcast came from American composers.

Everybody's Music (CBS, 1936–1938). An outgrowth of the older *Columbia Symphony Orchestra* broadcasts mentioned above, the show consisted of maestro Howard Barlow again conducting the Columbia house orchestra. Although the title, *Everybody's Music*, might suggest a dilution of content into semiclassics and even pop materials, that did not happen. Barlow stuck to the classical repertoire, and the Sunday afternoon show remained rigorously traditional, although he did occasionally include contemporary composers, such as Aaron Copland.

The Firestone Hour (NBC, 1928–1954; ABC, 1954–1957). One of the longest-running shows on radio, *The Firestone Hour* (it later became *The Voice of Firestone*, the name most people recall) reflected the elitist cultural attitudes of the Firestone family and even included several members as occasional speakers on the show. Among the many soloists who appeared regularly in the 1930s were Vaughn De Leath, a singer credited with helping to introduce the crooning style to radio, Lawrence Tibbett and Richard Crooks, two popular male singers, plus a number of opera stars. William Daly or Alfred Wallenstein usually conducted the Firestone Symphony Orchestra. The thirties mark the high point of popularity for the show, with an audience in the millions listening to the Firestone offering. In 1949, NBC simulcast the show for television, one of the first programs to employ this technology. *The Voice of Firestone* left radio in 1957, but continued on TV until 1963.

The Ford Sunday Evening Hour (CBS, 1934–1942). A concert-oriented show that featured different conductors each week, it allowed the Ford Motor Company to present its products in a dignified, cultural setting. Since the personnel constantly changed, the show tended to showcase a mix of musical styles and soloists. Just as the Firestone family played a role in *The Firestone Hour*, Henry Ford himself took an interest in the production, to the point of hiring most of the players from the Detroit Symphony Orchestra as regulars on the *The Ford Sunday Evening Hour*.

General Motors Concerts (NBC, 1929–1937). Even an industrial giant like General Motors felt the compulsion to be associated with high culture. Stars like Lauritz Melchior, Yehudi Menuhin, and Kirsten Flagstad graced the stage, treating audiences to the best in music; apparently, high expenses brought about the show's demise in the recession of 1937–1938.

The Metropolitan Opera (NBC, 1931–1958; CBS, 1958–1960; consortium, 1960–present). Preceded by the Chicago Civic Opera (Westinghouse, 1921–1926; NBC, 1926–1932). Far and away the longest-running show on radio, the Metropolitan Opera broadcasts have covered the history of American broadcasting. They came to the air waves after NBC engineered a $100,000 contract for exclusive radio rights to the famed New York opera company. In a series of firsts, the Saturday afternoon fixture long enjoyed but one sponsor, Texaco; and, from 1931 until his death in 1975, it had but one host, Milton Cross. Texaco no longer underwrites the show, but it continues on the air through foundation support.

Virtually everyone who was or is anyone in the world of opera has at one time or another appeared on *The Metropolitan Opera*. Given the show's longevity, probably only a few operas of any merit remain to be performed on this venerable showcase for the genre. The live broadcasts parallel the Met's regular season, and so *The Metropolitan Opera* can be heard from November to April, but fans eagerly await those brief five months.

In a nation that critics claim dislikes opera, the long-running success of the Metropolitan broadcasts would suggest that at least a small cadre of devoted listeners exists for this musical form. Certainly, millions have been exposed to Verdi, Puccini, Wagner, and innumerable other composers, and have heard most of the great operatic voices of the twentieth century. Whether the current consortium of stations and foundations will see fit to carry it seventy years into the twenty-first century is anyone's guess, but at present it seems in no danger of being canceled.

The Minneapolis Symphony Orchestra (NBC, 1933–1936). Another program of symphonic music in an increasingly crowded network schedule, Eugene Ormandy served as the symphony's conductor in the years before he took over the job with the Philadelphia Orchestra.

The NBC Symphony Orchestra (NBC, 1937–1954). This orchestra, created by NBC in order to secure the services of famed conductor Arturo Toscanini (1867–1957), illustrates the importance networks placed on having prestigious personalities and shows on their schedules. Toscanini, already renowned for his work with the New York Philharmonic and archrival CBS earlier in the decade, had retired when NBC made him an offer he could not refuse: his own show, featuring a top-notch orchestra. The fiery conductor could choose the musicians, and cost was not to be an object. Further, Toscanini did not have to lead the orchestra on a weekly basis; NBC agreed to ten performances each season, with guest conductors filling in for the remaining openings. This meant that *The NBC Symphony Orchestra* had, in addition to Toscanini, leaders like Dimitri Mitropoulos, Fritz Reiner, Artur Rodzinski, Leopold Stokowski, and George Szell mounting the podium (see *New York Philharmonic Orchestra*, below).

Arturo Toscanini (1867–1957) conducting the National Broadcasting Company Symphony Orchestra in 1938. The famed conductor, who two years earlier had apparently retired at the height of his career, was lured back to the podium by NBC with the promise of his own orchestra. Employing top-flight musicians, the network created the NBC Symphony, and its Saturday and Sunday evening broadcasts, with Toscanini wielding the baton, are considered among the most popular performances of classical music in radio history. [Library of Congress, Prints & Photographs Division]

Since NBC employed the musicians who played with the symphony, network administrators expected them to extend their talents to other broadcast assignments. They played the background music in dramas and variety shows, and demonstrated techniques on NBC's popular *Music Appreciation Hour* (see below). They may have been hired for the orchestra, but the network kept them busy with a variety of tasks.

Over the years, the show transcended mere symphonic performances; it became one of NBC's top-rated productions and ran on either Saturday or Sunday evenings, a choice time. Broadcast live from New York City, the network used its largest studio, giving the orchestra an audience of over 1,000 people. Because federal law prohibited selling tickets for public broadcasts, NBC gave away seats to the Toscanini performances. Invariably, lines formed and patrons filled the studio. No other radio show featuring classical music ever engendered such a level of public interest. In 1938, a *Fortune* magazine poll indicated that almost 40 percent of the population had heard of Toscanini, through either his CBS or NBC appearances. Probably no other individual or orchestra in the realm of classical music had that kind of name recognition. On the other hand, 85 percent of all record purchases at the time of the poll went for swing discs, so knowing about someone may not be enough.[3]

The New York Philharmonic Orchestra (CBS, 1927–1963). In 1930, CBS gained the rights to broadcast performances by the New York Philharmonic, one of the leading American orchestras. This step also meant they had, as maestro, Arturo Toscanini, arguably the best-known symphonic conductor in the world, who had led the aggregation since 1928. The relationship continued until 1936, when Toscanini retired. That same year, John Barbirolli assumed leadership of the orchestra, but the withdrawal of the colorful and temperamental Toscanini meant a loss both to the music world in general and to radio, CBS in particular. Although the network continued the New York Philharmonic broadcasts until 1963, the show never again had quite the stature it had enjoyed during the Toscanini years.

The Palmolive Hour (NBC, 1927–1931). An early trailblazer among the rash of shows that would feature classical programming during the 1930s, *The Palmolive Hour* consisted more of musical variety than straight "serious" music. Gus Haenschsen led a multitalented orchestra that had to play everything from jazz to operatic passages. NBC saw value—and prestige—in such a venture, and the show's success led to many efforts by stations and networks to bring high culture to radio.

The Philadelphia Symphony Orchestra (CBS, 1931–1937; NBC, 1937–1938; CBS, 1939–1940). Under the colorful leadership of Leopold Stokowski until 1935, and then the baton of Eugene Ormandy, the Philadelphia Symphony had the well-deserved reputation of being one of America's finest orchestras. In the competition to acquire broadcasting rights to as many aggregations as possible, it seemed to matter little to network executives at both NBC and CBS that they many times competed against themselves.

The Radio City Music Hall of the Air (NBC, 1932–1942). Broadcast directly from NBC's New York headquarters, this entry in the classical sweepstakes featured Erno Rapee as conductor. Although the orchestra existed for radio, it nonetheless provided yet another choice for listeners, and strengthened the network's lead over CBS for the most classical programming.

The Rochester Civic Orchestra (NBC, 1929–1942). A long-running series by an orchestra not as well known as some broadcasting over NBC at the time, the show developed a loyal audience. Guy Fraser Harrison led the Rochester group for more than a decade.

The Rochester Philharmonic Orchestra (NBC, 1929–1930; 1935–1937; 1939–1942). A mix of orchestral and operatic works, this series further emphasized NBC's commitment to classical broadcasting. After 1935, the colorful Jose Iturbi served as leader of the orchestra.

Waltz Time (NBC, 1933–1948). A show identical in many ways to *The American Album of Familiar Music* (NBC, 1931–1950), this nostalgic offering featured the old songs and melodies beloved by many. Frank Munn, "the Golden Voice of Radio" and a typical tenor of the time, sang many of the sentimental numbers to good effect. Not strictly classical, but not really pop-oriented either, *Waltz Time* effectively blended elements of both high and popular culture.

As the above listing of classically oriented radio shows demonstrates, American commercial radio devoted considerably more time to such performances than might be expected. Listenership—how many people actually tuned in—becomes another question altogether. From the information available, more listeners than might be expected had their dials turned to stations carrying classical music, but accurate statistics are hard to come by. In the eyes of stations and their sponsors, however, enough people listened to justify the expense. For both groups, the question of vanity and prestige also enters the equation. They clearly liked the veneer of quality, of class, that having a Toscanini or a Koussevitzky conduct a nationally known symphony bestows. Plus they saw themselves doing their civic duty of providing quality broadcasting, a gesture they hoped would cause the FCC to smile benignly on them. Whether a perceived need to provide the very best in programming or a self-serving gambit, the fact remains that the 1930s were rich times indeed for classical music on radio.

In addition to the many shows listed above—and the listing must by no means be thought exhaustive or complete—several other radio productions also approached serious music, albeit by different means, and one in particular deserves mention.

The Music Appreciation Hour

In 1928, NBC—far and away the leader in hours of network time devoted to classical music during the 1930s—premiered *The Music Appreciation Hour*.

This unique show would run until 1942 and make its host, Walter Damrosch, a household name. At first, it came on the air at 11:00 A.M. every Friday, an ideal time for classroom use. *The Music Appreciation Hour* changed to 2:00 P.M. Fridays in 1937, but continued to be broadcast during the normal school day.

Damrosch (1862–1950) was born into a musical family; his father had been a noted conductor. Following in his father's footsteps, Damrosch took the reins of the New York Symphony and toured with it extensively. He also composed operas, and delved into American literature for inspiration. In 1896 he wrote an opera based on Nathaniel Hawthorne's *The Scarlet Letter*; in 1937 he used Edward Everett Hale's *The Man without a Country* as another source. Neither composition attracted much attention, but they certified his broad interest in music.

Despite his lack of acclaim as a composer, Damrosch continued working in the musical field. He soon became an apostle of radio as a teaching tool. Starting with classrooms in New York City, his presentations were soon heard across the country. If a rural school lacked a receiver, students and teachers would gather around an automobile equipped with a radio and listen there. Given his celebrity, Damrosch even landed a small role in a Bing Crosby movie entitled *The Star Maker* (1939). He found wartime cutbacks in broadcast time discouraging, and he retired in 1942. Throughout the 1930s, however, he spoke to students about good music, illustrating his lectures with recorded and live examples. His personality and well-modulated voice seemed ideally suited to radio, and he reached audiences measured in the millions.[4]

NOTED CONDUCTORS OF THE 1930s

A number of orchestral conductors rose to some celebrity during the 1930s. More often than not, radio served as the vehicle that carried them to success. The following list is arranged alphabetically.[5]

Arthur Fiedler (1894–1979)

After a cosmopolitan boyhood spent in Boston, Fiedler went to Austria, but left Europe in 1914 with the outbreak of World War I. He became associated with the Boston Symphony Orchestra in 1915, and formed the Boston Sinfonietta in 1924 with twenty-five fellow musicians. This chamber group toured in New England, bringing live performances to rural areas; the activity propelled Fiedler toward one of his lifelong goals: to enlarge the audience for classical music in any way possible.

By 1929, Fiedler was conducting outdoor public concerts in Boston. His success with these led to his being appointed, in 1930, the conductor of a revitalized Boston Pops Orchestra, a position he would retain until his death in 1979. This aggregation had been founded in 1885, but languished during the 1920s. When Fielder took over, he expanded the repertoire of the orchestra, and began to include medleys of popular classical themes, show tunes, and even occasional popular songs. Although this nontraditional approach did not make everyone happy, Fiedler persevered, successfully bridging the gaps between musical genres. The income generated by these activities helped underwrite the budget for the more elite and conservative Boston Symphony Orchestra. Fiedler also branched out into radio and recording, further enlarging his audience. Despite the economic constraints of the Depression, he attracted a large, enthusiastic following for classical and semi-classical music.

Andre Kostelanetz (1901–1980)

A number of personalities made names for themselves via the semiclassical route, among them conductor Andre Kostelanetz. A kind of musical drifter in the constantly fluctuating schedules maintained by network radio during the 1930s, he fronted many orchestras and appeared on many shows. Under contract to CBS throughout the decade, he presented both classical and what has been called "light classical," or "semiclassical," music. Such pieces tend to be briefer, less complex compositions with strong melody components couched in lush, string-filled arrangements that appeal to a broader audience than more "serious" music. This approach turned out to be Kostelanetz's preferred area of music. In time, he led a sixty-five-piece orchestra for CBS, complementing the instrumentation with renowned vocal soloists. Despite the lack of a regular show under his own name, he developed something of a following and remained busy, doing one appearance after another and frequently recording.

A publicity still of Leopold Stokowski (1882–1977), a colorful conductor who worked diligently to expand the audience for classical music. Leader of the Philadelphia Symphony Orchestra from 1912 until 1936, Stokowski could be found working in movies, doing guest appearances, and anything else that might draw listeners. His striking looks and regular media exposure made him something of a celebrity throughout the decade. [Library of Congress, Prints & Photographs Division]

Leopold Stokowski (1882–1977)

Born in England to parents of Irish and Polish extraction, Stokowski proved to be a child prodigy. Accepted into the Royal College of Music at age thirteen, he moved to the United States in 1905 to take over the musical responsibilities at New York's St. Bartholomew's Church. He remained there until 1908, and then moved on to the position of conductor for the Cincinnati Symphony Orchestra in 1909. He continued to advance, and became leader of the mighty Philadelphia Orchestra in 1912, a position he would retain until 1936.

With Philadelphia as a secure home base, Stokowski commenced his life-long efforts to attract people to classical music. He tinkered with scores to increase their crowd appeal, and mastered much of the existing knowledge about lighting, design, acoustics, and electronics, always striving to create better sound for the audience.

His moves at inclusiveness raised many hackles, and Stokowski came to represent the eccentric artistic personality. A shock of white hair and a commanding presence added to the imagery. He championed young composers and avant-garde works, much to the consternation of many critics and symphony donors.

Stokowski closed out the decade by working with Walt Disney on the film *Fantasia* (1940). He also appeared in several films, notably *The Big Broadcast of 1937* and *One Hundred Men and a Girl* (1937). As founder of the All-American Youth Orchestra (AAYO), a group of young musicians who shared many of Stokowski's views, he received backing from Columbia Records, who promised to record the youthful aggregation. The advent of World War II blocked the AAYO, but its creation further enhanced Stokowski's reputation.

Arturo Toscanini (1867–1957)

(See the above entries on the NBC Symphony Orchestra and the New York Philharmonic for information on Toscanini.)

NOTED COMPOSERS OF THE 1930s

By and large, most classical music had a limited following during the Depression, especially that attempted by contemporary American composers. In the latter half of the decade, the big dance bands and the nation's fascination with swing proved irresistible in terms of public music preferences. With only a couple of exceptions, the mass audience rejected modernist compositions, finding them too complex, too technically advanced, and generally non-melodic. Nevertheless, a handful of American composers soldiered on, and a few of them even received some public recognition for their efforts. The list below is arranged alphabetically.[6]

Aaron Copland (1900–1990)

Possibly the best-known of the decade's composers, Copland owed much of his success to exposure on radio, recordings, and on film. Like his contemporary, Ferde Grofé (see below), he experimented with jazz in the 1920s, reaching out for a more accessible form of classical music, and he finally began to achieve the popularity he desired during the 1930s. His *El Salon Mexico* (1936), *Music for Radio (Prairie Journal)* (1937), and *Billy the Kid* (1938), along with two film scores, *The City* (1939; shown continuously at the New York World's Fair) and *Of Mice and Men* (1939), all received favorable public hearings.

One of the first American composers to write for the movies, Copland also wrote for another new medium, radio. CBS commissioned his *Music for Radio*, and the piece had its premiere on *Everybody's Music*, a network show that showcased the Columbia Symphony Orchestra under the baton of Howard Barlow. His film scores repeat the nostalgia for American themes that *Music for Radio* displays. Later, in the early 1940s, this vernacular approach reached its zenith with his justly famous and popular ballets *Rodeo* (1942) and *Appalachian Spring* (1944).

George Gershwin (1898–1937)

Hardly a classical composer in the traditional sense, Gershwin enjoyed occasional forays into "serious music." He often returned to earlier works in new settings. For example, his justly famous *Rhapsody in Blue*, a work he had composed in 1924 as "An Experiment in Modern Music," received a number of performances during the 1930s. Although his concerts enjoyed good attendance, the numbers could not compare to the thousands who would jam a swing concert. Further, in any discussions of Gershwin and classical music, most people think of *Rhapsody in Blue* and little else. He also wrote *Concerto in F* (1925) and *An American in Paris* (1928) in the twenties, compositions seldom heard in the years following their introductions.

Undaunted, Gershwin kept on writing. In early 1932, the Boston Symphony Orchestra under Serge Koussevitzky premiered his often-overlooked *Second Rhapsody* (also called *Manhattan Rhapsody, New York Rhapsody*, and *Rhapsody in Rivets*), a composition that furthered Gershwin's investigations into the marriage of blues, jazz, and traditional composing. Following a 1932 visit to Cuba, he scored a Latin-influenced work entitled *Rhumba*. After a successful 1932 concert with the New York Philharmonic that featured an all-Gershwin program including *Rhumba*, he gave the piece a new title he felt better described it, *Cuban Overture*.

Two years later, Gershwin tinkered with one of the best-known songs from his 1930 musical *Girl Crazy*. He took the up-tempo "I Got Rhythm" and in 1934 wrote *Variations on "I Got Rhythm,"* an intriguing effort that revealed much about his compositional techniques. Aside from an occasional orchestral performance, however, the *Variations* elicited little critical acclaim or public acceptance. Most people preferred the Gershwin who composed popular standards, not the composer who wrote "serious music."

A significant exploration of mixed musical genres came with Gershwin's *Porgy and Bess* (1935; libretto by Ira Gershwin, with DuBose Heyward). Billed as a "folk opera," *Porgy and Bess* includes many short, popular songs that have stood on their own for decades as standards. Such well-known melodies as "Summertime," "I Got Plenty o' Nuttin'," and "It Ain't Necessarily So" attracted appreciative audiences outside the confines of the extended work. With the exception of *Rhapsody in Blue*, *Porgy and Bess* stands as George Gershwin's most successful effort to go beyond the popular idiom. Since it contains so many melodies considered "nonclassical," however, and because of the unresolved debate about whether it is truly an opera or just another Broadway musical dressed in operatic conventions, *Porgy and Bess* remains difficult to place in the Gershwin canon (for more on the popular side of George Gershwin, see Chapter 3).[7]

Ferde (Ferdinand) Grofé (1892–1972)

Like Aaron Copland, Ferde Grofé proved an exception during the 1930s. Something of a musical genius, 1907 found him performing professionally as a pianist and violinist at social gatherings. From these beginnings, Grofé moved to vaudeville, and then to playing on film sets or at clubs. Bandleader Paul Whiteman heard Grofé in 1920, and persuaded him to join his organization as an arranger. This exposure to a large orchestra that played tight, precise arrangements led him toward the concept of symphonic jazz, the marriage of two seemingly opposed musical forms. In 1924, Grofé did the orchestral arrangement of George Gershwin's *Rhapsody in Blue* for its premiere at Aeolian Hall with the Whiteman aggregation.

Its success led Grofé to compose on his own; the popular *Grand Canyon Suite* (1931), a musical exposition on a natural wonder of America, was one of his early compositions. A section of the suite, entitled "On the Trail," became familiar to millions. Philip Morris cigarettes took this piece and made it a corporate signature on radio; the clop-clop of mules' hooves as they descend the canyon immediately identified the orchestration as Grofé's and—more importantly—the tobacco company's theme.

A scene from the 1935–1936 Theatre Guild production of *Porgy and Bess*. The George Gershwin–Ira Gershwin–DuBose Heyward folk opera featured an all-black cast and blended many musical forms. Frankly experimental for its day, *Porgy and Bess* attracted a popular following, and much of its music could be heard on radio and in recordings. [Library of Congress, Prints & Photographs Division]

In 1932, Grofé broke with Whiteman and branched out on his own. He worked as a radio arranger and received several commissions. He and an all-electric ensemble played at the New York World's Fair of 1939–1940. Playing Grofé's own work, the group performed on four "Novachords," electronic organs that simulated various orchestral sounds and thus served as precursors to the modern synthesizer. In addition, a Hammond organ, an instrument introduced to the public in 1935, rounded out the quintet.

Grofé often used recognizable, accessible content in his work and it brought him his modest success. *Yankee Doodle Rhapsody* (*American Fantasie*) (1936), *6 Pictures of Hollywood* (1938), and *Tin Pan Alley: The Melodic Decades* (1938) stand out among his other works of the 1930s.

Howard Hanson (1896–1985)

After a whirlwind of activity as a youth, Hanson, at the age of twenty-three, began serving as dean of the Conservatory of Fine Arts at the College of the Pacific, making him the youngest dean in the United States. As his career ascended, he continued to compose, and his *Nordic Symphony* (1922) brought him considerable recognition. It also helped in his 1924 appointment as Director of the Eastman School of Music at the University of Rochester, a prestigious position. He would remain with Eastman for the next forty years.

By the 1930s, Hanson enjoyed a solid reputation as one of the best of the younger generation of American composers. In 1930, he completed his *Symphony No. 2, "The Romantic."* Well-named, it reflected many of Hanson's romantic tonalities that would color his subsequent work. By 1933, he had finished his *Symphony No. 3*.

While writing symphonic works, Hanson also composed a three-act opera, *Merry Mount*, its libretto loosely based on an 1835 Nathaniel Hawthorne short story, "The Maypole of Merry Mount." It premiered at New York's Metropolitan Opera in 1934 and received fifty curtain calls, a record for the august venue. *Merry Mount* has remained Hanson's best-known work, although he continued to compose for many years thereafter.

Roy Harris (1898–1979)

In retrospect, Roy Harris proved important in establishing modern American symphonic music as equal to European efforts in the same realm. Esteemed by peers as both a teacher and composer, the Boston Symphony's Serge Koussevitzky championed him during the 1930s and introduced his *Third Symphony in One Movement* in 1939. Like Copland and Grofé, Harris tried using American folk music, dance rhythms, and even a bit of jazz in his writing. Because of its complexities, his music has not been much performed over the years, further distancing him from any potential audience. Two of his compositions, *Sad Song* (1938) and *Soliloquy and Dance* (1938), did attract some attention, but he never achieved anything approaching public popularity.

Walter Piston (1894–1976)

Even more daunting than Harris was Walter Piston, a "composer's composer." Also a teacher and textbook author, Piston brought a precision and clarity to his work that put him firmly in the modernist camp.

He gained some national recognition through Serge Koussevitzky, the leader of the Boston Symphony, but he remained unknown outside orchestral circles. His *The Incredible Flutist* (1938), a ballet suite introduced by the Boston Pops, probably stands as his most successful work from the 1930s.

Richard Rodgers (1902–1979)

Famous for his collaborations with Lorenz Hart and Oscar Hammerstein II, Richard Rodgers explored the extended, not-quite-classical format with a ballet, *Slaughter on Tenth Avenue*. Written for the play *On Your Toes* (1936), the number has become much beloved by symphony and pops orchestras. It has entered the standard repertoire of many such organizations, and is a perennial crowd-pleaser (for more on the popular compositions of Richard Rodgers, see Chapter 3).

Roger Sessions (1896–1985)

Another name known primarily by an elite group of classical music lovers, Sessions escaped notice by the general public. Born a prodigy, he had composed his first opera at age fourteen (it was never published). After graduating from Harvard in 1915, Sessions chose the academic life. He taught on and off at Princeton from 1935 to 1965.

The composer worked in a difficult modernist idiom, and his most significant works did not appear until after the 1940s. Perhaps his violin concertos of 1930–1935 can be counted among his more accessible efforts of the Depression era. But even then, there existed few derivative qualities in his work, and most of his compositions have a dense, complex texture that both orchestras and the public found difficult and unappealing. Although he was much admired by his peers, few of his works, then or now, ever receive public performance.

William Grant Still (1895–1978)

Still, a black American, occupies a unique place among composers of the 1930s. Serious musical composition during the 1930s was almost exclusively a white domain. Those blacks who succeeded in music usually had to pursue their careers in popular realms, such as jazz, swing, blues, or spirituals. According to an unspoken assumption, the doors to classical music stayed closed to blacks. And so it fell to someone like William Grant Still to open some of those doors.

Early in his life, he worked in various Ohio dance bands, and finally found work arranging for the great blues writer W. C. Handy. Still stayed with Handy from 1916 until 1934; he also did some arranging for other bands, including the little-known Willard Robison group. Robison, who was white, expanded Still's duties to include leading his radio aggregation, the Deep River Orchestra. Later in the 1930s, Still turned to arranging for the theater and working for small record labels oriented to black consumers, such as Black Swan.

His experiences led him to associations with Sophie Tucker, Paul Whiteman, and Artie Shaw. For Shaw, Still wrote the 1940 arrangement for "Frenesi," a number that became one of the biggest sellers of the entire Swing Era.

Even as he made a living in the popular field, Still also worked on his own compositions. In 1931, his *African-American Symphony* received its premiere. A mix of classicism and blues themes, it gained him some notice. In later editions of the work, he added verses by poet Paul Lawrence Dunbar to introduce each section. *Lenox Avenue* (1937) stands as a musical portrait of Harlem. A love for opera led him to compose *Blue Steel* (1935) and *Troubled Island*

Although not as well known to the general public as are many other composers of the period, William Grant Still (1895–1978) nonetheless established a strong reputation in the field of classical music. His *African-American Symphony* premiered in 1931, and went through several revisions during the decade. In a white-dominated profession, his compositional voice proved an exception, one of the few black Americans to achieve success, albeit limited, in the field. [Library of Congress, Prints & Photographs Division]

(1938; did not get publicly performed until 1949), two operas that explore themes like voodoo and the culture of Haiti, the "troubled island" of the title. For the general public, however, Still has remained an unknown composer.

Virgil Thomson (1896–1989)

Thomson was born in Kansas City, a heritage that would be reflected in his music. A true modernist, spare and direct in his phrasing, he and Aaron Copland (see above) had the ability to evoke regional American scenes that audiences found attractive.

This emphasis on region first found expression in *Symphony on a Hymn Tune*, an extended work he wrote in 1928. At about the same time, Thomson completed *Four Saints in Three Acts*, an opera that did not receive its premiere until 1934. These two works established his reputation, and he moved onto his most widely known compositions shortly thereafter.

In 1936, the Works Progress Administration (WPA), working through the Resettlement Administration, commissioned Thomson to score a documentary film directed by Pare Lorentz. The picture turned out to be *The Plow that Broke the Plains* (1936), a powerful essay about farming, conservation, and the efforts by the WPA to see that another Dust Bowl did not occur. Thomson's evocative score added to the drama, and the agency asked him to collaborate on a second picture with Lorentz.

In 1937, *The River* had its release. Another strong piece of filmmaking, this time involving the Tennessee Valley Authority and the reclamation of damaged land, *The River* has come down to the present as possibly the best documentary of the decade. Unforgettable in its imagery, both visual and musical, it captured the efforts of the caring government to lend assistance to people in need and led directly to the formation of the United States Film Service. These pictures also marked the first time the government actively promoted its programs via the film medium.

THE FEDERAL MUSIC PROJECT

Throughout the 1930s, and especially during the first half of the decade, musicians found it difficult to land steady employment. Even in the heyday of the Swing Era, with bands seemingly playing everywhere, many sidemen

felt the brunt of recession and straitened conditions. Added to the glum economic picture were the continuing inroads being made by radio, records,
jukeboxes, and sound movies. Opportunities for live performance and a
steady paycheck improved only slightly in the late 1930s; most players received little for any recording sessions in which they participated. The picture would not appreciably brighten until the American Federation of
Musicians (AFM) staged a prolonged strike that included a recording ban
from 1942 to 1944. Outside the scope of this study, it resulted in the rewrit-
ing of some of the rules for compensation and royalties, and a fairer deal for
those performing on records.

   In the late 1920s, a decline in once-booming record sales signaled the beginning of hard times for musicians, regardless of the music they played. The
Depression only exacerbated the situation, sending record sales spiraling
downward (see Chapter 1), and lessening opportunities for live appearances.
Places like hotels, restaurants, and theaters canceled orchestra contracts. To
cut their own costs, radio stations, which in the 1920s had often kept a band
on retention for studio performance, released these groups and instead relied on recordings for their music.

   The AFM estimated that upwards of two-thirds of the nation's musicians
needed jobs by 1933. Further research suggested that among those still working, most received less-than-average pay. As opera companies, symphonies,
and other musical venues closed their doors, more and more musicians had
to rely on jobs other than musical ones to make ends meet.

   Aware of the dire straits facing Americans in all occupations, in 1933 the
federal government created some emergency aid programs designed to alle-
viate the situation. The Federal Emergency Relief Administration (FERA)
came into being that same year to provide temporary aid to the unemployed,
and its largesse included musicians. FERA did not create specifically musical projects, but it did employ musicians (among many others) in its programs. A confusing program, FERA had no centralized supervision, and its
eligibility rules varied from state to state. Phased out in 1934, the program
had assisted only a handful of musicians with its scattershot approach to aid.

   While FERA struggled, some in government envisioned a heightened role
for relief agencies. In 1935, President Roosevelt received legislation that
would permit direct aid in the area of the arts. Until this proposal began to
make the rounds, the arts usually ended up as the orphans in any discussions
about economic relief. Reflecting a belief that persists into the present day,
many legislators considered the arts unsuitable recipients of government aid.

The arts, went the thinking, should prosper or fail on their own merits and fell outside the responsibilities of government.

Despite widespread opposition to funding the arts, the proposed legislation moved ahead. In 1935, the Works Progress Administration (WPA), one of the crown jewels of President Roosevelt's New Deal, came into being. With Harry Hopkins as its chief administrator, the WPA moved rapidly to provide aid to a wide spectrum of unemployed workers, including those in the arts. Hopkins, along with his aide, Jacob Baker, saw the WPA and its programs as an unprecedented opportunity to involve government in, and give direction to, the nation's cultural life.

The WPA created the Federal Arts Project, or Federal One, in August 1935. An umbrella title, Federal One consisted of four satellite agencies that would administer economic aid in the broad area of the arts: the Federal Writer's Project (FWP), the Federal Art Project (FAP), the Federal Theater Project (FTP), and the Federal Music Project (FMP).

The charge given these four "alphabet agencies" (a term used to identify many New Deal organizations, most of which went by their initials instead of their full names) was one unique in American history. Hopkins and Baker, as spokesmen for the WPA, asked each agency to employ as many artists as possible, each in his or her respective fields. Eligibility would be based on a person's presence on existing relief rolls. In addition—and the part of the charge that proved most problematic for many critics—the agencies were to create arts programs that would meet the artistic needs of the American people. The question that immediately arose in an area as subjective as art involved deciding who would determine the "artistic needs" of "the people." Should government be a party to such decisions? These doubts wracked the program from its onset, and would eventually contribute to its demise, an ending that commenced in 1939 for the music and theater portions. The writers and art sections disappeared in the early 1940s.

In September of 1935, President Roosevelt allocated over $27 million for the enterprise, an enormous sum for any project, especially one dealing with the arts. For many critics of the New Deal, this kind of money went for "social engineering," with no guaranteed results. But Hopkins and Baker were visionaries, and they saw this project as one that could go a long way toward defining American culture. They chose Henry Alsberg to head up the writers' section, Holger Cahill the arts, Hallie Flanagan the theater, and Nikolai Sokoloff for the music section.

Sokoloff (1886–1965) had been born in Russia and studied violin as a child.

At thirteen, he entered the Yale University music school on a special scholarship awarded to gifted youngsters. Within three years he had joined the Boston Symphony; in 1907 he returned to Europe for more study. A regular traveler between Europe and the United States, Sokoloff became conductor of the Cleveland Symphony Orchestra in 1918, a position he would hold until 1933.

He retired to Connecticut in 1933 and proceeded to organize a small orchestra that gave outdoor concerts in the area. Harry Hopkins tapped him for the leadership of the Federal Music Project in the midst of this semi-retired life, and Sokoloff readily agreed.

A man of strong opinions, Sokoloff displayed no hesitation in making his ideas known. His European background and training had instilled in him a decided preference for the established classics, and he had little patience with most contemporary composers, feeling they wasted their time in experimentation. These prejudices extended into the popular realm of music; for example, he argued (unsuccessfully) that non-classically trained musicians should not be paid as much as those who attended conservatories and the like.

As director, Sokoloff created an advisory committee that would give him counsel on how best to spend the federal monies the FMP had received. Given Sokoloff's background, it should come as no surprise that most of the advisory committee's members came from the realm of "serious," or classical, music. Of all those serving on the committee, perhaps the leading proponent of more popular formats was Joseph Weber, the president of the American Federation of Musicians, a group that represented most of the people playing in dance bands, pit orchestras, or otherwise laboring in the field of popular music. At the time of his appointment, unemployment had struck two-thirds of the union's membership, so Weber understood the concerns of working musicians. But Weber's voice served as a minority one; despite his pleas, the FMP directed a considerable portion of its energies and budget to more elitist areas of music. But preferences aside, it also provided work for thousands of otherwise unemployed musicians—and all, regardless of background or training, received equal wages, except for music teachers, who had to accept a lower pay scale.

By November, after just three short months, the FMP had already located jobs for over 900 individuals; after only six months, it had put at least 15,000 un- or underemployed musicians to work, making it the largest employer in the Federal Arts Project. Historians estimate the agency underwrote a quarter of a million public concerts attended by some 150 million people, usually charging a nominal admission of twenty-five cents. As a rule, the FMP emphasized performance more than it did composing; when the project began, only eleven recognized symphony orchestras existed in the United States. At its peak, the FMP funded thirty-four new orchestras across the country. It also put together thousands of radio broadcasts that reached millions of listeners.

The agency singled out many composers and commissioned new works, especially if their music employed distinctly American themes. One of its accomplishments involved the creation of the Composers Forum Laboratory in the fall of 1935. This forum originated in New York City, but soon branches appeared in Boston, Chicago, and Los Angeles. It encouraged composers to submit their latest work to a committee made up of musicians and project leaders. Selected compositions underwent rehearsal and enjoyed public performance. Audiences for these new works would be encouraged to evaluate them, a boon for composers. Limited to larger cities, the Composers Forum nonetheless opened a small door to those who wrote music.

Many younger American composers saw their works performed for the first time through the auspices of the FMP. The organization also reached out to the fringes of American music of the day, urging the participation of women, blacks, and other underrepresented groups. At the same time, the FMP had to be careful that it did not appear to be favoring any segment of society. In retrospect, the FMP did a good job of satisfying its many sponsors and critics. Alone among the federal arts agencies, it avoided any hint of scandal during its brief life.

It also stressed instruction in music and music appreciation, funding over a million classes that allowed some 14 million students to take lessons under government auspices. The FMP sponsored broad research on several areas of music, eventually compiling the Index of American Composers, as well as recording American blues and folk music. It catalogued 5,000 works by 1,500 composers and accumulated a priceless store of blues and folk recordings; the Library of Congress eventually housed both collections. Overall, the Federal Music Project stands as one of the few times that government interested itself in the arts and supported them enthusiastically.

Ideologically, Sokoloff and the FMP had to face the questions of classical versus popular music, and modern compositions as opposed to more traditional ones. These issues carried political implications with them. Many lawmakers wanted the FMP (and the other arts projects, as well) to stress American artists to the virtual exclusion of anyone foreign. At the same time,

The Federal Music Project (FMP) sponsored numerous orchestras and concerts. The posters advertising these activities tended to have a distinctive, 1930s style about them. Most of the posters were products of the Federal Art Project (FAP), a sister organization created by the government to create jobs during the Depression. Note the admission prices on this 1937 example; even with money adjusted for subsequent inflation, the FMP encouraged attendance by everyone and not a favored few. [Library of Congress, Prints & Photographs Division]

some members of Congress and their constituents spoke suspiciously about anything "modern," that somehow contemporary works spread the seeds of discontent and radicalism. So Sokoloff and his advisors had to walk a narrow line, attempting to keep enough people happy that the complaints of others would not jeopardize the FMP's mission.

In 1938, Charles Seeger, a man who had worked earlier with John and Alan Lomax (see Chapter 5) collecting folk materials, became the deputy director of the FMP. Seeger oversaw the folk and social music division of the agency and promoted indigenous folk expression and musical education. He worked diligently to preserve ethnic music, but his efforts came late in the program's life. Budget-cutting, under the threat of imminent war, began in earnest in 1939. Officials renamed the Federal Music Project as the WPA Music Program, but a year later Congress moved to end the agency altogether.[8]

World War II effectively canceled most ongoing cultural projects underwritten by the U.S. government. Budgets had been slashed in 1939, and Congress looked increasingly askance at any government involvement in the arts.

Outstanding Musical Artists from the 1930s

BANDLEADERS

This listing barely scratches the surface, since so many different bands came and went during the decade. What follows includes only the better-known leaders of the period, and deliberately omits those who lacked widespread popular success. More inclusive listings can be found on the Internet and in numerous books devoted to the big bands of the 1930s.[1]

Armstrong, Louis ("Satchmo," "Pops") (1901–1971)

An undisputed genius of jazz, Armstrong distinguished himself during the 1920s with his virtuoso trumpet work, both as leader and sideman. His gravelly voice and ability to improvise on lyrics practically defined the art of jazz singing. The 1930s saw him fronting several innovative bands, including two years in Europe (1933–1935). He also toured and recorded as a solo performer, creating a lasting body of impressive work. A favorite with audiences everywhere, Armstrong moved easily between the role of talented musician and that of popular entertainer, although in neither did he lose his zest for superlative playing. Many of his recorded efforts in the first half of the 1930s survive as pioneering excursions into swing, predating the popular white bands of the latter half of the decade. Whether hamming it up in the movies with the likes of Bing Crosby (*Pennies from Heaven*, 1936) or taking a flawless trumpet solo in front of a big band, Armstrong evolved into one of the great artists of the twentieth century. Capable of playing in almost any style, he could rise above even the most mediocre material and infuse it with both consummate showmanship and the essence of swing.

Arnaz, Desi (1917–1986)

Cuban by birth, Arnaz moved to Miami and joined the successful Xavier Cugat band in 1937. In Florida clubs, the group received billing as "Desi Arnaz and His Xavier Cugat Orchestra." In time, he broke with Cugat and formed his own Latin band. In the late 1930s, Arnaz introduced a new dance, the Conga; it proved so popular that for the remainder of the decade he advertised his band as "Desi Arnaz and His La Conga Orchestra."

Arnheim, Gus (1917–1986)

Arnheim fronted the Cocoanut Grove Orchestra from Los Angeles during the decade. The band's popular theme was "Sweet and Lovely" (1931; music by Gus Arnheim, Harry Tobias, and Jules Lemare) and the group briefly boasted both Russ Columbo and Bing Crosby as vocalists. Over the years, the Arnheim aggregation established a reputation as a solid swing band.

Barnet, Charlie (b. Charles Daly; 1913–1991)

Progressive both socially and in their musical arrangements, Barnet's 1930s orchestras borrowed freely from leaders like Duke Ellington and Jimmie Lunceford. Barnet displayed no hesitation in hiring black musicians, one of the first white bandleaders to do so. He also featured clarinetist Artie Shaw in 1934, and the Modernaires singing group in 1936. The band enjoyed a big 1939 hit with "Cherokee" (music by Ray Noble).

Basie, Count (b. William Bassie; 1904–1984)

Pianist and arranger with the Bennie Moten Band from Kansas City, Basie assumed leadership of the orchestra in 1935, following Moten's death. An accomplished pianist, in 1935 an admiring radio announcer christened Basie "Count." The nickname stuck, and the orchestra turned out to be a commercial success. Stars like Lester Young on tenor saxophone, Buck Clayton on trumpet, Jo Jones on drums, and Jimmy Rushing and Helen Humes on vocals comprised part of the lineup during the 1930s, certainly one of the most jazz-inflected bands of the era. "One O'Clock Jump" (1937; music by Count Basie), the band's up-tempo theme, typified its hard-swinging Kansas City style.

Bernie, Ben (b. Bernard Anzelevitz; 1894–1943)

Calling his band "Ben Bernie and All the Little Lads" and himself "The Ol' Maestro," Bernie had wide popular success leading a sweet band throughout the 1920s, 1930s, and into the 1940s. Recordings, network radio, and movies featured him, and he developed a trademark expression of "Yowsah,

Bands of every description traveled the United States during the 1930s, playing mainly for dancers. A typical orchestra of the period would be that led by Ben Bernie (1894–1943), the "Ol' Maestro," as his legions of fans called him. With his trademark cigar clamped in his mouth, he led a sweet band throughout the decade, and proved a natural for radio, hosting network shows on both NBC and CBS that dispensed dance music, humor, and lots of celebrity guests. [Library of Congress, Prints & Photographs Division]

yowsah" to accompany his performance. Although his music sounded innocuous at best, dancers and audiences liked his traditional approach, and people always clamored for the band's theme, "It's a Lonesome Old Town" (1931; music by Charles Kisco, lyrics by Harry Tobias).

Calloway, Cab (1907–1994)

During the 1920s, Calloway played in various New York nightspots and appeared in the black revue, *Hot Chocolates* (1929). In 1930, he got a chance to perform in Harlem's famed Cotton Club as Cab Calloway and His Orchestra; a solid success there established his fame. Film and radio soon beckoned, making him one of the first black entertainers to cross the invisible color line maintained by network radio. "Minnie the Moocher" (1931; words and music by Cab Calloway, Barney Bigard, and Irving Mills), Calloway's novelty theme, featured him doing scat singing, and made him known as "The Hi-De-Ho Man," a name taken from the lyrics and one that stuck through much of his long career. He even published a *Hepster's Dictionary* in 1936, a kind of insider's guide to the argot of jazz and swing then growing popular among fans. A best seller, it went through several reprintings. Despite the jive talk, clowning, and many theatrics—not the least of which included outlandish clothing—the orchestra and its irrepressible leader had a reputation as a disciplined, driving group that contained many fine soloists.

Clinton, Larry (1909–1985)

Active as an arranger for, among others, the Dorsey Brothers and the Casa Loma Orchestra in the first part of the decade, Clinton organized his own band in 1937. He frequently borrowed from classical composers for his work; for example, the popular "My Reverie" (1938; music by Claude Debussy, lyrics and arrangement by Larry Clinton) came from a melody by Debussy, but with added lyrics sung by vocalist Bea Wain. The orchestra's biggest hit was 1937's "The Dipsy Doodle" (music by Larry Clinton). The title comes from the sports world, such as a pitcher's screwball or a football player's evasive run, and the tune quickly became the group's theme.

Crosby, Bob (1913–1993)

The younger brother of crooner Bing Crosby, he found an appreciative public as the affable, nonplaying leader of a group called The Bobcats. Mainly a Dixieland band, the Bobcats scored some recording successes, especially with "South Rampart Street Parade" (1938; traditional) and a curious piece, "Big Noise from Winnetka" (1938), a jazzy number written and performed by bassist Bob Haggart and drummer Ray Bauduc as a duet. Audiences liked the interplay between the two musicians and it became a regular part of the Bobcats' repertoire.

Cugat, Xavier (1900–1990)

Remembered today mainly as a colorful bandleader who helped familiarize mass audiences with Latin rhythms, during the 1930s he and his orchestra were considered an important component of popular music. Seen in many films of the era, and an effective showman and self-promoter, Cugat came to be called "The Rhumba King."

Dorsey, Jimmy (1904–1957)

During the 1920s, saxophonist Jimmy Dorsey played with many different bands. In 1934, partnered with his brother Tommy, he formed the Dorsey Brothers Orchestra. Glenn Miller, destined to lead one of the most popular swing bands of all time, served as an important arranger and trombonist for the group. Personal rivalries between the brothers brought about the dissolution of the orchestra, and Jimmy took most of the members and formed the Jimmy Dorsey Orchestra. In the late 1930s, he added vocalists Bob Eberly and Helen O'Connell, and their duets on such numbers as "Amapola" (written in 1924, revived 1940; words and music by Joseph M. Lacalle) helped gain the band a broad measure of popularity.

Dorsey, Tommy (1905–1956)

A skilled trombonist, Dorsey established a reputation in the late 1920s as a talented sideman and soloist. In 1928, he co-led the Dorsey Brothers Orchestra with his brother Jimmy (see above), an aggregation that played mainly for recordings. With the rise of swing, the two formed a dance band in 1934. After a falling-out with his sibling, he organized the Tommy Dorsey Orchestra in 1935, featuring vocalist Jack Leonard. A string of hits followed, including "Marie" (1937; written 1928, words and music by Irving Berlin) and "Song of India" (1935; from Rimsky-Korsakov; arranged by Tommy Dorsey, E. W. "Red" Bone, and Carmen Mastren). His popular theme, "I'm Getting Sentimental Over You" (1932; music by George Bassman, lyrics by Ned Washington), led to his being dubbed "That Sentimental Gentleman of Swing." In early 1940, Tommy Dorsey hired an aspiring young vocalist named Frank Sinatra away from the Harry James band. The sensitive ballad arrangements of Axel Stordahl and Sinatra's interpretative crooning helped immensely to carry the band's unique sound to an adoring public, and launched the singer's career.

Duchin, Eddie (1910–1951)

Leader of a sweet society band, pianist Duchin achieved widespread exposure thanks to radio broadcasts from New York's Central Park Casino the Waldorf-Astoria, plus numerous recordings. As a bandleader, however, his image remained that of someone who played for the wealthy and socially prominent but added little to the music of the day.

Ellington, Duke (b. Edward Kennedy Ellington; 1899–1974)

Called "the Duke" because of his suave elegance, Ellington ranks as one of America's greatest composers. Also an exceptional pianist, arranger, and bandleader, he reached a creative peak during the 1930s that would extend for many years thereafter. His orchestras featured talented sidemen like Bubber Miley, Johnny Hodges, Ben Webster, "Tricky Sam" Nanton, Cootie Williams, and Harry Carney, and included Adelaide Hall and Ivie Anderson doing the vocals. One enduring hit after another flowed from his pen during the 1930s—"Mood Indigo" (1931), "It Don't Mean a Thing (If It Ain't Got that Swing)" (1932), "Sophisticated Lady" (1933; lyrics by Mitchell Parish), "Solitude" (1934), "Azure" (1937), and many others too numerous to mention—ensuring Ellington a secure place among the all-time favorites of the decade. Although his bands swung with the best of them, Ellington's individualism and his flair for texture and tonality placed him on a unique plane; no one else duplicated his orchestra's sound, and his always-innovative compositions and arrangements—for example, "Creole Rhapsody" (1931), "Stompy Jones" (1934), "Reminiscin' in Tempo" (1935), "Ko-Ko" (1940)—put him far ahead of his contemporaries.

Fields, Shep (1910–1981)

Playing primarily in New York–area clubs and hotels from 1934 on, Fields's orchestra came to be known as Shep Fields and His Rippling Rhythm. Fields achieved his "rippling rhythm," a definite crowd-pleasing device, by standing close to a microphone and blowing air through a straw into a glass of water. Corny as it might seem, it became the trademark of the band for many years. The orchestra enjoyed a big hit in 1936 with "Plenty of Money and You" (music by Harry Warren, lyrics by Shep Fields).

Garber, Jan (1894–1977)

Inspired by the popularity of the Guy Lombardo Orchestra (see below), Garber organized a sweet band in the 1930s that emulated the sound of the Royal Canadians. A commercial success, Garber became known as "the Idol of the Air Lanes," thanks to his many radio broadcasts. He gained recognition for promoting the concept of the "one-night stand" for a band—playing only one evening at a venue and then moving on to another.

Goodman, Benny (1909–1986)

A superb clarinetist, Goodman led some of the most popular swing orchestras and groups of the 1930s. He began playing professionally in the 1920s, and worked with several groups, including the Ben Pollack orchestra. He organized his first band in 1932 to accompany crooner Russ Columbo. Goodman formed his first swing-oriented group in 1934 and immediately gained some limited recognition. The *Let's Dance* program on NBC radio (1934–1935) gave him wider exposure, leading to a national tour that culminated with a broadcast from Los Angeles' Palomar Ballroom that many credit with sparking the Swing Era. He continued touring, appeared on radio (*Camel Caravan*) and in films (*Big Broadcast of 1937, Hollywood Hotel*), and cut studio recordings for several labels. During the decade, Goodman's bands featured such contemporary stars as Gene Krupa (drums), Teddy Wilson (piano), Lionel Hampton (vibes), Harry James (trumpet), and Fletcher Henderson (arrangements). Dubbed "The King of Swing" because of his popularity and commercial success, Goodman proved an innovator, leading racially mixed groups during a time of forced segregation, and playing a phenomenally well-received swing concert at New York's Carnegie Hall in 1938. Because of his enormous popularity, he probably did more to make swing a national trend during the 1930s than any other musician.

Gray, Glen (1906–1963)

A saxophonist, Gray began his career with a Detroit dance orchestra that in the 1920s called itself the Orange Blossoms. In 1929, the Orange Blossoms became the Casa Loma Orchestra, and Gray later assumed nominal leadership of the group. By 1937, his name came first, Glen Gray and the Casa Loma Orchestra. Through dances and recordings, the band gained considerable popularity, especially with "hot," or "killer-diller," up-tempo numbers like "No Name Jive" (1940; music by Larry Wagner). Many of the band's hits came from the pen of arranger Gene Gifford. He could write a syrupy ballad, such as "Smoke Rings" (1932; music by Gene Gifford, lyrics by Ned Washington), the group's theme, and turn around and create something frenetic like "White Jazz" (1933).

Hawkins, Erskine (1914–1993)

One of a handful of black bandleaders to succeed commercially during the 1930s, Hawkins first achieved fame with his 'Bama State Collegians, a band that toured extensively in the South. By the late 1930s, the 'Bama Collegians had become the Erskine Hawkins Orchestra, and boasted a big hit with "Tuxedo Junction" (1939; music by Erskine Hawkins, William Johnson, Julian Dash, and Buddy Feyne), a number famously covered by Glenn Miller.

Heidt, Horace (1901–1986)

After a career with vaudeville bands in the 1920s, Heidt formed a group known variously as Horace Heidt and His Musical Knights and Horace Heidt and His Brigadeers. By the mid-1930s, he worked regularly on network radio, doing shows that mixed humor, music, contests for prizes, and even occasional animal acts. The best-known of these was called *Pot o' Gold*

(1939–1941). Although his band never reached the top ranks, he did employ some women musicians, an unusual practice in those days.

Herman, Woody (b. Woodrow Charles Herman; 1913–1987)

A clarinetist with the Isham Jones Orchestra in the mid-1930s, Herman took over leadership when Jones became ill in 1938. Soon the Herman aggregation called itself "The Band that Plays the Blues," and included "Blue Prelude" (1933; music by Gordon Jenkins and Joe Bishop), "Blues on Parade" (1939; music by Toby Tyler), and "Blue Flame" (1940; music by James Noble and Joe Bishop) among its themes. Although the famous "Herman Herds" would come later, during the last years of the decade, the orchestra established a solid following, and even enjoyed a big hit in 1939 with "Woodchopper's Ball" (music by Woody Herman and Joe Bishop). In addition to his considerable clarinet skills, Herman was also an accomplished vocalist, frequently singing while his band played behind him.

Hines, Earl ("Fatha") (1903–1983)

A splendid pianist, Hines also fronted an outstanding band during the 1930s. He played from 1928 to 1938 at Chicago's Grand Terrace Ballroom, and had the good fortune of being broadcast nightly over network radio from that location. One of his best-known compositions was "Rosetta" (1933; music by Earl Hines and Henri Woode), and he cashed in on the boogie-woogie craze with "Boogie-Woogie on the St. Louis Blues" (originally written in 1914 by W. C. Handy; arranged by Earl Hines) in 1940.

Hutton, Ina Ray (1916–1984)

"The Blonde Bombshell of Rhythm" first caught the public eye in 1934, when Ina Ray Hutton and Her Melodears began touring and playing as an all-girl orchestra. Women musicians were virtually absent from popular music in the 1930s, so Hutton's band challenged the rules. But in the crowded music field of the day, everyone had to have a gimmick (see Phil Spitalny, below). She enjoyed modest success, but finally broke up the group in 1939 and began leading a traditional all-male orchestra.

James, Harry (1916–1983)

After a stint with the Ben Pollack Orchestra, trumpeter James joined Benny Goodman's band in 1936. His instrumental pyrotechnics electrified everyone, and he emerged as an important soloist. By the end of 1938, his fame assured, James left Goodman and formed his own successful band. He is also remembered for hiring a young singer named Frank Sinatra in 1939; overnight, Sinatra captured an adoring public and a new era in big bands and vocalists had commenced.

Kaye, Sammy (1910–1987)

The leader of a sweet band, Kaye always tried to please his patrons. His orchestra motto read, "Swing and Sway with Sammy Kaye," and the emphasis focused more on swaying than it did on swinging. At dances, he promoted "So You Want to Lead a Band?" a gimmick that allowed audience members to come onstage and attempt to wield a baton. People enjoyed these moments, and it quickly became a regular part of his performances. Although most critics dismissed him and his band, countless fans did not; Kaye's business acumen paid off and he retired a wealthy man.

Kemp, Hal (1904–1940)

Leader of another sweet orchestra, Kemp's bands tended to play hotels and large supper clubs. The talented John Scott Trotter turned out many of the group's arrangements, and he perfected the soft, bouncy sound that characterized Kemp's aggregation. Skinnay Ennis and Nan Wynn sang the vocals, and they complemented the band by crooning the numbers rather than belting them. Kemp composed the popular "When the Summer Is Gone" (1937), and the song became the band's theme. The group enjoyed its biggest hit with "Got a Date with an Angel" (1931; music by Jack Waller and Joseph Turnbridge, lyrics by Clifford Grey and Sonnie Miller).

King, Wayne (1901–1985)

Nicknamed "the Waltz King," King made a name for himself and his band starting in 1927. At that time, he began an eight-year association with Chicago's Aragon Ballroom, a successful run that led to recordings and several network radio shows. A typical set might include such sweet numbers as "Good Night, Sweetheart" (1931; words and music by Ray Noble, James Campbell, and Reg Connelly) or "I Don't Know Why (I Just Do)" (1931; music by Fred E. Ahlert, lyrics by Roy Turk). Although he played more than just waltzes, his traditional approach to music and dancing assured him a large popular following.

Kirby, John (1908–1952)

A bassist, and leader of a sextet that achieved considerable popularity, the group billed itself as "the Biggest Little Band in the World." Comprised of top musicians, including Charlie Shavers on trumpet and Buster Bailey on clarinet, the members could read and play virtually anything. After 1937, Kirby featured his wife, Maxine Sullivan, as the vocalist, and the band produced polite but swinging renditions of contemporary pop songs.

Kirk, Andy (1898–1992)

Kirk led the Kansas City-based Clouds of Joy Orchestra, and he employed pianist Mary Lou Williams as his primary arranger. This collaboration brought about such hits as "Froggy Bottom" (1930; music by Mary Lou Williams), "Roll'em" (1933; music by Mary Lou Williams), and "The Lady Who Swings the Band" (1936; music by Saul Chaplin, lyrics by Sammy Cahn). The group had been formed in 1929; it survived until 1948, an unusually long life for such an aggregation. Kirk's theme, "Until the Real Thing Comes Along" (1936; music by Saul Chaplin and Alberta Nichols, lyrics by Sammy Cahn, Mann Holiner, and L. E. Freeman), became a popular hit.

Kyser, Kay (1906–1985)

A band leader since 1926, Kyser showed a certain flair for attracting audiences. He used a vocalist to sing the title of upcoming numbers and employed a perky vocal chorus; the sidemen would occasionally do hokey instrumental routines, and it all coalesced into a successful band. He is best remembered for his network radio broadcasts of *Kay Kyser's Kollege of Musical Knowledge*, a musical quiz show. Kyser, the "Old Professor," would dress in academic regalia, including a mortarboard, and the players dressed as undergraduates complete with beanies. Taking someone from the audience, Kyser would ask easy questions about popular music. It proved a perfect vehicle for radio, and ran from 1937 until 1949. With listeners everywhere, Kyser soon found himself a household name, and even appeared in several Hollywood movies, including *That's Right, You're Wrong!* (1939) and *Scatterbrain* (1940). Comic vocalist Ish Kabibble (b. Merwyn A. Bogue) only added to the lighthearted tone of things, as their biggest hit, "Three Little Fishes" (1939; words and music by Saxie Dowell), demonstrated. Despite all the humor, the Kyser band could handle most musical numbers ably and enjoyed continuing success well into the 1940s.

Lewis, Ted (1892–1971)

Already an internationally known entertainer by the time the 1930s rolled around, Ted Lewis harked more to vaudeville than to the band business. He nonetheless fronted a band throughout the decade, an approach that allowed him to endlessly perform his trademark numbers of "When My Baby Smiles at Me" (1919; music by Ted Munro, lyrics by Ted Lewis and Andrew B. Sterling) and "Me and My Shadow" (1927; music by Dave Dreyer and Al Jolson, lyrics by Billy Rose) and to ask of his audience, "Is everybody happy?"

Lombardo, Guy (1902–1977)

For many people raised during the twentieth century, New Year's Eve would not be complete without hearing Guy Lombardo and His Royal Canadians playing the traditional "Auld Lang Syne," either in a posh night club or on the radio. Both the melody and the holiday were associated with this band, a band that promised "The Sweetest Music This Side of Heaven." It all began in the 1920s when the Lombardo brothers—Lebert, Carmen, Victor, and Guy—moved from Canada to the United States. With Guy as the leader, the band achieved remarkable success, performing stylized dance tunes like "You're Driving Me Crazy" (1930; words and music by Walter Donaldson), "Annie Doesn't Live Here Anymore" (1933; music by Harold Spina, lyrics by Johnny Burke and Joe Young), and "Boo Hoo" (1937; words and music by Carmen Lombardo, John Jacob Loeb, and Ed Heyman). Almost all of the orchestra's numbers concluded with a cymbal shot, a trademark. They landed a contract to play at and broadcast from the Roosevelt Grill in New York's Hotel Roosevelt, a job that endured for the next 33 years and made their orchestra a household name.

Lopez, Vincent (1895–1975)

Leader of yet another sweet orchestra, pianist Lopez played standards and stuck with the melody. As such, he gained considerable popularity in the New York area, eventually spending a good part of the 1930s broadcasting from the Hotel Taft. An astute businessman, Lopez even had several "Vincent Lopez Orchestras" working during the 1930s; he would make contracts for dances and such, and then send a band led by someone other than himself to fulfill the agreements. Of course, the band would play the regular Lopez arrangements and employ the same voicings, a practice not unheard of in large metropolitan areas with busy social calendars.

Lunceford, Jimmie (1902–1947)

A hard-swinging outfit from Memphis, the Jimmie Lunceford band made the big time in 1933 when it played Harlem's Cotton Club. With infectious arrangements by Sy Oliver, the group developed a distinctive ensemble sound appreciated by both listeners and dancers. "Tain't What'cha Do, It's the Way That'cha Do It" (1939; music by Sy Oliver, lyrics by Trummy Young) proved to be a hit for the orchestra.

Martin, Freddy (1906–1983)

The leader of a popular sweet band during the 1930s and after, Martin's style tended to be melodic and uncomplicated. He featured many vocals, often by Helen Ward or Buddy Clark, two fine big-band singers from that era. Although most of what he played in the thirties consisted of innocuous dance music, by the onset of the 1940s Martin moved in the direction of popularizing classical music; he is best remembered for a rendition of Tchaikovsky's Piano Concerto that came out on record as "Tonight We Love" (1941; music adapted by Freddy Martin and Ray Austin, lyrics added by Bobby Worth). It soon became the band's theme.

McCoy, Clyde (1903–1990)

Active by the late 1920s as a bandleader, trumpeter McCoy achieved remarkable success through the clever use of a mute that produced a distinctive "wah-wah" sound. In 1931, he parlayed this novelty into a multimillion-selling hit, "Sugar Blues" (1923; music by Clarence Williams, lyrics by Lucy Fletcher), a tune with which he would be forever associated. His bands remained popular throughout the decade.

McKinney's Cotton Pickers Orchestra

A pioneer big band, the group gained its name from drummer William McKinney (1895–1969), who originally formed it in 1922. At first a traditional band, it began to experiment with swing arrangements in 1927, when trumpeter/arranger Don Redman joined the aggregation. The orchestra reached its greatest popularity in the late 1920s and early 1930s and musical historians consider it a significant forerunner of the big swing bands that dominated the later thirties.

Miller, Glenn (1904–1944)

Miller, a so-so trombonist, played in and arranged for a variety of orchestras such as Ben Pollock, the Dorsey Brothers, Red Nichols, and Ray Noble during the 1930s; he finally formed his own group in 1937. This first effort produced a mediocre band that lacked a distinctive sound and crowd appeal. The following year, he organized a new aggregation that showed a hint of things to come. Miller employed excellent sidemen (and rarely soloed himself), and had the good fortune to land Ray Eberle, Marion Hutton, and the Modernaires as his vocalists. His personable manner and engaging theme, "Moonlight Serenade" (1939; music by Glenn Miller, lyrics by Mitchell Parish), charmed dancers, and he was soon playing casinos, hotels, ballrooms, and packing in the audiences. In 1940, the band recorded its biggest hit, "In the Mood" (1939; music by Joe Garland, lyrics by Andy Razaf) and saw *The Chesterfield Show* debut on network radio. These two events furthered his fame, and the Glenn Miller Orchestra stood poised, at the end of the decade, to become one of the most popular dance bands ever.

Millinder, Lucky (b. Lucius Venable Millinder; 1900–1966)

Although his bands never reached the top, they served as important training grounds for several generations of musicians. He led his first group from 1931 to 1934, at which time he began fronting the Mills Blue Rhythm Band. That aggregation broke up in 1938 and Millinder again assembled groups under his own name. Popular in Harlem, Millinder's bands from 1940 onward paved the way for many of the changes then taking place in jazz.

Moten, Bennie (1894–1935)

A bandleader and entrepreneur from Kansas City, Moten in the 1920s put together a superb orchestra that highlighted some of the best black musicians in the country. In 1932 and with a secure reputation, he named the group Bennie Moten's Kansas City Orchestra. A failed tonsillectomy in 1935 left the band briefly leaderless, but pianist Count Basie took over. With vocalist Jimmy Rushing belting the blues, and an endless array of instrumental soloists providing swinging backgrounds, the Moten band quickly became the Count Basie Orchestra and its success continued unabated through the rest of the decade.

Nelson, Ozzie (b. Oswald George Nelson; 1906–1975)

Better remembered today as the good-natured father who led the Nelson family and starred in *The Adventures of Ozzie and Harriet*, a long-running radio (1944–1954) and later television comedy (1952–1966), Ozzie Nelson also led a band during the 1930s. In fact, his wife Harriet served as the vocalist for a while. Nelson's band never achieved the popularity of Benny Goodman's or Glenn Miller's, but it represented just how many orchestras dotted the musical landscape during the Swing Era.

Nichols, Red (b. Ernest Loring Nichols; 1905–1965)

Nichols, a cornetist, played with many bands during the 1920s and 1930s. His own groups were dubbed "Red Nichols and His Five Pennies," although most of them had more than five sidemen. Nichols tended to favor traditional jazz, or Dixieland, over the polished swing of the 1930s. Nonetheless, some of the best musicians of the era sat in with the cornetist on his many recordings.

Norvo, Red (b. Kenneth Norville; 1908–1999)

A talented musician who played an unusual instrument—the xylophone—Norvo, between 1936 and 1939, had one of the better small bands in the country. Sometimes introduced as "Mr. and Mrs. Swing," the title referred to Norvo and his wife, vocalist Mildred Bailey. In dozens of recordings, the couple produced a unique body of work, a mix of jazz, swing, and popular elements that attracted a small but enthusiastic audience.

Pollack, Ben (1903–1971)

In a career that dated back to the early 1920s, Pollack led a fine jazz-based orchestra in the early 1930s that nurtured many of the players who would come to dominate the Swing Era. Among the more famous alumni from his band were Benny Goodman and Glenn Miller. Pollack himself played drums, and he drove his groups with authority, although he never achieved the commercial success that many of his former sidemen later enjoyed.

Reisman, Leo (1897–1961)

A classically trained violinist, Reisman in the 1920s determined to lead a proper, "high society" orchestra, one that would play for refined dancing. By the 1930s, he had achieved his goal, and moved to New York's posh Waldorf-Astoria for an extended stay. Vocalists Lee Wiley, Fred Astaire, and Dinah Shore performed under his leadership early in their careers. Reisman also enjoyed slots on network radio, appearing consistently from 1931 until 1938.

Scott, Raymond (1908–1994)

Leader of a quintet that attracted considerable attention in the mid-1930s, Scott scored unique music that can be best described as "novelty tunes," although "inspired lunacy" has also been employed. Consisting of complex arrangements usually played at breakneck tempos, the group is erroneously remembered today for providing the wacky backgrounds for many Warner Brothers cartoons. In reality, Scott never wrote for the studio; arranger Carl Stalling took Scott's material and worked it liberally into the "Merrie Melodies and Looney Tunes" soundtracks. But numbers like "The Toy Trumpet" (1936), "Powerhouse" (1937), "Twilight in Turkey" (1937), and "In an 18th Century Drawing Room" (1939) drew appreciative audiences and sold well as recordings.

Shaw, Artie (1910–2004)

The Artie Shaw orchestra established a reputation as one of the most popular bands of the later 1930s. In the early years of the decade, Shaw had free-lanced with different groups and did not go out on his own until 1936. An excellent clarinetist, Shaw scored a tremendous hit with Jerry Gray's arrangement of Cole Porter's "Begin the Beguine" in 1938, a recording that shot him and his orchestra into the upper echelons of popular music. The band's moody theme, "Nightmare" (1937, composed by Shaw himself), hinted at more modern music to come, but spirited renditions of Rudolf Friml's "Indian Love Call" (1924), "Back Bay Shuffle" (1938; music by Theodore McCrae) and "Frenesi" (1940; music by Alberto Dominguez, lyrics by Ray Charles and S.K. Russell) kept the orchestra in the spotlight. Commercial success guaranteed Shaw top musicians and vocalists, including among the latter Helen Forrest, Billie Holiday, Kitty Kallen, and Tony Pastor.

Sissle, Noble (1889–1975)

Sissle co-authored, with pianist Eubie Blake, the successful 1921 Broadway musical *Shuffle Along*; that success gave Sissle, who was black, entrée into the white-dominated entertainment field. By the 1930s, he had gained recognition as a leader in vaudeville, musicals, and the nightclub circuit. His band appeared in a variety of venues otherwise closed to black artists, making Sissle something of a pioneer. In 1937, he introduced a young Lena Horne as his band's vocalist.

Spitalny, Phil (1905–1970)

Leader of a band that featured women as its players, Spitalny's group received billing as "Phil Spitalny and His All-Girl Orchestra." Like Ina Ray Hutton (see above), this maestro had a gimmick that worked for over ten years. Thanks to good promotion, Spitalny landed a radio show entitled *The Hour of Charm*; it ran on network radio from 1934 to 1948. All of the musicians went by first names only—"Vivien," "Lola," "Velma," "Connie," and so on. A regular feature included "Evelyn and Her Magic Violin," a segment that allowed Evelyn Klein to talk about and play her 1756 violin. Much of what the Spitalny group did consisted of musical hokum, but it also brought about modest success for this unusual band.

Waller, Fats (b. Thomas Waller; 1904–1943)

Waller's band, Fats Waller and His Rhythm, proved enormously popular throughout the 1930s. The band—more accurately a sextet, for the most part—played clubs and recorded innumerable tunes, ranging from novelty and swing to jazz. The combination of Waller's stride piano and infectious humor, along with the lyrics of collaborator Andy Razaf, made for a string of hits, such as "Ain't Misbehavin'" (1929), "Honeysuckle Rose" (1929), "Black and Blue" (1929), "Keepin' Out of Mischief Now" (1932), and countless others.

Waring, Fred (1900–1984)

A native of Pennsylvania, Waring in the 1920s created an unusual combination of orchestra and glee club/chorus that he called Fred Waring and His Pennsylvanians. Using lush arrangements of old standards and patriotic songs, he built an enduring reputation as a purveyor of nostalgia and Americana and was fondly called "America's Singing Master." The 1930s found Waring established on network radio; *The Fred Waring Show* ran consistently from 1933 until 1949, and he also took his orchestra and chorus to Broadway and to films. Hardly a dance band, Waring's orchestra and massed voices combined music with entertainment and show business.

Webb, Chick (1902–1939)

A superb drummer, Webb led, from 1931 until 1935, the house band at New York's Savoy Ballroom, a Harlem mecca for swing and jazz. The aggregation featured compositions and arrangements by Edgar Sampson (including, naturally, his own "Stompin' at the Savoy," 1936), and served as a proving ground for a host of future stars. In 1934, Webb hired Ella Fitzgerald as the band's vocalist; in fact, she led the band after Webb's 1939 death, keeping it going for three years, but she finally went out on her own.

Weems, Ted (1901–1963)

Weems fronted a band that featured singers more than it did instrumentalists. Crooner Perry Como stands out as the most famous alumnus of the group; he would rise to enormous heights of popularity in the decades to come. In the 1930s, however, Como was on the way up, and vocalizing for the Weems orchestra got him his start. The band also featured a whistler, Elmo Tanner, who recorded "Heartaches" (music by Al Hoffman; lyrics by John Klenner) in 1931. Mildly popular initially—Guy Lombardo and His Royal Canadians also recorded it—Tanner and Weems re-recorded it several years later and it became a popular favorite. Then, in 1947, a new generation of listeners rediscovered the tune, and the old recording enjoyed renewed success, making it one of one of the biggest hits of the year.

Welk, Lawrence (1903–1992)

Although he soared to great fame as a television bandleader in the 1960s, Welk had actually led orchestras since the 1920s, and attracted wide attention in 1934 with "Beer Barrel Polka" (music by Jaramir Vejvoda, lyrics by Lew Brown and Wladimire A. Timm). His admittedly corny approach to presentation and his penchant for polkas made him an easy target for critics, but generations of Americans have loved his showmanship, and he and his orchestra, almost alone among the many musicians of the era, live on through endless syndicated replays of his long-running television series, *The Lawrence Welk Show* (1955–1982).

Whiteman, Paul (1890–1967)

Whiteman organized his first band in 1918, and by the 1920s had been dubbed "The King of Jazz," a press agent's title that stayed with him until his death. He began recording in 1920 and became widely known as a result. His orchestras hardly qualify as jazz or swing aggregations, but he did hire some of the best people in the business. Names like the Dorsey Brothers, Bing Crosby, Mildred Bailey, Johnny Mercer, and other musical celebrities at one time or another worked for "Pops" Whiteman. He strove to make jazz "respectable," that is, acceptable to more educated and socially elite patrons, and even commissioned George Gershwin to write his famous *Rhapsody in Blue* (1924) for a concert he was planning. But the later 1930s and the emphasis on swing found Whiteman's rather pompus, overarranged style out of date. He soldiered on, performing in movies and on radio in addition to clubs and shows, but his bands no longer attracted as great a following, and many saw him as a relic of the Roaring Twenties.

VOCALISTS

Most of the bands of the 1930s featured vocalists, both male ("boy singers") and female ("canaries"). In fact, with the widespread availability of radio and recordings, these singers could sometimes be identified more readily than the orchestras backing them. Usually younger than either the leaders or most of the sidemen, vocalists attained increasing importance and popularity, a situation that would intensify in the 1940s. The listing below briefly describes some of those singers who achieved acclaim in the 1930s.[2]

Anderson, Ivie (1905–1949)

After a career of clubs and shows, Anderson joined Duke Ellington in 1931, his first full-time vocalist. She remained with the band until 1942, and fans remember her both for ballads and up-tempo numbers, especially "Rose of the Rio Grande" (1938; music by Harry Warren and Ross Gorman, lyrics by Edgar Leslie) and "It Don't Mean a Thing (If It Ain't Got That Swing)" (1932; words and music by Duke Ellington and Irving Mills), a tune she introduced, thus helping with the popularization of the term "swing."

Astaire, Fred (1899–1987)

Usually thought of as one of the best dancers and most popular movie stars of the era, Fred Astaire also enjoyed a successful career as a vocalist. Most of what he sang came from his films, especially those musicals in which he co-starred with Ginger Rogers. His taste in music proved as impeccable as his dancing, and major composers, such as Irving Berlin, Jerome Kern, and George Gershwin regularly provided scores for his movies. For example, in *Top Hat* (Irving Berlin, 1935) he performs "Top Hat, White Tie, and Tails"; in *Swing Time* (1936; Jerome Kern and Dorothy Fields) the number is "The Way You Look Tonight"; and in *A Damsel in Distress* (1937; George and Ira Gershwin), he sings "I Can't Be Bothered Now" and his dancing can also be heard on the recording. Over the span of the decade, Astaire had numerous other hits, a testament to his singing abilities and the popularity of his movies.

Bailey, Mildred (1907–1951)

The first woman to be a featured vocalist behind a famous band, Bailey rose to fame singing with Paul Whiteman from 1929 to 1934. She was often called "The Rockin' Chair Lady" because of her hit version of Hoagy Carmichael's "Rockin' Chair" in 1932. The following year she married band-leader/xylophonist Red Norvo, and the couple, dubbed "Mr. and Mrs. Jazz," enjoyed modest success in clubs and on radio and recordings.

Boswell, Connee (b. Connie Boswell; 1907–1976)

With her sisters Martha and Helvetia ("Vet"), she formed, in the early 1930s, the Boswell Sisters vocal trio, a jazz-oriented group that helped popularize up-tempo swing numbers. They enjoyed a popular hit in "Life Is Just a Bowl of Cherries" (1931; music by Ray Henderson, lyrics by Lew Brown) in 1933. In many ways, the Boswells presaged the style taken by another trio, the Andrews Sisters, in the 1940s. In 1935, Connee Boswell became a soloist, despite the challenge of being wheelchair-bound. Her interpretation of "The Nearness of You" (1938; music by Hoagy Carmichael, lyrics by Ned Washington) reached the charts. In the meantime, she performed with Tommy Dorsey, Benny Goodman, Bing Crosby, and many other headliners.

Carlisle, Una Mae (1918–1956)

A prolific songwriter in addition to being an accomplished singer, Carlisle toured with Fats Waller. The two recorded "I Can't Give You Anything but Love" (1928; music by Jimmy McHugh, words by Dorothy Fields) in 1939, and she had a minor hit with her own composition, "Walkin' by the River" (1940; lyrics by Robert Sour).

Clark, Buddy (b. Walter Clark; 1912–1949)

Clark began his career with Benny Goodman on his *Let's Dance* radio series. The exposure led him to Hollywood where he dubbed his voice for non-singing actors. His style grew out of the crooning developed by Bing Crosby and Rudy Vallee and adapted particularly well to the medium of radio. He worked on the network show *Your Hit Parade* in the late 1930s, as well as making a number of recordings. Never a big star, he typified the hard-working band singer.

Cox, Ida (1896–1967)

Hardly a household name in the 1930s, Cox began her career as a church singer and performer in minstrels. She graduated to theaters and stage productions around 1910. The thirties saw her leading her own tent show acts. In 1939, she sang in John Hammond's Carnegie Hall extravaganza, *From Spirituals to Swing*. This exposure led to some recording activity for the blues veteran, but she never achieved the fame she deserved.

Ennis, Skinnay (1909–1963)

A regular with the Hal Kemp orchestra from 1925 until 1938, Ennis also did some comedy routines on radio. He is best remembered for his hit with Kemp, "Got a Date with an Angel" (1931; music by Jack Waller and Joseph Turnbridge, lyrics by Clifford Grey and Sonnie Miller).

Fitzgerald, Ella (1917–1996)

In 1934, while performing in an amateur show at Harlem's Apollo Theater, scouts spotted Fitzgerald's considerable talents and she soon thereafter joined the Chick Webb band. "A-Tisket, A-Tasket" (1938; words and music by Al Feldman and Ella Fitzgerald), recorded with Webb in 1938, became her first major hit. The following year saw Fitzgerald take over leadership of the Webb orchestra when he died. Although her years of superstardom still lay ahead, she had already mastered her distinctive "scat" style of singing, a technique that involves improvising on lyrics and instrumental passages using nonsense syllables, often phrasing them in a manner similar to musical instruments instead of traditional vocal inflections.

Garland, Judy (1922–1969)

A teenaged star in the movies, Garland first attracted musical attention in *Broadway Melody of 1938* (1937) when she sang "Dear Mr. Gable/You Made Me Love You" (1913; music by James V. Monaco, lyrics by Joseph McCarthy) to a photograph of Clark Gable. She followed that success with "Zing! Went the Strings of My Heart" (1935; words and music by James F. Hanley) in the movie *Listen, Darling* (1938). Her casting as Dorothy in *The Wizard of Oz* (1939) assured her stardom, especially her rendition of Harold Arlen's "Over the Rainbow" (lyrics by E.Y. Harburg). She had two more hits from *Andy Hardy Meets Debutante* (1940), one of the pictures in the popular Andy Hardy series, "I'm Nobody's Baby" (1921; music by Lester Santly and Milton Ager, lyrics by Benny Davis) and "Alone" (1935; music by Nacio Herb Brown, lyrics by Arthur Freed). From then on she emerged as one of the country's most popular entertainers.

Holiday, Billie ("Lady Day") (1915–1959)

Critic John Hammond discovered Billie Holiday while working the Harlem club scene. He set up her recording debut with Benny Goodman in 1933; from there she appeared with Teddy Wilson, Count Basie, Artie Shaw, and a number of pick-up swing groups. Unfortunately, her personal life often attracted as much attention as her splendid jazz singing. Insiders, however, early on recognized Holiday as one of the finest interpreters of lyrics and their connection to the music. She can be heard on "Your Mother's Son-in-Law" (1933; music by Alberta Nichols, lyrics by Mann Holiner) with the early Goodman band, "Any Old Time" (1938; words and music by Artie Shaw) with Artie Shaw, and on "Strange Fruit" (1939; words and music by Lewis Allan [Abel Meeropol]), a controversial anti-lynching song. The major recording companies and radio networks refused to touch "Strange Fruit," fearing an audience backlash, but the small Commodore label fortunately recorded it, thereby saving it for posterity.

Humes, Helen (1913–1981)

Humes began recording as a teenager in the late 1920s doing blues and up-tempo numbers. A decade later found her singing with Count Basie's orchestra, although the bandleader usually limited her to ballads (Jimmy Rushing did most of the blues for the band). She remained with Basie from 1938 until 1942, and gained recognition as an outstanding vocalist. Her distinctive style can be heard on numbers like "Blame It on My Last Affair" (1939; music by Henry Nemo, lyrics by Irving Mills) and "My Heart Belongs to Daddy" (1939; words and music by Cole Porter).

Robeson, Paul (1898–1976)

Hardly a band singer, or even a popular entertainer in the broad sense of the term, Robeson excelled at acting, and his concert singing electrified audiences for several decades. The son of an escaped slave, he led in everything he attempted, from athletics to academics. Although trained as a lawyer, racial prejudice ended that career. He became a noted Broadway performer (*Show Boat*, 1932) and Shakespearean actor (*Othello*, 1930), starred in a number of films (*The Emperor Jones*, 1933, *Song of Freedom*, 1936, *Proud Valley*, 1939, others), and recorded frequently. His rendition of Earl Robinson's "Ballad for Americans" (1938; lyrics by John Latouche) on both CBS radio and at the 1939–1940 New York World's Fair became legendary for its power (see Chapter 5). In time, his activist stands on civil rights brought him under the scrutiny of Congress. Continual persecution for his outspoken views led to depression and eventual seclusion. During the 1930s and 1940s, however, Paul Robeson gained recognition as a leading voice for equality, and stages around the world served as his podium.

Rushing, Jimmy ("Mr. Five-by-Five") (1903–1972)

Jimmy Rushing will always be associated with Count Basie. From 1927 onward, or back in the days before Basie led a band, Rushing performed with both Bennie Moten and Walter Page's Blue Devils, the predecessors of the Basie aggregation. With his burly frame (thus his nickname) and manner of shouting the blues, Rushing proved a real crowd pleaser, and he remained with Basie until 1948. During that time, he recorded such classics as "Good Morning Blues" (1937; music by Count Basie and Eddie Durham, lyrics by Jimmy Rushing), "Sent for You Yesterday" (1938; music by Eddie Durham, lyrics by Jimmy Rushing), and "Evil Blues" (1939; music by Count Basie and Harry Edison, lyrics by Jimmy Rushing).

Sinatra, Frank (1915–1998)

Although his fame touched only the very last years of the decade, Sinatra's success and popularity as a "boy singer" marked the end of the dominance of the bands and their leaders and the gradual ascendancy of the vocalist as the star attraction. Stories of Sinatra's dedication to his craft have long circulated; his apprenticeship under Harry James and, later, Tommy Dorsey, set the stage for the smitten teens who could not resist the kid from Hoboken. Little survives from those early years; he recorded "All or Nothing at All" (1939; words and music by Arthur Altman and Jack Lawrence) with the James band in mid-1939 and a handful of tunes in 1940 with Tommy Dorsey, such as "I'll Never Smile Again" (1940; words and music by Ruth Lowe), but little else. As Sinatra's fame grew, a new code of behavior came into effect between fans and their favorite singers: the vocalist took center stage; the band and its leader had become secondary.

Smith, Bessie (1894–1937)

Nicknamed "The Empress of the Blues," Smith enjoyed her greatest fame in the 1920s, but she continued as a strong force in American blues music until her death in 1937. Capable of filling a theater with her powerful voice without the aid of amplification, her music nonetheless had a dated quality in the Swing Era. She tried to change, but a deadly automobile accident prevented her from completing a comeback.

Smith, Kate (1907–1986)

Kate Smith first began to attract attention in the mid-1920s; she would remain a favorite for the next fifty years. A native of North Carolina, promoters billed her as "The Songbird of the South," and she soon had a continuing series of her own radio shows. Her broadcasts ran under varying titles, beginning in 1931 with *Kate Smith Sings* and continuing virtually without interruption until 1952. Her rendition of "When the Moon Comes Over the Mountain" (1931; music by Harry Woods, lyrics by Howard Johnson) made her a star of the first rank; the song became her theme and hit after hit followed. In 1938, composer Irving Berlin gave her exclusive rights to the words and music to "God Bless America" (written in 1918, at the close of World War I for a musical entitled *Yip, Yip, Yaphank*, but dropped from the score). With World War II on the horizon, Smith's strong, optimistic singing of the song lifted people's spirits, making it a kind of second National Anthem.

Sullivan, Maxine (1911–1987)

Best known for her swinging interpretations of old folk songs, such as "Loch Lomond" (1937; traditional), "Annie Laurie" (1938; traditional), and "Darling Nellie Gray" (1938; traditional), Sullivan brought her artistry to many other styles of music as well. Married to bandleader John Kirby, the couple had a popular CBS radio show, *Flow Gently, Sweet Rhythm*, in 1939–1940. They were the first black artists to host a jazz-oriented series.

Tibbett, Lawrence (1896–1960)

Although opera singers have usually failed to appeal to the general American public, Lawrence Tibbett proved the exception. A bass-baritone with the Metropolitan Opera Company from 1923 until 1950, Tibbett took the lead in Hollywood's *The Rogue Song* (1930). Audiences loved him; nominated for an Academy Award (Best Actor), he went on to star in a number of other movies. Tibbett branched out into radio and recording, moves that further broadened his popularity. A white performer, he gained part of his fame as an interpreter of black spirituals, often in blackface. Taking the role of Porgy, he did the first recording of Gershwin's *Porgy and Bess* in 1935, and his interpretation of "I Got Plenty o' Nuttin'" (1935; music by George Gershwin, lyrics by Ira Gershwin and DuBose Heyward) became a hit.

Turner, Joe ("Big Joe") (1911–1985)

Teamed with pianist Pete Johnson in 1938's historic *From Spirituals to Swing*, the exposure made the duo overnight hits, although they had actually worked together for many years prior to the concert. A true blues shouter, Turner went on to considerable popularity in subsequent years. His best-known efforts with Johnson include 1938's "Roll'em Pete" (music by Pete Johnson, lyrics by Joe Turner) and "Cherry Red" (1939; music by Pete Johnson, lyrics by Joe Turner), both boogie-woogie classics.

Ward, Helen (1916–1998)

The quintessential big band singer, Ward toured and recorded with Benny Goodman during the mid-thirties. Able to sing just about anything in the band's book, she projected professionalism, whether in a crowded dancehall or a stuffy recording studio. She can be heard with Goodman in such numbers as "All My Life" (1935; music by Sam H. Stept, lyrics by Sidney D. Mitchell) and her biggest hit with the band, "Goody, Goody" (1936; music by Matty Malneck, lyrics by Johnny Mercer).

A publicity shot of band vocalist Helen Ward (1916–1998) with clarinetist Benny Goodman (1909–1986), the "King of Swing." Ward exemplified the attractive and talented "girl singer" that accompanied most big bands during the 1930s; Goodman, of course, led one of the most successful orchestras around, and Ward performed ably with him. Together they cut many records, including "It's Been So Long" (1936; music by Walter Donaldson, lyrics by Harold Adamson), "Too Good to be True" (1928; music by Ray Henderson, lyrics by Buddy DeSylva and Lew Brown), and "All My Life" (1936; music by Sam H. Stept, lyrics by Sidney D. Mitchell). [Library of Congress, Prints & Photographs Division]

Wiley, Lee (1915–1975)

    If Helen Ward epitomizes the band singer, Wiley does the same for cabaret singers. Possessed of a distinctive, husky voice, as well as striking good looks, she seems the ideal person to be singing ballads in a smoky night-club. Her numerous recordings with some of the best names in jazz reinforce the image. She enjoyed her first hit in 1931, a rendition of "Time On My Hands" (1930; music by Vincent Youmans, lyrics by Harold Adamson and Mack Gordon). In addition, she pioneered in the making of "concept albums"—recordings based on certain themes or the works of specific songwriters. In 1939 she began the first of a series of albums dedicated to composers; in time, the albums would include the Gershwins, Cole Porter, Rodgers and Hart, and Harold Arlen (1939–1943).

SONGWRITERS, LYRICISTS, AND ARRANGERS

What follows consists of a brief listing of some of those people who composed the melodies, put memorable words to the music, and possessed the skills necessary to arrange words and music in such ways that bands and vocalists could have their own distinctive sound. Often overlooked by the public, this group of individuals created some of the most enduring American music of the 1930s or any other time. As a rule, they resided behind the scenes; the public knew little about them and only a handful achieved any celebrity; instead, millions knew their music.[3]

Arlen, Harold (b. Hyman Arluck; 1905–1986)

    Arlen first appeared on the music scene in the 1920s; by 1930 he was writing songs for the Cotton Club and for Broadway, and soon had composed such standards as "I Gotta Right to Sing the Blues" (*Earl Carroll's Vanities,* 1932; lyrics by Ted Koehler), "Stormy Weather" (1933; lyrics by Ted Koehler), and "Last Night When We Were Young" (1936; lyrics by E. Y. Harburg). His greatest popular fame came in 1939 with the release of MGM's *The Wizard of Oz*. Arlen wrote the score, and it included many favorites; "Over the Rainbow" (1939; lyrics by E. Y. Harburg), especially as sung by Judy Garland, probably remains the best remembered piece from the picture.

Berlin, Irving (b. Israel Baline; 1888–1989)

    One of the handful of composers/songwriters to escape anonymity, Berlin achieved a certain celebrity with the general public. Given his extraordinary long life, Berlin wrote for most of the twentieth century, composing over 1,000 songs, hundreds of which went on to become hits, and many of those now considered standards. He personified Tin Pan Alley; he could work in virtually any format and he usually wrote his own lyrics. Unable to read music (an arranger would transcribe his ideas to paper), Berlin composed for the theater, the movies, and general popular consumption. The 1930s proved a banner decade for him, with dozens of standards coming from his prolific imagination. "Easter Parade" (*As Thousands Cheer*, 1933), "Top Hat, White Tie, and Tails" (*Top Hat*, 1935), "Cheek to Cheek" (*Top Hat*, 1935), and "Let Yourself Go" (*Follow the Fleet*, 1936) serve only as examples of his variety. Fred Astaire, one of his favorite vocalists, incidentally sang all of the foregoing, a tribute to Berlin's skills and Astaire's taste. "God Bless America," Berlin's well-loved ode to patriotism, had been originally written in 1918; it reappeared, literally pulled out of a trunk, as the shadows of World War II began to stretch across the nation. The song caught the national imagination in 1939, especially in the recorded version by Kate Smith.

Cahn, Sammy (1913–1993)

An often-overlooked lyricist, Cahn established himself with Hollywood in the mid-thirties, although most of his best work would not gain notice until the 1940s or later. With the swing craze reaching its peak in the last years of the decade, Cahn began to attract notice with soundtrack songs from films like *Manhattan Merry-Go-Round* (1938; music by Saul Chaplin) and *52nd Street* (1937; music by Walter Bullock). His first hit occurred when he scored the English words for "Bei Mir Bist Du Shoen" (1938; music by Sholom Secunda), an old Yiddish song that achieved great popularity when the Andrews Sisters recorded it. As Cahn carefully points out in his lyrics, the title means "you are grand." This number proved so successful that it appeared in two films, *Love, Honor and Behave* and *Prisoner of Swing* (both 1938).

Carmichael, Hoagy (b. Howard Hoagland Carmichael; 1899–1981)

Throughout much of his long career, the Indiana-born Carmichael composed for, and also appeared in, a number of films as an actor, singer, and pianist. Best known for "Star Dust" (1927; lyrics by Mitchell Parish added in 1929), possibly the most recorded title in the history of popular American music, he also composed such evergreens as "Rockin' Chair" (1930), "Lazy River" (1931; lyrics by Sidney Arodin), "Lazybones" (1934; lyrics by Johnny Mercer), and "The Nearness of You" (1938; lyrics by Ned Washington). His lanky looks, plus his laconic manner, made him a recognizable Hollywood character actor and he appeared in fourteen films. Being on screen gave him the opportunity to perform his music before a huge captive audience.

Donaldson, Walter (1893–1947)

As the composer of "Yes, Sir, That's My Baby" (1925; lyrics by Gus Kahn) and "My Blue Heaven" (1927; lyrics by George Whiting), plus dozens of other pop tunes, Donaldson was already a well-known songwriter when the 1930s began. He enlarged on his fame by creating two big hits for Guy Lombardo and His Royal Canadians: "Little White Lies" and "You're Driving Me

Crazy! (What Did I Do?)," both written in 1930. At this time, he moved to Hollywood and churned out song after song for the movies. In 1933, he wrote "Dancing in the Moonlight" (lyrics by Gus Kahn) for *The Prizefighter and the Lady*; three years later he earned an Academy Award nomination for Best Song with "Did I Remember?" (lyrics by Harold Adamson) in the film *Suzy* (1936).

Dubin, Al (1891–1945)

A Swiss-born lyricist, Dubin came to Hollywood in the early 1930s. He teamed up with composer Harry Warren to create a remarkable series of standards during the decade, beginning with the score for the musical hit *42nd Street* (1933). The powerful "Remember My Forgotten Man" (1933; music by Harry Warren) in the film *Gold Diggers of 1933* established his credentials to write timely lyrics. Among his other works with Warren are "Boulevard of Broken Dreams" (*Moulin Rouge*, 1933), "I Only Have Eyes for You" (*Dames*, 1934), and the novelty number, "Flagenheimer's Odorless Cheese" (*Broadway Gondolier*, 1935).

Duke, Vernon (b. Vladimir Dukelsky; 1903–1969)

A Russian-born songwriter, Duke pursued both popular music and classical composition, retaining his birth name of Dukelsky until 1955 for his ballets, concertos, and oratorios. From 1921 onward, he used the more familiar "Vernon Duke" for his lighter work. On the popular side, Duke achieved renown on Broadway with "April in Paris" (1932; lyrics by E. Y. Harburg) and two songs from the *Zigfield Follies of 1934*, "I Like the Likes of You" and "What Is There to Say?" (both with lyrics by E. Y. Harburg). In 1936 he penned both music and lyrics for the haunting "Autumn in New York" and collaborated with lyricist Ira Gershwin for "I Can't Get Started." He continued his dual careers until his death in 1969.

Ellington, Duke (b. Edward Kennedy Ellington; 1899–1974)

Although Ellington certainly ranks as one of the premier American composers and arrangers, his orchestra clearly served as his primary method of expression. Therefore, he can be found under the "Bandleader" section above, but also see "Strayhorn, Billy" below.

Fields, Dorothy (1905–1974)

In a profession long dominated by men, Dorothy Fields managed to overcome gender biases and rose to become an outstanding songwriter. But she also proved the exception; most women languished in the music business, and few achieved any measure of success. A lyricist, she first collaborated with composer Jimmy McHugh, creating such standards as "On the Sunny Side of the Street" (*Lew Leslie's International Revue*, 1930), "Don't Blame Me"

On the left, composer Vernon Duke (1903–1969); on the right, lyricist Ira Gershwin (1896–1983). Both masters of their musical crafts, they also worked together on a number of occasions. Duke first attempted classical composition, but found his strength lay in more popular genres. Gershwin, of course, usually collaborated with his brother George, but took time in 1936 to set words to a Vernon Duke melody. "I Can't Get Started," one of the classics of the 1930s, resulted from that joint effort. [Library of Congress, Prints & Photographs Division]

(*Clowns in Clover*, 1933), and "I'm in the Mood for Love" (*Every Night at Eight*, 1935). Soon she worked with additional songwriters, especially Jerome Kern in Hollywood, a union that resulted in "Never Gonna Dance" (*Swing Time*, 1936) and "You Couldn't Be Cuter" (*Joy of Living*, 1938), among many others.

Friml, Rudolf (1879–1972)

Born in Czechoslovakia, Friml came to the United States in 1906. He made his mark composing in a form unfamiliar to most Americans, the operetta. Actress/singer Jeanette MacDonald frequently starred in Friml musicals, and he reached his largest audiences doing film scores; he even adapted his previous stage works to screen. For example, his *The Vagabond King* (1925) became a movie with the same name in 1930. His best-known work, *Rose Marie* (play, 1924; film, 1936), stars MacDonald and Nelson Eddy, the second operetta in a long-running series by the two actors. Friml's *The Firefly* (1912) went to Hollywood in 1937, and served as another MacDonald vehicle. The film also includes "The Donkey Serenade" (music by Rudolf Friml and Herbert Stothart, lyrics by Bob Wright and Chet Forrest), a popular favorite that actually came from a 1923 song he called "Chansonette."

Gershwin, George (1898–1937)

One of the giants of American music, Gershwin excelled in all areas of popular song. A skilled pianist and composer, he usually worked in partnership with his brother, lyricist Ira Gershwin. Their collective talents resulted in dozens of classics—"Bidin' My Time" (*Girl Crazy*, 1930), "Let's Call the Whole Thing Off" (*Shall We Dance*, 1937), "A Foggy Day (in London Town)" (*A Damsel in Distress*, 1937), "Love Is Here to Stay" (*The Goldwyn Follies*, 1938)—that ranged from songs for theater, movies, and recordings, to the opera *Porgy and Bess*, composed in 1935. In that last effort, DuBose Heyward, the librettist, contributed some lyrics, but Ira Gershwin wrote most of the words to the score. A man of wide-ranging genius, George Gershwin also wanted to create more serious music, and works like *Rhapsody in Blue* (1924), his famous concert work, resulted. During the 1930s, he continued to follow that urge with *Second Rhapsody for Piano and Orchestra* (1931) and *Variations on "I Got Rhythm"* (1934).

Gershwin, Ira (1896–1983)

A brilliant lyricist, Ira Gershwin is often thought of as George Gershwin's brother. But without Ira's ability to create memorable words for George's music, it seems unlikely that George Gershwin would rank as high on the pantheon of American songwriters as he does. The melodies of "But Not for Me" (*Girl Crazy*, 1930), "Who Cares?" (*Of Thee I Sing*, 1931), and "I Was Doing All Right" (*Goldwyn Follies*, 1938) certainly linger in the mind, but the words bring the music to life, the recalled snippets of a line or two that allow the song to live on in memory. After George's untimely death, Ira continued to write, working with many different composers.

Gifford, Gene (1908–1970)

Best remembered as the chief arranger for the Casa Loma Orchestra, Gifford represents those composer/arrangers who worked to give a band a distinctive "sound." In Gifford's case, his approach involved the use of riffs, or repeated musical phrases, and it proved so successful in the Swing Era that others frequently imitated his techniques. He proved particularly good at up-tempo pieces, as attested by the popularity of the Casa Lomans' performances of his "Maniac's Ball" (1932), "Black Jazz" (1932), and "White Jazz" (1933).

Gray, Jerry (1915–1976)

Gray joined the Artie Shaw band in 1938 as an arranger. That same year, he took Cole Porter's 1935 "Begin the Beguine" and completely altered the Latin-influenced song into a smooth swing tune designed for American dancers. An overwhelming success, it made Gray an in-demand arranger. He continued with Shaw, contributing arrangements of such numbers as "Lover Come Back to Me" (1939; originally 1928, music by Sigmund Romberg, lyrics by Oscar Hammerstein II) and "Non-Stop Flight" (1938). In 1939, he moved to the Glenn Miller Orchestra and began creating arrangements that catapulted the Miller aggregation to the top of all the bands. One of his first contributions was an interpretation of "In the Mood" (1938), a song written by Joe Garland. In 1939, in an RCA Victor Bluebird recording, "In the Mood" proved a tremendous hit, and Gray would continue with the Miller band for a number of years.

Grofé, Ferde (b. Ferdinand Rudolf von Grofé; 1892–1972)

Grofé stands among a tiny group of serious composers who also had a popular following during the 1930s. He first came into prominence when he orchestrated George Gershwin's *Rhapsody in Blue* for the Paul Whiteman orchestra (1924). He continued working with Whiteman, helping to write arrangements for *The King of Jazz* (1930), a big Hollywood musical that included Gershwin performing his by-now famous *Rhapsody*. In 1931, Whiteman premiered Grofé's *Grand Canyon Suite*, a classical composition that attempts to musically picture the canyon. People liked his approach and the suite received considerable acclaim. The best-known section is "On the Trail," where the clop-clop-clop of donkey hooves can be heard. That work gained Grofé much radio exposure, conducting jobs, and arranging, making him one of the most visible serious musicians of the period.

Hammerstein, Oscar, II (1895–1960)

Perhaps best known by modern audiences for his longtime (1943–1960) collaboration with composer Richard Rodgers, Oscar Hammerstein had years earlier established a significant reputation on Broadway as a lyricist. Working with composer Jerome Kern (see below), the two practically defined the modern stage musical with *Show Boat* (1927). They continued their collaboration in an on-again, off-again way with hits like "I've Told Ev'ry Little Star" and "The Song Is You" (both *Music in the Air*, 1932), and "All the Things You Are" (*Very Warm for May*, 1939). When not working with Kern, Hammerstein teamed up with Rudolf Friml for the operetta *Rose Marie* (stage, 1924; film, 1936), creating such popular favorites as "Indian Love Call." He worked in a similar manner with Sigmund Romberg for *May Wine* (1935), contributing the words for "Once Around the Clock." He even provided lyrics for the zany Olsen-Johnson comedy *Hellzapoppin'* (1938). By and large, however, Hammerstein's career coasted during the 1930s; not until he and Richard Rodgers formed their partnership in the early 1940s would he achieve the heights for which he has become most famous.

Harburg, E. Y. ("Yip") (1896–1981)

"Yip" Harburg wrote the powerful story of Depression loss that unfolds in "Brother, Can You Spare a Dime?" (1932; music by Jay Gorney). But it was also Harburg who penned the hilarious stanzas for "Lydia, the Tattooed Lady" (*At the Circus*, 1939; music by Harold Arlen). The topical distance between the two songs could not be greater, and it shows how thoroughly professional, how multitalented, were the men (and occasional women) working in Tin Pan Alley during the thirties. Harburg would also create the lovely lyrics that grace "April in Paris" (*Walk a Little Faster*, 1932; music by Vernon Duke) and "What Is There to Say?" (*Ziegfeld Follies of 1934*; music by Vernon Duke), and contributed to dozens of other melodies of the decade.

Hart, Lorenz (1895–1943)

Best known as the lyricist half of Rodgers and Hart, he teamed up with composer Richard Rodgers in 1920 (see below). Although success eluded the pair for several years, in 1925 they achieved some fame for *Garrick Gaieties*, and thereafter found themselves in demand for Broadway shows and Hollywood movies. The partnership dissolved in the early 1940s, but music lovers have been left with a body of work that is often wry, always sophisticated, and reflective in many ways of the era. A sampling of Hart's memorable lyrics set to Rodgers' music might include "Ten Cents a Dance" (*Simple Simon*, 1930), "Blue Moon" (one of their few songs written neither for stage nor screen, 1935), "It's Easy to Remember" (*Mississippi*, 1935), and "The Lady Is a Tramp" (*Babes in Arms*, 1937).

The songwriting team of Richard Rodgers (1902–1979; left) and Lorenz Hart (1895–1943; right) created one stage and screen hit after another throughout the 1920s and 1930s. Masters of sophisticated songs long favored by vocalists and instrumentalists alike—"Ten Cents a Dance," "Little Girl Blue," "My Funny Valentine," and "The Lady Is a Tramp" have certainly stood the test of time—they lifted the popular standard to a new level of maturity. [Library of Congress, Prints & Photographs Division]

Henderson, Fletcher (1898–1952)

A distinguished black bandleader in his own right, Henderson reached his largest audiences working as an arranger for Benny Goodman and other white-led orchestras. Because his band did not succeed commercially, Henderson fell into financial straits and had to sell many of his arrangements to Goodman. In that roundabout manner, Henderson's music reached far more people than it might otherwise have done. For example, Jelly Roll Morton wrote and recorded "King Porter Stomp" in 1923; ten years later, Henderson did an arrangement of it for his own band, but it went nowhere in sales. Then, in 1935, the Goodman band, using Henderson's arrangement, recorded "King Porter Stomp" and it became a big hit. For many reasons— and race is primary among them—Fletcher Henderson could never achieve the commercial success of a Goodman or a Miller, yet his brilliant arrangements helped define the swing style of the 1930s.

Kern, Jerome (1885–1945)

With stage hits like *Sunny* (1925), *Show Boat* (1927), and *Sweet Adeline* (1929) behind him, Jerome Kern entered the 1930s as the dean of American theater composers. But like so many others at the time, Kern turned increasingly from Broadway to Hollywood, focusing on film scores for much of the decade. He nonetheless completed the music for a number of outstanding stage musicals during the 1930s, including *Music in the Air* (lyrics by Oscar Hammerstein II) and *Roberta* (lyrics by Otto Harbach). Among his many memorable movie melodies, "A Fine Romance" and "The Way You Look Tonight" (both from *Swing Time*, 1936; lyrics by Dorothy Fields) could more than show Kern's range and versatility. In addition, he also created the film scores for several of his stage hits that Hollywood adapted for the screen.

Loesser, Frank (1910–1969)

Only twenty years old when the decade began, Frank Loesser can be counted as something of a latecomer to the 1930s. But he made up for any lost time by joining Paramount Studios and writing the lyrics to dozens of songs featured in movies from 1938 to 1940. He put words to "Two Sleepy People" (*Thanks for the Memory*, 1938; music by Hoagy Carmichael), "See What the Boys in the Backroom Will Have" (*Destry Rides Again*, 1939; music by Fred Hollender), and "I Hear Music" (*Dancing on a Dime*, 1940; music by Burton Lane) during a sustained burst of creativity. Greater fame awaited Loesser, but he had established himself in a brief period of time.

McHugh, Jimmy (1895–1969)

McHugh began his career in music as a song plugger, but quickly moved to composing his own music. By 1924 he had his first hit, "When My Sugar Walks Down the Street" (lyrics by Gene Austin). He began collaborating with lyricist Dorothy Fields in 1928, a partnership that would last well into the 1930s. "Exactly Like You" (1930) and "I Feel a Song Coming On" (1935) were among their successes, but he also worked with many other lyricists and enjoyed a string of successes in the 1940s.

Mercer, Johnny (1909–1976)

A composer and a lyricist of some note, and also an accomplished popular singer, Mercer quickly rose to modest fame in the 1930s. "Lazybones" (1933; music by Hoagy Carmichael) served as his breakthrough work, and he followed that with a string of hits including "I'm an Old Cowhand" (*Rhythm on the Range*, 1936), "Too Marvelous for Words" (*Ready, Willing, and Able*, 1937; music by Richard Whiting), "Jeepers, Creepers" (*Going Places*, 1939; music by Harry Warren), and the swing classic, "And the Angels Sing" (1939; music by Ziggy Elman). Before the end of his long career in the 1970s, Mercer had written the words to over 1,500 songs.

Mundy, Jimmy (1907–1983)

An arranger who began his professional career working with pianist Earl Hines from 1932 to 1936, Mundy joined the Benny Goodman band in 1936 and stayed until 1939. During his tenure, he contributed dozens of arrangements to Goodman, then riding on a crest of unparalleled popularity. Numbers like the show-stopping "Sing, Sing, Sing" (1936; original music by Louis Prima and Andy Razaf) owe their excitement to Mundy's skills. Originally two distinct melodies, plus riffs from several soloists, "Sing, Sing, Sing" dates from the early 1930s. Mundy combined these disparate elements into the familiar, lengthy swing anthem that belongs to Goodman alone. Other Mundy big-band hits followed—often referred to as "killer-dillers," since they thrilled listeners and dancers with their up-tempo sense of excitement—such as "Bugle Call Rag" (originally 1923; music by Jack Pettis, Billy Meyers, and Elmer Schoebel) and "Airmail Special" (1941; music by Benny Goodman, Charlie Christian, and Jimmy Mundy).

Noble, Ray (1903–1978)

An Englishman of many talents, bandleader and composer Ray Noble spent most of his working life in the United States. He led a good dance band in the early 1930s and it included some of the best sidemen of the day. But he will probably be remembered for several standards he wrote, such as "The Very Thought of You" (1934), "Cherokee" (1939), and that sentimental favorite with which many orchestras choose to end a dance, "Goodnight, Sweetheart" (1931; with James Campbell and Reg Connelly).

Oliver, Sy (b. Melvin James Oliver; 1910–1988)

Oliver contributed memorable arrangements to both the Jimmie Lunceford and the Tommy Dorsey bands. He first attracted attention with Lunceford, contributing such charts as "Four or Five Times" (1927; music by Byron Gay, lyrics by Marco H. Hellman), "For Dancers Only" (1937; music by Don Raye, Vic Schoen, and Sy Oliver), and the band's trademark "Tain't What'cha Do, It's the Way That'cha Do It" (1939; music by Sy Oliver, lyrics by Trummy Young). In 1939, he joined Dorsey as chief arranger, and there he established a reputation for creating crisp, swinging versions of many songs. Among his earliest hits with the band was "Easy Does It" (1939; music by Sy Oliver), and in time he virtually defined the musical style of the Dorsey orchestra.

Parish, Mitchell (1900–1993)

A lyricist, Parish built his fame on taking the instrumental melodies of others and putting appropriate words to them. The best example of this skill rests with Hoagy Carmichael's "Star Dust," a tune composed in 1927. But "Star Dust" got lost among a plethora of similar medium-tempo songs, and not until 1929 did Parish write the words that made it one of the all-time great standards. His lyrics slowed the music down and gave it a dreamy, ethereal quality. His reputation assured, Parish went on to add words to Duke Ellington's "Sophisticated Lady" (1933), one of the few times someone outside the tight circle of the Ellington orchestra had a major hand in creating the music. "Stars Fell on Alabama" (1934) was composed by Frank Perkins, but the Parish lyrics make it memorable. A song long associated with big-band swing is "Don't Be That Way" (1934; music by Edgar Sampson and Benny Goodman). Popular for dancing, it took on a second life when Parish wrote lyrics for it in 1938. In a similar vein, "Stairway to the Stars" (1935; music by Matty Malneck and Frank Signorelli), first appeared as an instrumental. It did little until Parish worked his magic in 1939, whereupon it proved a big hit for Glenn Miller and his band. Finally, Miller's own theme song, "Moonlight Serenade" (1939; music by Glenn Miller) features a set of Mitchell Parish lyrics.

Porter, Cole (1891–1964)

Another major figure in American popular music, Porter composed a collection of unforgettable tunes for which he provided his own sophisticated lyrics. The Broadway stage and the movies served as his bailiwick, and each year saw new Porter scores. Some 1930s samplings from those scores would include the controversial "Love for Sale" (*The New Yorkers*, 1930), "Night and Day" (*Gay Divorce*, 1932), "Anything Goes" (*Anything Goes*, 1934), the hugely successful "Begin the Beguine" (*Jubilee*, 1935), and "My Heart Belongs to Daddy" (*Leave It to Me!* 1938). His career went on long after the 1930s, and he consistently added laurels to his already distinguished crown.

Razaf, Andy (b. Andreamentania Paul Razafkeriefo; 1895–1973)

Best known as the lyricist partner of pianist Fats Waller, Razaf had created, by the beginning of the 1930s, a memorable body of work. He did not slow down, however, but instead collaborated with a number of musicians, including Waller, and proceeded to write such hits as "Blue Turning Grey Over You" (1930; music by Fats Waller), "Memories of You" (*Lew Leslie's Blackbirds of 1930*; music by Eubie Blake), "Christopher Columbus" (1936; music by Leon Berry), and the dancer's delight, "Stompin' at the Savoy" (1936; music by Edgar Sampson, Benny Goodman, and Chick Webb, lyrics by Andy Razaf).

Redman, Don (1900–1964)

Although he led his own big band from 1931 to 1940, it did not prosper and had few recording opportunities. He did, however, gain his own radio show in the late 1930s, the first black bandleader to do so. Redman will be remembered as one of the fathers of swing because of his compositions and arrangements. What he pioneered in the 1920s and 1930s with bands like Fletcher Henderson, McKinney's Cotton Pickers, plus his own group, became the basics of swing composition and arranging. His theme song, "Chant of the Weed" (1932), stands as a harmonically complex work, suggesting some of the more difficult Duke Ellington compositions of the era. Despite his adventuresome arrangements, he remained more of a favorite among his colleagues than he did the general public, although that same public bought and danced to music much influenced by Don Redman.

Rodgers, Richard (1902–1979)

One of the most esteemed American composers of the twentieth century, Rodgers in reality enjoyed two careers: his long-time partnership with Lorenz Hart (see above), and his equally rewarding association with Oscar Hammerstein II (see above) following Hart's death in 1943. During the 1930s, Rodgers and Hart could do no wrong as far as the stage and screen were concerned. The two penned a remarkable number of songs destined to become standards, and each tune contained a blend of witty, sophisticated lyrics and a memorable melody. Hummable, hard-to-forget music seemed to flow naturally from Rodgers' pen, a characteristic he would successfully carry on when he later teamed with Hammerstein. For the thirties, the insouciant "I've Got Five Dollars" (*America's Sweetheart*, 1931) perfectly captured the era, along with such melodic classics as "Lover" (*Love Me Tonight*, 1933), "My Romance" (*Billy Rose's Jumbo*, 1935), "There's a Small Hotel" (*On Your Toes*, 1935), and "My Funny Valentine" (*Babes in Arms*, 1936).

Romberg, Sigmund (1887–1951)

A Hungarian by birth, Romberg emigrated to the United States in 1909, but it was not until 1917 that he began to garner some acclaim. Like his counterpart, Rudolf Friml (see above), he often worked in the operetta format. He, too, went on to Hollywood, helping to fashion many of his plays into movies, although some did not make the transition until well after the 1930s. He saw *The New Moon* (1928) filmed twice; once in 1930 with Lawrence Tibbett and Grace Moore, and again in 1940 with Jeanette MacDonald and Nelson Eddy. It includes the popular "Stout-Hearted Men." (lyrics by Oscar Hammerstein II). *Maytime* (1917) reached screens in 1937, once more featuring the team of Eddy and MacDonald. He even scored an original movie, *The Night Is Young*, in 1935. It features "When I Grow Too Old to Dream" (lyrics by Oscar Hammerstein II), a hit song for Nelson Eddy.

Sampson, Edgar (1907–1973)

Yet another arranger who learned his craft with the Fletcher Henderson orchestra (1931–1933), Sampson went on to acclaim working with Chick Webb until 1937 at the famous Savoy Ballroom. During this time, he wrote several swing standards, among them "Blue Lou" (1935; music by Edgar Sampson and Irving Mills), "Stompin' at the Savoy" (1936; music by Edgar Sampson, Benny Goodman, and Chick Webb, lyrics by Andy Razaf), and "Don't Be that Way" (1938; music by Benny Goodman and Edgar Sampson, lyrics by Mitchell Parish). Benny Goodman, who always recognized good writing and arranging, had popular hits of these numbers, and helped make Sampson a major figure during this period.

Schwartz, Arthur (1900–1984)

Educated as an attorney, Schwartz practiced law during the day but lived for the theater and music in his free time. By the late 1920s, he pretty much forsook his law books and embarked on a songwriting career. Frequently teamed with lyricist Howard Dietz, he also collaborated with many other distinguished lyricists. Among Schwartz's better-known works are "Something to Remember You By" (*Three's a Crowd*, 1930; lyrics by Howard Dietz), "Dancing in the Dark" (*The Band Wagon*, 1931; lyrics by Howard Dietz), "Alone Together" (*Flying Colors*, 1931; lyrics by Howard Dietz), and "Seal It with a Kiss" (*That Girl from Paris*, 1936; lyrics by Edward Heyman).

Strayhorn, Billy ("Swee'Pea") (1915–1967)

Duke Ellington's collaborator, arranger, and lyricist from 1938 onward, Strayhorn brought a new level of sophistication to one of the most polished orchestras of the decade. His remarkable lyrics to "Lush Life" (1938) stand among the most worldly wise as anything in American music, and had been initially written a year before he joined Ellington, which meant that Strayhorn was all of sixteen years old. He contributed the band's rousing theme, "Take the 'A' Train" in 1941, and many others, such as "Something to Live For" (1939) and "I'm Checking Out Goombye" (1939). Strayhorn helped fashion the distinctive sound of the orchestra for some thirty years; in many ways, he served as Ellington's indispensible right-hand man.

Warren, Harry (1893–1981)

Unlike many of his fellow songwriters, Warren devoted most of his career to movie songs. Keeping with tradition, however, he started out in New York City. With the 1922 publication of "Rose of the Rio Grande" (co-composer, Ross Gorman; lyrics by Edgar Leslie), he was on his way. In 1930, he wrote "Cheerful Little Earful" (lyrics by Ira Gershwin and Billy Rose) for the Broadway revue *Sweet and Low*. Already well-established in Hollywood by the early Thirties, the release of *42nd Street* in 1933 merely added new luster to his reputation. He went on to score forty films throughout the decade, and he teamed up with lyricist Al Dubin in thirty-three of them, including such hits as "42nd Street" (*42nd Street*, 1933), "The Gold Digger's Song (We're in the Money)" (*Gold Diggers of 1933*, 1933), and "Lullaby of Broadway" (*Gold Diggers of 1935*, 1935), the last of which won Warren his first of three Academy Awards for Best Song. "Hooray for Spinach" (*Naughty but Nice*, 1938; lyrics by Johnny Mercer) stands as possibly his most unusual title.

Washington, Ned (1901–1976)

A talented lyricist, Washington collaborated with some of the era's best composers, and enjoyed an especially rewarding partnership with Victor Young. Together, the two wrote "Can't We Talk It Over?" (1932), "A Ghost of a Chance," and "A Hundred Years from Today" (both 1933), along with many others. With other composers, Washington gave words to "I'm Getting Sentimental over Your" (1932; music by George Bassman), the Casa Loma Orchestra theme, "Smoke Rings" (1933; music by Gene Gifford), "The Nearness of You" (1940; music by Hoagy Carmichael), and the Academy Award–winning song from *Pinocchio*, "When You Wish Upon a Star" (1940; music by Leigh Harline).

Whiting, Richard A. (1891–1938)

Yet another writer of songs destined to become standards, Whiting spent most of his all-too-brief career in Hollywood. Working with the best lyricists in the business, he wrote such melodies as "Beyond the Blue Horizon" (*Monte Carlo*, 1930; lyrics by Leo Robin), the Shirley Temple classic "On the Good Ship Lollipop" (*Bright Eyes*, 1934; lyrics by Sidney Clare), "Too Marvelous for Words" (*Ready, Willing, and Able*, 1937; lyrics by Johnny Mercer), and probably the first popular song to feature the term in its title—but hardly in the way it would later be used—"Rock and Roll" (1934; lyrics by Sidney Clare). This last number appeared in the film *Transatlantic Merry-Go-Round* (1934), and features the Boswell Sisters in a rousing rendition. He also composed the unofficial anthem of the film industry, "Hooray for Hollywood" (lyrics by Johnny Mercer) in 1937. It highlighted the movie *Hollywood Hotel* (1937).

Youmans, Vincent (1898–1946)

An established Broadway composer by the early 1920s, Youmans hit the big time with *No, No, Nanette* (1925), especially "Tea for Two" (lyrics by Irving Caesar). With the onset of the thirties, he did the music for a show entitled *Smiles* (1930) that flopped, but out of it came "Time on My Hands" (lyrics by Harold Adamson and Mack Gordon). Like so many others, Youmans moved to Hollywood and enjoyed success with *Hit the Deck* (1930), a movie that includes "Sometimes I'm Happy" (lyrics by Irving Caesar). In 1933, he scored the music for the film *Flying Down to Rio*, the picture that almost overnight made the careers of Ginger Rogers and Fred Astaire. With Youmans' "The Carioca" (lyrics by Gus Kahn and Edward Eliscu), the two dancers stole the show and went on to rank among the biggest movie stars of the decade.

INSTRUMENTALISTS AND SIDEMEN

Given space limitations, the instrumentalists mentioned below include only those who had wide popular acclaim. Since hundreds of bands roamed the nation throughout the 1930s, a figure that translates as thousands of sidemen, any attempts at inclusiveness or commentary would necessitate a much lengthier text, something outside the scope of this book. In many cases, instrumentalists went on to lead bands of their own, but as a rule those efforts failed to meet commercial expectations. Details on who played what with whom and when can be found in numerous sources, and these selections should be considered as starting points and nothing more.[4]

Bassists and Guitarists

Blanton, Jimmy (1918–1942)—bass.

Christian, Charlie (1916–1942)—guitar.

Foster, Pops (1892–1969)—bass.

Gaillard, Slim (1916–1991)—guitar.

Green, Freddie (1911–1987)—guitar.

Guy, Fred (1899–1971)—guitar.

Haggart, Bob (1914–1998)—bass.

Hinton, Milt (1910–2002)—bass.

Lang, Eddie (1902–1933)—guitar.

Page, Walter (1900–1957)—bass.

Reinhardt, Django (1910–1953)—guitar.

Stewart, Slam (1914–1987)—bass.

Brass

Allen, Henry ("Red") (1908–1967)—trumpet.

Anderson, Cat (1916–1981)—trumpet.

Berigan, Bunny (1908–1942)—trumpet.

Cheatham, Doc (1905–1997)—trumpet.

Clayton, Buck (1911–1991)—trumpet.

Edison, Harry ("Sweets") (1915–1999)—trumpet.

Eldridge, Roy ("Little Jazz") (1911–1989)—trumpet.

Elman, Ziggy (1914–1968)—trumpet.

James, Harry (1916–1983)—trumpet.

Jenney, Jack (1910–1945)—trombone.

Manone, Wingy (1904–1982)—trumpet.

Nanton, Joe ("Tricky Sam") (1904–1948)—trombone.

Page, Hot Lips (1908–1954)—trumpet.

Shavers, Charlie (1917–1971)—trumpet.

Stewart, Rex (1907–1967)—trumpet.

Teagarden, Jack (1905–1964)—trombone.

Williams, Cootie (1910–1985)—trumpet.

Drummers

Bauduc, Ray (1906–1988).

Catlett, Sid ("Big Sid") (1910–1951).

Greer, Sonny (1895–1982).

Jones, Jo (1911–1985).

Krupa, Gene (1909–1973).

McKinley, Ray (1910–1995).

Rich, Buddy (1917–1987).

Singleton, Zutty (1898–1975).

Pianists

Blake, Eubie (1883–1983).

Davenport, Cow Cow (1894–1955).

Johnson, James P. (1891–1955).

Johnson, Pete (1904–1967).

Lewis, Meade Lux (1905–1964).

Powell, Mel (1923–1998).

Slack, Freddie (1910–1965).

Smith, Clarence ("Pinetop") (1904–1929).

Smith, Willie ("The Lion") (1887–1973).

Stacy, Jess (1904–1994).

Sullivan, Joe (1906–1971).

Tatum, Art (1909–1956).

Waller, Thomas ("Fats") (1904–1943).

Williams, Mary Lou (1910–1981).

Wilson, Teddy (1912–1986).

Yancey, Jimmy (1898–1951).

Zurke, Bob (1912–1944).

Reeds

Bechet, Sidney (1897–1959)—soprano saxophone.

Bigard, Barney (1906–1980)—clarinet.

Freeman, Bud (1906–1991)—tenor saxophone.

Hawkins, Coleman ("Hawk," "Bean") (1904–1969)—tenor saxophone.

Hodges, Johnny (1906–1970)—alto saxophone.

Johnson, Budd (1910–1984)—tenor saxophone.

Miller, Eddie (1911–1991)—tenor saxophone.

Russell, Pee Wee (1906–1969)—clarinet.

Smith, Willie (1910–1967)—alto saxophone.

Webster, Ben (1909–1973)—tenor saxophone.

Young, Lester ("Prez") (1909–1959)—tenor saxophone.

Vibraphonists and Xylophonists

Hampton, Lionel (1908–2002)—vibraphone.

Norvo, Red (1908–1999)—xylophone.

Violinists

Grappelli, Stephane (1908–1997).

Smith, Stuff (1909–1967).

Venuti, Joe (1894–1978).

Appendix: Timeline

1929   "Star Dust," a medium-tempo instrumental written by Hoagy Carmichael in 1927, receives a haunting set of lyrics by Mitchell Parish and becomes one of the most performed and recorded popular songs of all time.

A young and relatively unknown clarinetist named Benny Goodman begins recording with Red Nichols and His Five Pennies, a Dixieland band; he would continue to do so until 1933.

Record sales soar to $75 million for the year.

1930   The Ipana Troubadours, a singing group named after a tooth powder and featured on radio since 1926, scores a big hit with their rendition of "Three Little Words" (music by Harry Ruby, lyrics by Bert Kalmar).

"St. James Infirmary" (arranged by Joe Primrose), a much-recorded blues song from the turn of the century, enjoys new life in popular renditions by Louis Armstrong and Cab Calloway.

1931   On March 3, 1931, the United States Congress officially declares "The Star-Spangled Banner" to be the National Anthem.

1931   Ferde Grofé's *Grand Canyon Suite* is introduced by Paul Whiteman and his orchestra.

Metropolitan Opera broadcasts begin; they would continue without interruption into the present.

1932   The title to Duke Ellington's "It Don't Mean a Thing (If It Ain't Got That Swing)" has one of the first mentions of the word "swing."

In the Broadway revue *Americana*, "Brother, Can You Spare a Dime?" (music by Jay Gorney, lyrics by E. Y. Harburg), the song most closely associated with the Depression, gets introduced.

1933   *The National Barn Dance*, which debuted in 1924, is picked up by NBC network radio.

The movie *Flying Down to Rio* for the first time teams Fred Astaire and Ginger Rogers; they get to do "The Carioca" (music by Vincent Youmans, lyrics by Gus Kahn and Edward Eliscu) and steal the show; they would star in eight additional films during the 1930s.

As proof of the influence of movies on audiences, popular musicals like *42nd Street* and *Gold Diggers of 1933* spawn numerous recorded hits.

Record sales, after slumping since the stock market crash, bottom out at $5 million for the year, a drop of over 90 percent since 1929.

Western Union delivers the first singing telegram; it consists of the song "Happy Birthday," and the recipient is entertainer Rudy Vallee.

1934   *Billboard Magazine* begins tracking the airplay of pop songs; in 1938 it would add jukebox figures.

The first popular use of the word "jitterbug" occurs in a Cab Calloway tune of the same name recorded in 1934.

Muzak begins in Cleveland, Ohio, piping music directly into homes and businesses using telephone lines.

Decca Records enters the American music scene; it signs Bing Crosby as its first major artist.

1935   George Gershwin's *Porgy and Bess* opens; written as a "folk
                opera," it contains a wealth of popular standards and quickly
                endears itself with audiences and musicians alike.

                Your Hit Parade premieres on NBC network radio; it attempts
                to chart what songs are the most popular across the country.
                An immediate success, it will remain on radio until 1957.

1936   *The Kate Smith Hour*, a major variety show, makes its debut
                on the CBS network. The singer had previously performed
                on both NBC and CBS in other formats.

                Aaron Copland's *El Salon Mexico* helps establish him as a
                major American composer.

1937   Famed conductor Arturo Toscanini assumes leadership of
                the NBC Symphony Orchestra, an aggregation formed by the
                network to gain prestige and capitalize on Toscanini's con-
                siderable fame. The show would run until 1954.

                The Tanglewood music complex in Lenox, Massachusetts,
                opens.

                A number of contemporary American composers, such as
                Aaron Copland, Howard Hanson, Roy Harris, Walter Piston,
                and William Grant Still, have their compositions played on
                network radio.

1938   In January, Benny Goodman and his orchestra, plus guest
                artists like Count Basie, Buck Clayton, Johnny Hodges,
                Lester Young, and many others, perform at Carnegie Hall,
                the first jazz/swing concert ever held at the prestigious site.

                Arthur Fiedler, conducting the Boston Pops Orchestra,
                records "Jalousie" (1925; words and music by Jacob Gade and
                Vera Bloom), a period piece with tango overtones; it becomes
                the first million-selling recording of a light classic.

                A novelty song, "Chiquita Banana" (words and music by Len
                Mackenzie, Garth Montgomery, and William Wirges), as
                performed by Carmen Miranda decked out in an outlandish
                tropical fruit headdress, captures a large following.

                The Texas Wanderers, a country group, have an unexpected
                hit with "It Makes No Difference Now" (words and music by
                Floyd Tillman).

1939   "Ciribiribin" (1909; words and music by Rudolf Thaler and
            A. Pestalozza), a trumpet showpiece, becomes a major hit
            for Harry James.

            Because of her race, contralto Marian Anderson is denied
            the use of Constitution Hall by the Daughters of the Amer-
            ican Revolution; she instead sings at the Lincoln Memorial
            with the blessing of President Roosevelt. The integrated
            crowd is estimated to be 75,000 people.

            At Eleanor Roosevelt's invitation, the Coon Creek Girls, an
            old-time country string band, perform for the King and
            Queen of England.

1940   *Beat the Band*, a musical quiz show, premieres on NBC radio,
            while *Gene Autry's Melody Ranch*, a country-western variety
            series, does likewise on rival CBS.

            In light of the boogie-woogie craze, the Andrews Sisters
            make *Your Hit Parade* with "Beat Me, Daddy, Eight to the
            Bar" (music by Don Raye, lyrics by Hughie Prince and
            Eleanor Sheehy).

            The biggest-selling record of the year is Tommy Dorsey's
            rendition of "I'll Never Smile Again" (words and music by
            Ruth Lowe), a number that features his hugely popular vo-
            calist, Frank Sinatra. Unnoticed by most people, this success
            signaled a change: singers would become dominant in the
            1940s, replacing the bands themselves as the popular fa-
            vorites.

Notes

CHAPTER 1

1. Extensive statistics on the growth of radio can be found in Christopher H. Sterling and John M. Kitross, *Stay Tuned: A Concise History of American Broadcasting* (Belmont, CA: Wadsworth Publishing Company, 1990), 631–61.

2. Erik Barnouw, in *A History of Broadcasting in the United States. Vol. 1: A Tower in Babel* (New York: Oxford University Press, 1966), does a good job of chronicling the early days of radio. Sterling and Kitross also provide early technical background in their *Stay Tuned*, 62–99.

3. In a series of informative articles, Ian Whitcomb has written a history of crooning. They are "The First Crooners, Volume One: The Twenties," http://www.picklehead.com/ian/ian_txt_firstcrooners1.html and "The First Crooners, Volume Two: 1930–1934," http://www.picklehead.com/ian/ian_txt_firstcrooners2.html.

4. See Whitcomb, "The First Crooners, Volume Three: 1935–1940," http://www.picklehead.com/ian/ian_txt_firstcrooners3.html.

5. Allison McCracken, " 'God's Gift to Us Girls': Crooning, Gender, and the Re-Creation of American Popular Song, 1928–1933," *American Music* 17:4 (Winter 1999), http://www.findarticles.com/cf_dis/m2298/4_17/63583955/p2/article.jhtml.

6. A study of Columbo's life that links him also to crooning is Joseph Lanza and Dennis Penn, *Russ Columbo and the Crooner Mystique* (Los Angeles: Feral House, 2002).

7. Crosby's life is covered in Gary Giddins, *Bing Crosby: A Pocketful of Dreams; The Early Years, 1903–1940* (Boston: Little, Brown and Company, 2001).

8. See McCracken, " 'God's Gift to Us Girls.' "

9. The subject of programming popular music on 1930s radio is covered in John Gray Peatman, "Radio and Popular Music," in *Radio Research 1942–1943*, ed. Paul F. Lazarsfeld and Frank N. Stanton (New York: Duell, Sloan and Pearce, 1944), 335–93.

10. For a detailed listing of "Hit Parade" selections, see John R. Williams, *This Was "Your Hit Parade"* (Camden, ME: Courier-Gazette, 1973); the show itself is discussed in John Dunning, *On the Air: The Encyclopedia of Old-Time Radio* (New York: Oxford University Press, 1998), 738–40.

11. Lewis A. Erenberg, *Swingin' the Dream: Big Band Jazz and the Rebirth of American Culture* (Chicago: University of Chicago Press, 1998), 41–47.

12. See Duncan MacDougald Jr., "The Popular Music Industry," in *Radio Research 1941*, ed. Paul F. Lazarsfeld and Frank N. Stanton (New York: Duell, Sloan and Pearce, 1941), 65–109; and Russell Sanjek, *Pennies from Heaven: The American Popular Music Business in the Twentieth Century* (New York: Da Capo Press, 1996), 47–183.

13. The history of the recording industry is a complex and confusing one. Helpful resources include Michael Chanin, *Repeated Takes: A Short History of Recording and Its Effects on Music* (New York: Verso, 1995), 62–67; Andre Millard, *America on Record: A History of Recorded Sound* (New York: Cambridge University Press, 1995), 158–69; and Oliver Read and Walter L. Welch, *From Tin Foil to Stereo: Evolution of the Phonograph* (Indianapolis, IN: Howard W. Sams & Company, 1959), 399–407.

14. Sanjek, *Pennies from Heaven*, 117–211.

15. A detailed history of jukeboxes, with many illustrations, is John Krivine, *Jukebox Saturday Night* (London: New English Library, 1977). Another useful source is Vincent Lynch and Bill Henkin, *Jukebox: The Golden Age* (Berkeley, CA: Lancaster-Miller, 1981). Additional jukebox information can be obtained at http://www.nationaljukebox.com./history.html and http://www.tomszone.com.

CHAPTER 2

1. A good introduction to the construction of popular songs can be found in Allen Forte, *Listening to Classic American Popular Songs* [Includes CD] (New Haven, CT: Yale University Press, 2001), especially chapters 1 and 2.

2. The popular music business is chronicled in David Ewen, *The Life and Death of Tin Pan Alley: The Golden Age of American Popular Music* (New York: Funk and Wagnalls Company, 1964) and David A. Jasen, *Tin Pan Alley: The Composers, the Songs, the Performers and Their Times* (New York: Donald I. Fine, 1988).

3. Russell Sanjek, *Pennies from Heaven: The American Popular Music Business in the Twentieth Century* (New York: Da Capo Press, 1996), v–xv, 1–27, 66–142.

4. Duncan MacDougald Jr., "The Popular Music Industry," in *Radio Research 1941*, ed. Paul F. Lazarsfeld and Frank N. Stanton (New York: Duell, Sloan and Pearce,

1941), 65–109; and John Gray Peatman, "Radio and Popular Music," in *Radio Research 1942–1943*, ed. Paul F. Lazarsfeld and Frank N. Stanton (New York: Duell, Sloan and Pearce, 1944), 335–93.

5. Ewen, *The Life and Death of Tin Pan Alley*, 304–10.

6. Composer Alec Wilder has written a good study of standards. See *American Popular Song: The Great Innovators, 1900–1950* (New York: Oxford University Press, 1972).

7. Max Morath, *The NPR Curious Listener's Guide to Popular Standards* (New York: Berkley Publishing [Perigee Book], 2002), 1–6.

8. Discussions about accuracy when tracking popular music can be found in Mac-Dougald, "The Popular Music Industry," 65–109; and Joel Whitburn, *A Century of Pop Music* (Menomonee Falls, WI: Record Research, 1999), vii–x, 45–46.

9. The rankings for 1929 and the subsequent years listed in the chapter are taken from Whitburn, *A Century of Pop Music*.

10. Will Friedwald, *Stardust Melodies: A Biography of Twelve of America's Most Popular Songs* (New York: Pantheon Books, 2002), 212–41.

11. Gary Giddins' *Bing Crosby: A Pocketful of Dreams; The Early Years, 1903–1940* (Boston: Little, Brown and Company, 2001) includes a complete discography.

12. Friedwald, *Stardust Melodies*, 143–79.

CHAPTER 3

1. Good overviews of the Broadway musical of the 1930s can be found in Martin Gottfried, *Broadway Musicals* (New York: Harry N. Abrams, 1979) and Stanley Green, *Ring Bells! Sing Songs! Broadway Musicals of the 1930's* (New Rochelle, NY: Arlington House, 1971).

2. Much has been written about Irving Berlin. An introductory source is Lawrence Bergreen, *As Thousands Cheer: The Life of Irving Berlin* (New York: Viking-Penguin, 1990).

3. For additional information on the Gershwins, see David Ewen, *A Journey to Greatness: The Life and Music of George Gershwin* (New York: Henry Holt and Company, 1956) and Edward Jablonski, *Gershwin* (New York: Doubleday, 1987).

4. For additional information on Jerome Kern, see Gerald Bordman, *Jerome Kern: His Life and Music* (New York: Oxford University Press, 1980).

5. A colorful individual, much has been written about Cole Porter. Two possible sources are George Eells, *The Life That Late He Led: A Biography of Cole Porter* (New York: G. P. Putnam's Sons, 1967) and William McBrien, *Cole Porter: A Biography* (New York: Alfred A. Knopf, 1998).

6. Given their distinctive personalities, individual studies of both Hart and Rodgers are essential. Recommended are Dorothy Hart, *Thou Swell, Thou Witty: The*

Life and Lyrics of Lorenz Hart (New York: Harper & Row, 1976) and William G. Hyland, *Richard Rodgers* (New Haven, CT: Yale University Press, 1998). See also Samuel Marx and Jan Clayton, *Rodgers and Hart: Bewitched, Bothered, and Bedeviled* (New York: G. P. Putnam's Sons, 1976) for information on the writing team.

7. One way to better understand musicals is to hear the songs performed. Two useful and well-packaged collections of stage music are *American Musical Theater* [6 LPs], Smithsonian Collection of Recordings, R 036, 1989 and *Star Spangled Rhythm: Voices of Broadway and Hollywood* [4 CDs], Smithsonian Collection of Recordings, RD 111, 1997. Both sets include detailed pamphlets about the music.

8. Two Web sites that will provide more detailed information on these plays are (for *The Cradle Will Rock*) http://www.americancentury.org/cradleguide.htm and (for *Pins and Needles*) http://www.ibdb.com/show?ID=7102.

9. For more on this aspect of the music business, see Michael Chanin, *Repeated Takes: A Short History of Recording and Its Effects on Music* (New York: Verso, 1995), 54–62.

10. On the musical in general, see John Springer, *All Talking! All Singing! All Dancing! A Pictorial History of the Movie Musical* (Secaucus, NJ: The Citadel Press, 1966); on Berkeley in particular, see John Baxter, *Hollywood in the Thirties* (New York: A. S. Barnes & Company, 1968), especially 131–33.

11. For more on Berlin's movie career, see Bergreen, *As Thousands Cheer*.

12. For the Gershwins' movie contributions, see Edward Jablonski and Lawrence D. Stewart, *The Gershwin Years* (Garden City, NY: Doubleday & Company, 1958) and Deena Rosenberg, *Fascinating Rhythm: The Collaboration of George and Ira Gershwin* (New York: Penguin Books [Plume], 1991).

13. Bordman's *Jerome Kern* covers Kern's movie career.

14. For Porter and the movies, see Eells, *The Life That Late He Led* and McBrien, *Cole Porter*.

15. Details about the music Rodgers and Hart composed for the movies can be found in Hart's *Thou Swell, Thou Witty* and Hyland's *Richard Rodgers*.

16. A source for materials on underrepresented figures like McKinney is http://www.geocities.com/nina_mae_mckinney/. For more information on movies in general, see the *Internet Movie Database*, http://us.imdb.com/; it provides detailed statistics on thousands of films.

CHAPTER 4

1. For a usable definition of jazz, see Loren Schoenberg, *The NPR Curious Listener's Guide to Jazz* (New York: Berkeley Publishing [Perigee Book], 2002), 1–5. For swing, see Gunther Schuller, *The Swing Era: The Development of Jazz, 1930–1945* (New York: Oxford University Press, 1989), 222–25.

2. A good general jazz history can be found in Gary Giddens, *Visions of Jazz: The First Century* (New York: Oxford University Press, 1998), especially 67–230.

3. Max Harrison, "Swing Era Big Bands and Jazz Composing and Arranging," in *The Oxford Companion to Jazz*, ed. Bill Kirchener (New York: Oxford University Press, 2000), 277–91.

4. Both George T. Simon's *The Big Bands* (New York: The Macmillan Company, 1967) and Leo Walker's *The Wonderful Era of the Great Dance Bands* (Berkeley, CA: Howell-North Books, 1964) contain information on virtually every band, sweet or swing, that played during the 1930s.

5. Lewis A. Erenberg, *Swingin' the Dream: Big Band Jazz and the Rebirth of American Culture* (Chicago: University of Chicago Press, 1998) and David W. Stowe, *Swing Changes: Big-Band Jazz in New Deal America* (Cambridge, MA: Harvard University Press, 1994) present compelling arguments about the rise of swing and its connections to the Depression and the New Deal.

6. A good critical and biographical study of Duke Ellington is Stanley Dance's *The World of Duke Ellington* (New York: Charles Scribner's Sons, 1970).

7. Stanley Dance, *The World of Count Basie* (New York: Charles Scribner's Sons, 1980).

8. Fortunately, the concerts have been preserved on record, along with extensive liner notes. *From Spirituals to Swing* [3 CDs], Vanguard 70169, 1999.

9. Information on Glen Gray and the Casa Loma Band can be found at the *Big Bands Database Plus*, http://www.nfo.net/USA/index.html.

10. An informative biography of Goodman is James Lincoln Collier's *Benny Goodman and the Swing Era* (New York: Oxford University Press, 1989).

11. The complete Carnegie Hall Concert can be found on *Benny Goodman at Carnegie Hall: 1938* [2 CDs], Columbia/Legacy C2K 65143, 1999.

12. See George T. Simon, *Glenn Miller and His Orchestra* (New York: Thomas Y. Crowell Company, 1974).

13. The phenomenon of swing dancing is covered in Geoffrey C. Ward and Ken Burns, *Jazz: A History of America's Music* (New York: Alfred A. Knopf, 2000), 174–77, 217–21, 261.

14. John Dunning, *On the Air: The Encyclopedia of Old-Time Radio* (New York: Oxford University Press, 1998), 60–74.

15. The names of movies and the musicians who appeared in them can be found at David Meeker, *Jazz in the Movies* (New York: Da Capo Press, 1981) and Scott Yanow, *Swing: Great Musicians, Influential Groups* (San Francisco: Miller Freeman, 2000).

16. See Erenberg, *Swingin' the Dream: Big Band Jazz and the Rebirth of American Culture*, and Stowe, *Swing Changes*, for more on youth and new musical trends.

17. Quoted in Ward and Burns, *Jazz*, 246.

18. Stowe, *Swing Changes*, 46–49.

CHAPTER 5

1. Information on both shows can be found in John Dunning, *On the Air: The Encyclopedia of Old-Time Radio* (New York: Oxford University Press, 1998), 291–92, 478–80. A more detailed source is Charles K. Wolfe, *A Good-Natured Riot: The Birth of the Grand Ole Opry* (Nashville, TN: Vanderbilt University Press, 1999).

2. The life of Jimmy Rodgers is covered at http://www.nativeground.com/jimmyrodgers.asp/.

3. An excellent source about the Carter Family is Mark Zwonitzer, with Charles Hirshberg, *Will You Miss Me when I'm Gone? The Carter Family and Their Legacy in American Music* (New York: Simon & Schuster, 2002).

4. A detailed history of jukeboxes, with many illustrations, is John Krivine, *Jukebox Saturday Night* (London: New English Library, 1977). Another useful source is Vincent Lynch and Bill Henkin, *Jukebox: The Golden Age* (Berkeley, CA: Lancaster-Miller, 1981). Additional jukebox information can be obtained at http://www.nationaljukebox.com./history.html and http://www.tomszone.com.

5. Materials on singing cowboys in general can be found at http://www.allmusic.com/cg/amg.dll. For information specific to Gene Autry or to Roy Rogers, see http://www.ubl.artistdirect.com/music/artist/bio/. In addition, the *Internet Movie Database*, http://www.us.imdb.com, gives complete details on all of their films, including soundtracks.

6. A good synopsis of Western Swing and its performers is http://www.nfo.net/usa/weswing.html. A complete retrospective of Bob Wills's recorded work is *Bob Wills & His Texas Playboys* [4 CDs], Proper Records, Ltd., Properbox 32, 2001. This set also includes a booklet by Adam Koromorski that details the history of the group.

7. Robert Santelli and Emily Davidson, eds., *Hard Travelin': The Life and Legacy of Woody Guthrie* (Hanover, NH: Wesleyan University Press, 1999).

8. Sources that deal with protest music abound. See Timothy P. Lynch, *Strike Songs of the Depression* (Jackson: University Press of Mississippi, 2001); R. Serge Denisoff, *Great Day Coming: Folk Music and the American Left* (Baltimore, MD: Penguin Books, 1971); R. Serge Denisoff and Richard A. Peterson, eds., *The Sounds of Social Change* (New York: Rand McNally & Company, 1972). For the lyrics to some of this music, see Alan Lomax, *Hard Hitting Songs for Hard-Hit People* (New York: Oak Publications, 1967).

9. Information on Earl Robinson can be found at http://www.entertainment.msn.com/artist/ and http://www.historylink.org/output.cfm.

10. More on Cajun contributions to American music can be found in Barry Jean Ancelet, Jay D. Edwards, and Glen Pitre, *Cajun Country* (Jackson: University Press of Mississippi, 1991). See also http://www.cajunculture.com/other/musiccajun.htm.

11. The Library of Congress provides information on the Lomaxes at http://www.memory.loc.gov/ammem/lohtml/lojohnbio.html. Also, the Fall 2002 ISAM Newslet-

ter provides biographical data at http://www.depthome.brooklyn.cuny.edu/isam/
cohen1.html.

12. The blues have been written about widely. A good starting point is Paul Oliver,
ed., *The Blackwell Guide to Recorded Blues* (Cambridge, MA: Basil Blackwell, Ltd. [Black-
well Reference], 1991). An extensive bibliography and discography accompany the text.
Nelson George's *The Death of Rhythm and Blues* (New York: Pantheon Books, 1988)
has two chapters on the blues during the 1930s (3–58). A general history would be
Francis Davis, *The History of the Blues* (New York: Hyperion, 1995).

13. Timothy M. Kahil, "Thomas A. Dorsey and the Development and Diffusion of
Traditional Black Gospel Piano," in *Perspectives on American Music, 1900–1950*, ed.
Michael Saffle (New York: Garland Publishing, 2000), 171–91. See also http://www.
arts.state.ms.us/crossroads/music/gospel/mu2_text.html.

CHAPTER 6

1. A detailed history of the FCC and its radio impacts can be found in Erik
Barnouw's *A History of Broadcasting in the United States. Vol. 1: A Tower in Babel* (New
York: Oxford University Press, 1966), 200–219, 243–61. See also Christopher H. Sterling and John M. Kitross, *Stay Tuned: A Concise History of American Broadcasting* (Belmont, CA: Wadsworth Publishing Company, 1990), 94–137, 632–59.

2. Descriptions of these and other classically oriented radio shows can be found in
John Dunning's *On the Air: The Encyclopedia of Old-Time Radio* (New York: Oxford
University Press, 1998).

3. For more on Toscanini, see Mortimer H. Frank, *Arturo Toscanini: The NBC Years*
(Portland, OR: Amadeus Press, 2002), and Donald C. Meyer, "Toscanini and the NBC
Symphony Orchestra: High, Middle, and Low Culture, 1937–1954," in *Perspectives on
American Music, 1900–1950*, ed. Michael Saffle (New York: Garland Publishing, 2000),
301–22.

4. Sondra Wieland Howie, "*The NBC Music Appreciation Hour*: Radio Broadcasts
of Walter Damrosch, 1928–1942," *Journal of Research in Music Education* 51:1 (Spring
2003): 64–76.

5. Two good starting points for researching American conductors are John A. Garraty and Mark C. Carnes, eds., *American National Biography*, 24 vols. (New York: Oxford University Press, 1999) and Stanley Sadie, ed., *The New Grove Dictionary of Music
and Musicians*, 29 vols. (New York: Macmillan Publishers, 2001).

6. Two good, nontechnical starting points for researching American composers are
Sadie, *The New Grove Dictionary of Music and Musicians*, and Ronald L. Davis, *A His-
tory of Music in American Life. Vol. III: The Modern Era, 1920–Present* (Malabar, FL:
Robert Krieger Publishing Company, 1981), 97–239.

7. David Ewen, *A Journey to Greatness: The Life and Music of George Gershwin* (New

York: Henry Holt and Company, 1956) and Edward Jablonski, *Gershwin* (New York: Doubleday, 1987) both provide material on Gershwin and his place in American music.

8. For the complete story of the FMP, see Kenneth J. Bindas, *All of This Music Belongs to the Nation: The WPA's Federal Music Project and American Society* (Knoxville: University of Tennessee Press, 1995). Additional information can be found in Richard Crawford, *America's Musical Life* (New York: W. W. Norton & Company, 2001), especially pp. 580–96.

CHAPTER 7

1. The sources for information on the bands, both sweet and swinging, and the bandleaders of the era are plentiful. Among the best books on the subject, the following deserve mention: Scott Yanow, *Swing: Great Musicians, Influential Groups* (San Francisco, CA: Miller Freeman, 2000). Encyclopedic in its coverage, the Yanow text omits virtually no one. More folksy in tone, but nonetheless comprehensive, is George T. Simon's *The Big Bands* (New York: The Macmillan Company, 1967). As much pictorial as it is textual, Leo Walker's *The Wonderful Era of the Great Dance Bands* (Berkeley, CA: Howell-North Books, 1964) provides a glimpse of both the bands and their audiences. Another encyclopedic source can be found on the World Wide Web: *Big Bands Database Plus*, http://www.nfo.net/USA/index.html. This vast archive covers bands, leaders, sidemen, vocalists, and even composers, lyricists, and arrangers. Recorded compilations include *Big Band Jazz* [4 CDs], Smithsonian Collection RD 030, 1983, and *Swing That Music! The Big Bands, the Soloists, and the Singers* [4 CDs], Smithsonian Collection RD 102, 1993. Both sets include informative booklets of notes.

2. Many of the leading vocalists of the 1930s can be found discussed in the sources noted above (note 1). In fact, one of the best places for information on singers is the *Big Bands Database Plus*, http://www.nfo.net/USA/index.html. It even contains a separate section on the subject. Bruce Crowther and Mike Pinfold cover numerous vocalists in *Singing Jazz: The Singers and Their Styles* (San Francisco, CA: Miller Freeman, 1997). Another comprehensive text is Will Friedwald's *Jazz Singing: America's Great Voices* (New York: Da Capo Press, 1996). In a like manner, Leslie Gourse's *Louis' Children: American Jazz Singers* (New York: Quill, 1984) does a good job with the Swing Era.

3. Information about the many composers, lyricists, and arrangers who helped define the music of the era is as copious as that about bands and bandleaders. The reader is directed to Max Morath, *The NPR Curious Listener's Guide to Popular Standards* (New York: Berkley Publishing [Perigee Book], 2002), as a good starting point. A resource guide including books and Web addresses is an added plus. Other useful materials on the subject include *Composers & Lyricists Database*, http://www.nfo.net/cal/tr1.html;

David Ewen, *The Life and Death of Tin Pan Alley: The Golden Age of American Popular Music* (New York: Funk and Wagnalls Company, 1964); William G. Hyland, *The Song Is Ended: Songwriters and American Music, 1900–1950* (New York: Oxford University Press, 1995); David A. Jasen, *Tin Pan Alley: The Composers, the Songs, the Performers and Their Times* (New York: Donald I. Fine, 1988); Alec Wilder, *American Popular Song: The Great Innovators, 1900–1950* (New York: Oxford University Press, 1972); and William Zinsser, *Easy to Remember: The Great American Songwriters and Their Songs* (Jaffrey, NH: David R. Godine, 2000).

4. Individual studies exist for virtually every important sideman (and woman) ever to grace a bandstand during the 1930s. The works mentioned in note 1 (above) tend to cover band members as well as the many leaders and vocalists. For brief thumbnail sketches of innumerable instrumentalists, a good starting point is Leonard Feather and Ira Gitler, *The Biographical Encyclopedia of Jazz* (New York: Oxford University Press, 1999). The Smithsonian Institution has compiled several collections of music from the period; one of the best for identifying sidemen and soloists is *Swing That Music!* An informative booklet by critic Martin Williams accompanies the set.

Selected Bibliography

Allen, Bob, ed. *The Blackwell Guide to Recorded Country Music*. Oxford: Blackwell Publishers, 1994.

Allen, Frederick Lewis. *Only Yesterday*. New York: Harper & Row, 1931.

———. *Since Yesterday*. New York: Bantam Books, 1940.

American Heritage Editors. *The American Heritage History of the 20's & 30's*. New York: American Heritage Publishing Company, 1970.

American Musical Theater [6 LPs]. Smithsonian Collection of Recordings. R 036, 1989.

American Popular Song [7 LPs]. Smithsonian Collection of Recordings. R 031, 1984.

Ancelet, Barry Jean, Jay D. Edwards, and Glen Pitre. *Cajun Country*. Jackson: University Press of Mississippi, 1991.

An Anthology of Big Band Swing, 1930–1955. 2 CDs. Decca GRD 2-629, 1993.

"Autry, Gene." http://www.ubl.artistdirect.com/music/artist/bio/. Accessed April 12, 2004.

Awmiller, Craig. *This House on Fire: The Story of the Blues*. New York: Franklin Watts, 1996.

Barfield, Ray. *Listening to Radio, 1920–1950*. Westport, CT: Praeger Publishers, 1996.

Barnouw, Erik. *A History of Broadcasting in the United States*. Vol. 1: *A Tower in Babel*. New York: Oxford University Press, 1966.

———. *A History of Broadcasting in the United States*. Vol. 2: *The Golden Web*. New York: Oxford University Press, 1968.

Bastin, Bruce. *Red River Blues: The Blues Tradition in the Southeast*. Urbana: University of Illinois Press, 1986.

Baxter, John. *Hollywood in the Thirties*. New York: A. S. Barnes & Company, 1968.

Benny Goodman at Carnegie Hall: 1938 [2 CDs]. Columbia/Legacy C2K 65143, 1999.

Bergreen, Lawrence. *As Thousands Cheer: The Life of Irving Berlin*. New York: Viking-Penguin, 1990.

Best, Gary Dean. *The Nickel and Dime Decade: American Popular Culture during the 1930s.* Westport, CT: Praeger Publishers, 1993.

Big Band Jazz [4 CDs]. Smithsonian Collection of Recordings. RD 030, 1983.

Big Bands Database Plus. http://www.nfo.net/USA/index.html. Accessed January 17, 2004.

Bindas, Kenneth J. *All of This Music Belongs to the Nation: The WPA's Federal Music Project and American Society.* Knoxville: University of Tennessee Press, 1995.

———. *Swing, That Modern Sound.* Jackson: University Press of Mississippi, 2001.

Block, Geoffrey. *Enchanted Evenings: The Broadway Musical from* Show Boat *to* Sondheim. New York: Oxford University Press, 1997.

Bordman, Gerald. *Jerome Kern: His Life and Music.* New York: Oxford University Press, 1980.

Boyd, Jean A. "Western Swing: Working-Class Southwestern Jazz of the 1930s and 1940s." In *Perspectives on American Music, 1900–1950.* Ed. Michael Saffle. New York: Garland Publishing, 2000, 193–214.

"Cajun Music." http://www.cajunculture.com/other/musiccajun.htm. Accessed March 25, 2004.

Chanin, Michael. *Repeated Takes: A Short History of Recording and Its Effects on Music.* New York: Verso, 1995.

Clarke, Donald. *The Rise and Fall of Popular Music.* New York: St. Martin's Press, 1995.

Collier, James Lincoln. *Benny Goodman and the Swing Era.* New York: Oxford University Press, 1989.

Composers & Lyricists Database. http://www.nfo.net/cal/tr1.html. Accessed February 15, 2004.

Country Music Magazine Editors. *The Comprehensive Country Music Encyclopedia.* New York: Random House [Times Books], 1994.

The Cradle Will Rock. http://www.americancentury.org/cradleguide.htm. Accessed January 27, 2004.

Crawford, Richard. *America's Musical Life.* New York: W. W. Norton & Company, 2001.

Crowther, Bruce, and Mike Pinfold. *Singing Jazz: The Singers and Their Styles.* San Francisco, CA: Miller Freeman, 1997.

Csida, Joseph, and June Bundy Csida. *American Entertainment: A Unique History of Popular Show Business.* New York: Watson-Guptil Publications, 1978.

Dale, Rodney. *The World of Jazz.* New York: Elsevier-Dutton, 1980.

Dance, Stanley. *The World of Count Basie.* New York: Charles Scribner's Sons, 1980.

———. *The World of Duke Ellington.* New York: Charles Scribner's Sons, 1970.

Davis, Francis. *The History of the Blues.* New York: Hyperion, 1995.

Davis, Ronald L. *A History of Music in American Life: Volume III: The Modern Era, 1920–Present.* Malabar, FL: Robert Krieger Publishing Company, 1981.

Denisoff, R. Serge. *Great Day Coming: Folk Music and the American Left.* Baltimore, MD: Penguin Books, 1971.

Denisoff, R. Serge, and Richard A. Peterson, eds. *The Sounds of Social Change.* New York: Rand McNally & Company, 1972.

Dunning, John. *On the Air: The Encyclopedia of Old-Time Radio.* New York: Oxford University Press, 1998.

———. *Tune in Yesterday: The Ultimate Encyclopedia of Old-Time Radio, 1925–1976.* Englewood Cliffs, NJ: Prentice-Hall, 1976.

Eells, George. *The Life That Late He Led: A Biography of Cole Porter*. New York: G. P. Putnam's Sons, 1967.

Erdelyi, Michael. "The Relation between 'Radio Plugs' and Sheet Sales of Popular Music." *Journal of Applied Psychology* 24 (1940): 696–702.

Erenberg, Lewis A. *Swingin' the Dream: Big Band Jazz and the Rebirth of American Culture*. Chicago: University of Chicago Press, 1998.

Ewen, David. *All the Years of American Popular Music*. Englewood Cliffs, NJ: Prentice-Hall, 1977.

———. *A Journey to Greatness: The Life and Music of George Gershwin*. New York: Henry Holt and Company, 1956.

———. *The Life and Death of Tin Pan Alley: The Golden Age of American Popular Music*. New York: Funk and Wagnalls Company, 1964.

———. *Panorama of American Popular Music*. Englewood Cliffs, NJ: Prentice-Hall, 1957.

The Fabulous Swing Collection [CD]. Jazz Heritage 515799L, 1998.

Feather, Leonard. *The New Edition of the Encyclopedia of Jazz*. New York: Bonanza Books, 1962.

Feather, Leonard, and Ira Gitler. *The Biographical Encyclopedia of Jazz*. New York: Oxford University Press, 1999.

Forte, Allen. *Listening to Classic American Popular Songs* [Includes CD]. New Haven, CT: Yale University Press, 2001.

Frank, Mortimer H. *Arturo Toscanini: The NBC Years*. Portland, OR: Amadeus Press, 2002.

Friedwald, Will. *Jazz Singing: America's Great Voices*. New York: Da Capo Press, 1996.

———. *Stardust Melodies: A Biography of Twelve of America's Most Popular Songs*. New York: Pantheon Books, 2002.

From Spirituals to Swing [3 CDs]. Vanguard 70169, 1999.

Furia, Philip. *The Poets of Tin Pan Alley: A History of America's Great Lyricists*. New York: Oxford University Press, 1990.

Garraty, John A., and Mark C. Carnes, eds. *American National Biography*. 24 vols. New York: Oxford University Press, 1999.

George, Nelson. *The Death of Rhythm and Blues*. New York: Pantheon Books, 1988.

Giddins, Gary. *Bing Crosby: A Pocketful of Dreams; The Early Years, 1903–1940*. Boston: Little, Brown and Company, 2001.

———. *Visions of Jazz: The First Century*. New York: Oxford University Press, 1998.

Gleason, Ralph J., ed. *Jam Session: An Anthology of Jazz*. New York: G. P. Putnam's Sons, 1958.

Godfrey, Donald C., and Frederic A. Leigh, eds. *Historical Dictionary of American Radio*. Westport, CT: Greenwood Press, 1998.

"Gospel Music." http://www.arts.state.ms.us/crossroads/music/gospel/mu2_text.html. Accessed March 27, 2004.

Gottfried, Martin. *Broadway Musicals*. New York: Harry N. Abrams, 1979.

Gottlieb, William P. *The Golden Age of Jazz*. New York: Simon and Schuster, 1979.

Gourse, Leslie. *Louis' Children: American Jazz Singers*. New York: Quill, 1984.

Govenar, Alan. *Meeting the Blues*. Dallas, TX: Taylor Publishing Company, 1988.

Great Vocalists of the Big Band Era [6 LPs]. Columbia Special Products, CBS Records, 1978.

Green, Benny. *Let's Face the Music: The Golden Age of Popular Song.* London: Pavilion Books, 1989.

Green, Stanley. *Encyclopaedia of the Musical Film.* New York: Oxford University Press, 1981.

———. *Ring Bells! Sing Songs! Broadway Musicals of the 1930's.* New Rochelle, NY: Arlington House, 1971.

———. *Songs of the 1930's.* Winona, MN: Hal Leonard Publishing Company, 1986.

Greene, Hank. *Square and Folk Dancing.* New York: Harper & Row, 1942.

Hamm, Charles. Liner Notes. "American Song During the Great Depression." *Brother, Can You Spare a Dime?* LP. New World Records, 1977.

———. *Yesterdays: Popular Song in America.* New York: W. W. Norton & Company, 1979.

Harris, Rex. *Jazz.* New York: Penguin Books, 1952.

Harrison, Max. "Swing Era Big Bands and Jazz Composing and Arranging." In *The Oxford Companion to Jazz.* Ed. Bill Kirchener. New York: Oxford University Press, 2000, 277–91.

Hart, Dorothy. *Thou Swell, Thou Witty: The Life and Lyrics of Lorenz Hart.* New York: Harper & Row, 1976.

Haskins, Jim. *The Cotton Club.* New York: New American Library [Plume], 1977.

Henderson, Amy, and Dwight Blocker Bowers. *Red, Hot & Blue: A Smithsonian Salute to the American Musical.* Washington, DC: Smithsonian Institution Press, 1996.

Hentoff, Nat, and Albert McCarthy, eds. *Jazz.* New York: Grove Press, 1959.

Hentoff, Nat, and Nat Shapiro, eds. *The Jazz Makers.* New York: Grove Press, 1957.

Horowitz, Joseph. *Understanding Toscanini.* New York: Alfred A. Knopf, 1987.

Howie, Sondra Wieland. "*The NBC Music Appreciation Hour:* Radio Broadcasts of Walter Damrosch, 1928–1942." *Journal of Research in Music Education* 51:1 (Spring 2003): 64–76.

Hyland, William G. *Richard Rodgers.* New Haven, CT: Yale University Press, 1998.

———. *The Song Is Ended: Songwriters and American Music, 1900–1950.* New York: Oxford University Press, 1995.

Inge, Thomas M., ed. *Concise Histories of American Popular Culture.* Westport, CT: Greenwood Press, 1982.

———. *Handbook of American Popular Culture.* 3 vols. Westport, CT: Greenwood Press, 1981.

Internet Movie Database. http://imdb.com/. Accessed March 16, 2004.

Jablonski, Edward. *Gershwin.* New York: Doubleday, 1987.

Jablonski, Edward, and Lawrence D. Stewart. *The Gershwin Years.* Garden City, NY: Doubleday & Company, 1958.

Jasen, David A. *Tin Pan Alley: The Composers, the Songs, the Performers and Their Times.* New York: Donald I. Fine, 1988.

Jazz of the 1930s: Greatest Hits. CD. BMG 09026-68735-2, 1997.

The Jazz Singers [5 CDs]. The Smithsonian Collection of Recordings. RD 113, 1998.

Jones, Max, and John Chilton. *Louis: The Louis Armstrong Story.* Boston: Little, Brown and Company, 1971.

"Jukebox History." http://www.nationaljukebox.com/history.html. Accessed March 10, 2004.

"Jukeboxes." http://www.tomszone.com. Accessed March 10, 2004.

Kalil, Timothy M. "Thomas A. Dorsey and the Development and Diffusion of Traditional Black Gospel Piano." In *Perspectives on American Music, 1900–1950*. Ed. Michael Saffle. New York: Garland Publishing, 2000, 171–91.

Keepnews, Orrin, and Bill Grauer Jr. *A Pictorial History of Jazz*. New York: Crown Publishers, 1955.

Kennedy, Michael. *The Concise Oxford Dictionary of Music*. New York: Oxford University Press, 1980.

Kenney, William Howland. *Recorded Music in American Life: The Phonograph and Popular Memory, 1890–1945*. New York: Oxford University Press, 1999.

Kingsbury, Paul, and Alan Axelrod, eds. *Country: The Music and the Musicians*. New York: Abbeville Press, 1988.

Kirchner, Bill, ed. *The Oxford Companion to Jazz*. New York: Oxford University Press, 2000.

Krivine, John. *Jukebox Saturday Night*. London: New English Library, 1977.

Laforse, Martin W., and James A. Drake. *Popular Culture and American Life*. Chicago: Nelson-Hall, 1981.

Lanza, Joseph, and Dennis Penn. *Russ Columbo and the Crooner Mystique*. Los Angeles: Feral House, 2002.

Levin, Gail, and Judith Tick. *Aaron Copland's America: A Cultural Perspective*. New York: Watson-Guptill Publications, 2000.

Lomax, Alan. *Hard Hitting Songs for Hard-Hit People*. New York: Oak Publications, 1967.

"Lomax, John." http://www.memory.loc.gov/ammem/lohtml/lojohnbio.html and http://www.depthome.brooklyn.cuny.edu/isam/cohen1.html. Accessed April 20, 2004.

Lynch, Timothy P. *Strike Songs of the Depression*. Jackson: University Press of Mississippi, 2001.

Lynch, Vincent, and Bill Henkin. *Jukebox: The Golden Age*. Berkeley, CA: Lancaster-Miller, 1981.

Lynes, Russell. *The Lively Audience: A Social History of the Visual and Performing Arts in America, 1890–1950*. New York: Harper and Row, 1985.

MacDonald, J. Fred. *Don't Touch That Dial! Radio Programming in American Life, 1920–1960*. Chicago: Nelson-Hall, 1979.

MacDougald, Duncan, Jr. "The Popular Music Industry." In *Radio Research 1941*. Ed. Paul F. Lazarsfeld and Frank N. Stanton. New York: Duell, Sloan and Pearce, 1941, 65–109.

Maltby, Richard. *Passing Parade: A History of Popular Culture in the Twentieth Century*. New York: Oxford University Press, 1989.

Marquis, Alice G. *Hopes and Ashes: The Birth of Modern Times, 1929–1939*. New York: The Free Press, 1986.

Marx, Samuel, and Jan Clayton. *Rodgers and Hart: Bewitched, Bothered, and Bedeviled*. New York: G. P. Putnam's Sons, 1976.

Mattfeld, Julius. Variety *Music Cavalcade*. Englewood Cliffs, NJ: Prentice-Hall, 1962.

McBrien, William. *Cole Porter: A Biography*. New York: Alfred A. Knopf, 1998.

McCracken, Allison. " 'God's Gift to Us Girls': Crooning, Gender, and the Re-Creation of American Popular Song, 1928–1933." *American Music* 17:4 (Winter 1999), http://www.findarticles.com/cf_dis/m2298/4_17/63583955/p2/article.jhtml. Accessed March 20, 2004.

McCutcheon, Marc. *The Writer's Guide to Everyday Life from Prohibition through World War II*. Cincinnati, OH: Writer's Digest Books, 1995.

"McKinney, Nina Mae." http://www.geocities.com/nina_mae_mckinney/. Accessed March 1, 2004.

Meeker, David. *Jazz in the Movies*. New York: Da Capo Press, 1981.

Meyer, Donald C. "Toscanini and the NBC Symphony Orchestra: High, Middle, and Low Culture, 1937–1954." In *Perspectives on American Music, 1900–1950*. Ed. Michael Saffle. New York: Garland Publishing, 2000, 301–22.

Millard, Andre. *America on Record: A History of Recorded Sound*. New York: Cambridge University Press, 1995.

Millard, Bob. *Country Music: 70 Years of America's Favorite Music*. New York: Harper-Collins [HarperPerennial], 1993.

Morath, Max. *The NPR Curious Listener's Guide to Popular Standards*. New York: Berkley Publishing [Perigee Book], 2002.

Morgan, Elizabeth. *Socialist and Labor Songs of the 1930s*. Chicago: Charles H. Kerr Publishing Company, 1997.

Morris, Ronald L. *Wait Until Dark: Jazz and the Underworld, 1880–1940*. Bowling Green, OH: Popular Press, 1980.

Morthland, John. *The Best of Country Music*. Garden City, NY: Doubleday & Company [Dolphin], 1984.

Murray, Albert. *Stomping the Blues*. New York: Da Capo Press, 1976.

Nye, Russel. *The Unembarrassed Muse: The Popular Arts in America*. New York: The Dial Press, 1970.

Oermann, Robert K. *A Century of Country: An Illustrated History of Country Music*. New York: TV Books, 1999.

Oliver, Paul, ed. *The Blackwell Guide to Recorded Blues*. Cambridge, MA: Basil Blackwell, Ltd. [Blackwell Reference], 1991.

Panati, Charles. *Extraordinary Origins of Everyday Things*. New York: Harper & Row, 1987.

———. *Panati's Parade of Fads, Follies, and Manias*. New York: HarperCollins, 1991.

Peatman, John Gray. "Radio and Popular Music." In *Radio Research 1942–1943*. Ed. Paul F. Lazarsfeld and Frank N. Stanton. New York: Duell, Sloan and Pearce, 1944, 335–93.

Phillips, Cabell. *The* New York Times *Chronicle of American Life: From the Crash to the Blitz: 1929–1939*. New York: The Macmillan Company, 1969.

Pins and Needles. http://www.ibdb.com/show.asp?ID=7102. Accessed January 27, 2004.

Poor Man's Heaven [CD]. Bluebird 82876-50958-2, 2003.

"Popular Hits of the 1930s." http://www.songwritershalloffame.org/era_overview.asp?erald=2. Accessed March 15, 2004.

Prendergast, Roy M. *Film Music: A Neglected Art*. New York: W. W. Norton & Company, 1977.

RCA Victor Jazz: The First Half-Century, The Thirties. CD. Bluebird 66086-2, 1992.

Read, Oliver, and Walter L. Welch. *From Tin Foil to Stereo: Evolution of the Phonograph*. Indianapolis, IN: Howard W. Sams & Company, 1959.

"Robinson, Earl." http://www.entertainment.msn.com/artist/ and http://www.history link.org/output.cfm. Accessed April 20, 2004.

"Rodgers, Jimmy." http://www.nativeground.com/jimmyrodgers.asp/. Accessed March 22, 2004.

"Rogers, Roy." http://www.ubl.artistdirect.com/music/artist/bio/. Accessed April 12, 2004.

Rosenberg, Deena. *Fascinating Rhythm: The Collaboration of George and Ira Gershwin.* New York: Penguin Books [Plume], 1991.

Sadie, Stanley, ed. *The New Grove Dictionary of Music and Musicians.* 29 vols. New York: Macmillan Publishers, 2001.

Sanjek, Russell. *Pennies from Heaven: The American Popular Music Business in the Twentieth Century.* New York: Da Capo Press, 1996.

Santelli, Robert, and Emily Davidson, eds. *Hard Travelin': The Life and Legacy of Woody Guthrie.* Hanover, NH: Wesleyan University Press, 1999.

Santelli, Robert, Holly George-Warren, and Jim Brown, eds. *American Roots Music.* New York: Harry N. Abrams, 2001.

Scanlan, Tom. *The Joy of Jazz: The Swing Era, 1935–1947.* Golden, CO: Fulcrum Publishing, 1996.

Schoenberg, Loren. *The NPR Curious Listener's Guide to Jazz.* New York: Berkley Publishing [Perigee Book], 2002.

Schuller, Gunther. *The Swing Era: The Development of Jazz, 1930–1945.* New York: Oxford University Press, 1989.

Settel, Irving. *A Pictorial History of Radio.* New York: Grosset and Dunlap, 1967.

Shaw, Arnold. *Let's Dance: Popular Music in the 1930s.* New York: Oxford University Press, 1998.

Simon, George T. *The Big Bands.* New York: The Macmillan Company, 1967.

———. *Glenn Miller and His Orchestra.* New York: Thomas Y. Crowell Company, 1974.

Singers and Soloists of the Swing Bands [4 LPs]. Smithsonian Collection of Recordings. R 035, 1987.

"Singing Cowboys." http://www.allmusic.com/cg/amg.dll. Accessed February 23, 2004.

Springer, John. *All Talking! All Singing! All Dancing! A Pictorial History of the Movie Musical.* Secaucus, NJ: The Citadel Press, 1966.

Star Spangled Rhythm: Voices of Broadway and Hollywood [4 CDs]. Smithsonian Collection of Recordings. RD 111, 1997.

Stearns, Marshall. *The Story of Jazz.* New York: Oxford University Press, 1958.

Sterling, Christopher H., and John M. Kitross. *Stay Tuned: A Concise History of American Broadcasting.* Belmont, CA: Wadsworth Publishing Company, 1990.

Stowe, David W. *Swing Changes: Big-Band Jazz in New Deal America.* Cambridge, MA: Harvard University Press, 1994.

Swing That Music! The Big Bands, the Soloists, and the Singers [4 CDs]. Smithsonian Collection of Recordings. RD 102, 1993.

Tichi, Cecelia. *High Lonesome: The American Culture of Country Music.* Chapel Hill: University of North Carolina Press, 1994.

TIME-LIFE Books. *This Fabulous Century.* Vol. III: 1920–1930. NY: Time-Life Books, 1969.

TIME-LIFE Books. *This Fabulous Century.* Vol. IV: 1930–1940. NY: Time-Life Books, 1969.

TIME-LIFE Books. *This Fabulous Century.* Vol. V: 1940–1950. NY: Time-Life Books, 1969.

Toll, Robert C. *The Entertainment Machine: American Show Business in the Twentieth Century.* New York: Oxford University Press, 1982.

Tucker, Mark, ed. *The Duke Ellington Reader*. New York: Oxford University Press, 1993.

Tudor, Dean, and Nancy Tudor. *Grass Roots Music*. Littleton, CO: Libraries Unlimited, 1979.

Ulanov, Barry. *A History of Jazz in America*. New York: Da Capo Press, 1952.

Variety Books. *The* Variety *History of Show Business*. New York: Harry N. Abrams, 1993.

Vocalists Database. http://www.nfo.net/USA/voc.html. Accessed January 17, 2004.

Walker, Leo. *The Big Band Almanac*. Rev. ed. New York: Da Capo Press, 1989.

———. *The Wonderful Era of the Great Dance Bands*. Berkeley, CA: Howell-North Books, 1964.

Ward, Geoffrey C., and Ken Burns. *Jazz: A History of America's Music*. New York: Alfred A. Knopf, 2000.

Wecter, Dixon. *The Age of the Great Depression, 1929–1941*. Chicago: Quadrangle Books, 1948.

"Western Swing." http://www.nfo.net/usa/weswing.html. Accessed April 2, 2004.

Whitburn, Joel. *A Century of Pop Music*. Menomonee Falls, WI: Record Research, 1999.

Whitcomb, Ian. *After the Ball: Pop Music from Rag to Rock*. Baltimore, MD: Penguin Books, 1972.

———. "The First Crooners, Volume One: The Twenties." http://www.picklehead.com/ian/ian_txt_firstcrooners1.html. Accessed March 16, 2004.

———. "The First Crooners, Volume Two: 1930–1934." http://www.picklehead.com/ian/ian_txt_firstcrooners2.html. Accessed March 16, 2004.

———. "The First Crooners, Volume Three: 1935–1940." http://www.picklehead.com/ian/ian_txt_firstcrooners3.html. Accessed March 16, 2004.

Wiebe, Gerhart. "The Effect of Radio Plugging on Students' Opinions of Popular Songs." *Journal of Applied Psychology* 24 (1940): 721–27.

Wilder, Alec. *American Popular Song: The Great Innovators, 1900–1950*. New York: Oxford University Press, 1972.

Williams, John R. *This Was "Your Hit Parade."* Camden, ME: Courier-Gazette, 1973.

Williams, Martin T., ed. *The Art of Jazz*. New York: Oxford University Press, 1959.

———. *The Jazz Tradition*. New York: Oxford University Press, 1983.

Wills, Bob. *Bob Wills & His Texas Playboys* [4 CDs]. Proper Records, Ltd. Properbox 32, 2001.

Wolfe, Charles K. *A Good-Natured Riot: The Birth of the Grand Ole Opry*. Nashville, TN: Vanderbilt University Press, 1999.

The World of Swing. CD. Columbia Legacy CK 66080, 2000.

Yanow, Scott. *Swing: Great Musicians, Influential Groups*. San Francisco: Miller Freeman, 2000.

Young, William H., and Nancy K. Young. *The 1930s*. Westport, CT: Greenwood Press, 2002.

Zinsser, William. *Easy to Remember: The Great American Songwriters and Their Songs*. Jaffrey, NH: David R. Godine, 2000.

Zwonitzer, Mark, with Charles Hirshberg. *Will You Miss Me when I'm Gone? The Carter Family and Their Legacy in American Music*. New York: Simon & Schuster, 2002.

Broadway Show Title Index

Film Title Index

Radio Show Title Index

Song Title Index

General Index

Abbott, Bud, 105
Abbott, George, 83, 111
Academy Awards (Best Song), 55–56, 58, 61, 92, 103, 112, 224, 235
Acuff, Roy (and His Smoky Mountain Boys), 148
Adamson, Harold, 8, 108–9, 221–22, 224, 235
Ager, Milton, 46, 217
Ahlert, Fred E., 43, 207
Allan, Fleming, 154
Allan, Lewis (Abel Meeropol), 218
Allen, Gracie, 99
Allen, Henry ("Red"), 236
Alsberg, Henry, 194
Alter, Louis, 56
Altman, Arthur, 64, 219
American Federation of Musicians (AFM), 193, 195
Anderson, Cat, 236
Anderson, Ivie, 51, 140, 204, 215
Anderson, Marian, 242
Anderson, Maxwell, 59
Andrews Sisters, The (Patti, Maxine, La Verne), 53, 59, 114, 216, 223, 242

Arden, Eve, 85
Arlen, Harold, 33, 36, 69; compositions, 47, 51, 113–14, 222, 228; *The Wizard of Oz*, 61–62, 114, 217, 222
Armstrong, Harry, 76
Armstrong, Louis, 87, 199–200; blues, 166, 239; films, 99, 113–14, 140
Arnaz, Desi, 111, 200
Arnheim, Gus, 11, 127, 200
Arnold, K., 156
Arodin, Sidney, 223
ASCAP, 30
Astaire, Fred, 54–56, 58, 215–16; Broadway, 79; dancer, 49, 96–97, 99, 102, 112; films, 50, 96–99, 102, 106, 108, 112, 236, 240; recordings, 57; vocalist, 49, 53, 212, 223
Austin, Gene, 6, 230
Austin, Ray, 210
Autry, Gene, 152–54
Azpiazu, Don, 48

Bacon, Lloyd, 13
Bailey, Buster, 207

About the Authors

WILLIAM H. YOUNG is a freelance writer and independent scholar. He recently retired from teaching English, American Studies, and popular culture at Lynchburg College in Virginia, where he taught for thirty-six years. Young has published books and articles on various subjects of popular culture, including the recent Greenwood volume, *The 1950s*, with his wife Nancy.

NANCY K. YOUNG is an adjunct professor for the Counselor Education Program in the School of Education and Human Development at Lynchburg College.